IMAGES
of America

Capitol Park and Spanish Town

I0806185

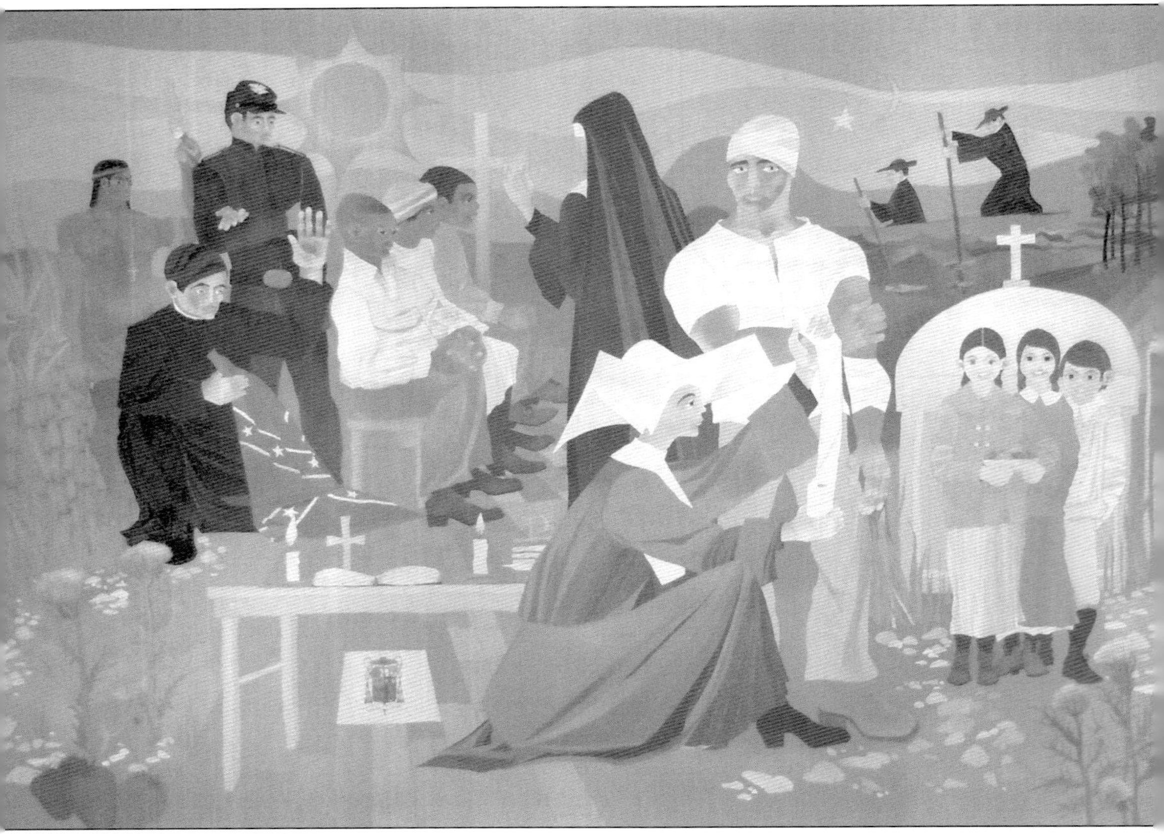

History of the Diocese of Baton Rouge, by muralist Adalie Brent, is representative of much of the history of Capitol Park and Spanish Town. Native Americans, early European settlers, Civil War soldiers, newly freed slaves, and others are represented in the work, which now hangs at the office of the Diocese of Baton Rouge. (Courtesy of the family of Adalie Brent.)

On the Cover: From 1927 until 1957, Catholic High School occupied a campus on the north side of North Street between Third and Fourth Streets. By the 1930s, enrollment had risen to more than 600. Then as now, the school boasted a large number of extracurricular activities, including an outstanding marching band. In this photograph from 1941, the band is posed on the steps of the State Capitol. (Courtesy of Catholic High School.)

IMAGES
of America

CAPITOL PARK AND SPANISH TOWN

Matt Isch
Foreword by Jay Dardenne

ARCADIA
PUBLISHING

ISBN 978-1-4671-1696-1

Published by Arcadia Publishing
Charleston, South Carolina

Printed in the United States of America

Library of Congress Control Number: 2015960613

For all general information, please contact Arcadia Publishing:
Telephone 843-853-2070
Fax 843-853-0044
E-mail sales@arcadiapublishing.com
For customer service and orders:
Toll-Free 1-888-313-2665

Visit us on the Internet at www.arcadiapublishing.com

Contents

FOREWORD

One of the hidden charms of downtown Baton Rouge is the fact that it celebrates and memorializes the mixed French and Spanish influence on the development of the Capital City. Few Baton Rougeans focus on the fact that North Boulevard is the dividing line, or in the Louisiana vernacular, the "neutral ground," between the French influence in Beauregard Town and the Spanish influence in the aptly named Spanish Town, north of North Street.

The collection of photographs in this book by Matt Isch is a tribute to the eclectic history, the functionality, and the livability of this unique area of our city that dates back to the community's earliest days.

Matt first visited the State Capitol with his parents when he was nine years old. He fell in love with the building, and in the course of working in the legislature and offices in Spanish Town, he became a student of Louisiana history and a Spanish Town devotee.

For contemporary Louisianians, it's hard to imagine the Capitol Park area as anything but a home to the nation's tallest state capitol. Prior to the capitol's construction in 1932, the entire Spanish Town area was a sprawling university environment. The streets of Spanish Town were occupied by students, professors, classroom buildings, and fraternity houses. Today, the area is a blend of the old and the new. Contemporary state office buildings surround a thriving residential area that is home to an assortment of characters, state employees, lobbyists, and downtown enthusiasts. It is also home to the unique spectacle known as Spanish Town Mardi Gras, when the neighborhood welcomes thousands of revelers who come to enjoy the antics and the creative political spoofs of the Krewe of Spanish Town.

This book brings to life a small, but significant, sliver of Baton Rouge around which the city developed.

—Jay Dardenne
January 2016

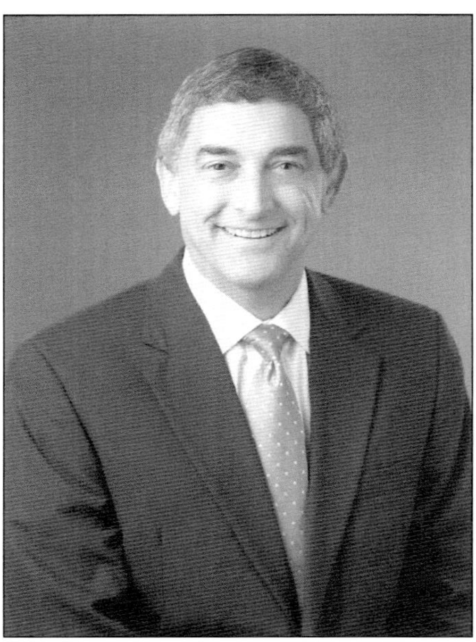

Jay Dardenne is a former Baton Rouge Metro councilman, state senator, secretary of state, and lieutenant governor.

ACKNOWLEDGMENTS

The photograph below is the first that I collected for this book. I took it myself shortly before noon on March 10, 1980, from my office window on the sixth floor of the Louisiana State Capitol. Six floors below, David C. Treen was about to be inaugurated as the 51st governor of Louisiana and its first Republican governor since Reconstruction. Over the next four years, I would have the opportunity to travel to every corner of Louisiana with the governor as a special assistant, and during that time, I fell in love with the story of Louisiana.

In assembling the other 200 or so photographs and images in the book, there are many people who deserve special thanks. Chief among them are Charlene Bonnette and the staff of the Louisiana Collection of the State Library of Louisiana, Melissa Eastin and the staff of the Baton Rouge Room of the East Baton Rouge Parish Library, Anna Gospodinovich and the staff of the Louisiana State Museum, Tara Zachary Laver and the staff of the Hill Memorial Library at LSU, Carolyn Bennett and the staff of the Foundation for Historical Louisiana, and Larry Murray and Mary Jane Marcantel at the Historic Spanish Town Civic Association.

Sincere thanks also go to Margie Alexander at Catholic High School, Smiley Anders, Lynne Barre at the Franciscan Missionaries of Our Lady, Cathy Berry, Winnie Byrd, Peggy Duerr, Anne Dunn, Marie Force at Delta Air Lines, Kaye French, Darryl Gissel, Anna and Jason Hart, Amy Jones at the Diocese of Baton Rouge, Su King, Donna LaFleur, Joanna Brent Leake, Janice McDonald, Cheryl McCormick and Derrell Cohoon, Rev. Fred Jeff Smith and the Shiloh Missionary Baptist Church, Nina Carazo Snapp, Fr. Frank Uter, Adam Watson at the Archives of Florida, and Elizabeth Weinstein.

Finally, this book would not be possible without the guidance of Liz Gurley at Arcadia Publishing and Jay Dardenne. Endless thanks to both of you.

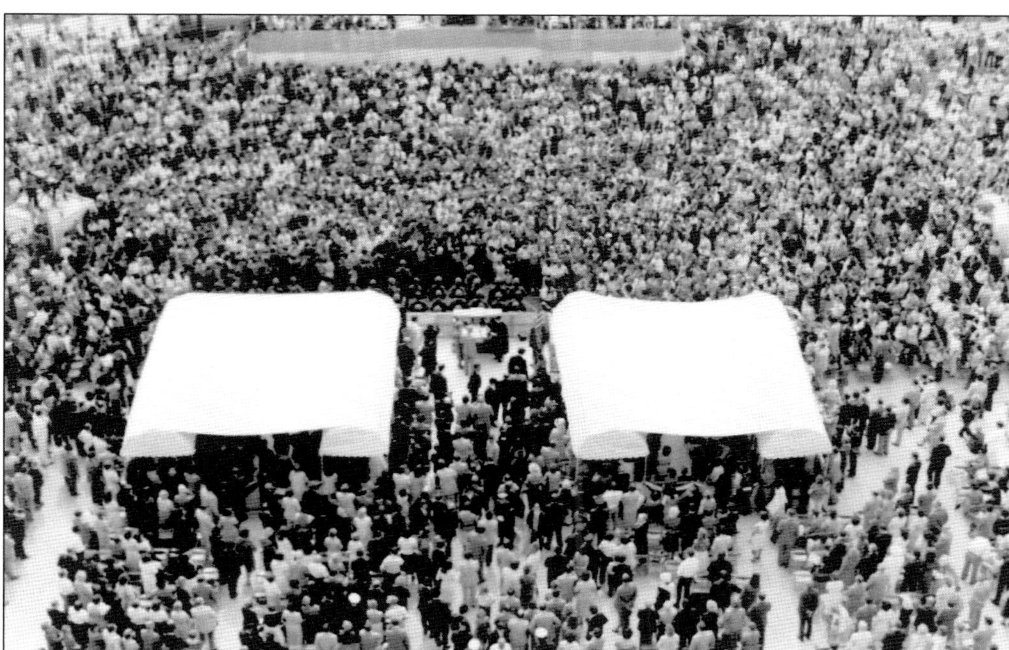

INTRODUCTION

After days of sailing from the mouth of the Mississippi River, Pierre LeMoyne, Sieur d'Iberville, and his brother Jean Baptist LeMoyne de Bienville, finally spotted high land along the east bank of the river on March 17, 1699. They tied up along the muddy bank and spied either a red cypress tree or a reddish pole adorned with fish and other dead animals that stood where a small bayou drained into the great river. Members of the Bayougoula tribe who met them told them that the pole marked the boundary of the hunting lands between themselves and the Houmas tribe. According to Fr. Anastase Douay, chaplain of the expedition, the tribes called the site Isse Trouma, or Istrouma, meaning "red stick."

The French would translate the phrase to *baton rouge*. D'Iberville himself was rather less impressed with Isse Trouma. He described the village as "107 huts and 2 temples, and . . . about 200 to 250 men and a few women and children. The smallpox, which they still had in the village had killed about ¼ of the people. They place the bodies of the dead on platforms around the village, quite close . . . raised 7 feet above. . . . This stinks badly and attracts many buzzards to the neighborhood."

Over the years, claims for the location of Istrouma have been made for a number of sites along the river from the bluff where the Old State Capitol now stands in downtown to Scott's Bluff near Southern University, but based on Douay's description, the strongest claim belongs to a site near what is now the Capitol Annex in Capitol Park.

Another version of the first European landing in what would become Baton Rouge tells another story altogether. About the same time that the d'Iberville expedition was plying the Mississippi River, another French expedition was sailing upriver to the settlement at Natchez. Le Page du Pratz, a French sailor, wrote that the sailors had not seen high ground for days until they arrived at the bluffs at Baton Rouge. When the crew had an opportunity to go ashore and stretch their legs, the ship's carpenter spied a huge cypress on the bluff and exclaimed, "*Monsieur le Capitaine, regardez donc ce joli baton rouge!*" (Captain, just look at that pretty red stick!) He boasted that if he were allowed to cut down the tree, he could build two boats, one of 16 tons and one of 14 tons. The captain demurred, and the cypress was spared. Du Pratz further embellishes the story to say that the great tree in question stood at what is now the intersection of North and Third Streets until it was taken down in 1837.

While both of these stories are problematic in different ways, they do share a common setting. Both Istrouma and Du Pratz's cypress at the intersection of North and Third Streets lay in the area now referred to as Capitol Park and Spanish Town.

The history of Baton Rouge and Louisiana has been unfolding in these 75 mostly square blocks for almost 10,000 years. Artifacts found in and around the ceremonial mound that remains near the Arsenal in Capitol Park date to 8,000 BCE.

In the 1700s, the French granted large swatches of the land along the river to planters and established a crude earthwork fort just south of the current site of the Pentagon Barracks. The Treaty of San Ildefonso in 1762 and the Treaty of Paris in 1763 ended the colonial aspirations of the French in Louisiana. New Orleans was ceded to the Spanish and the lands around Baton Rouge were relinquished to the British.

The British bolstered the ramparts of the mostly neglected French blockhouse and renamed it Fort New Richmond, but it was still far from imposing. One of its British defenders described it as "a miserable fortlet," and little resistance was offered when the Spanish governor of New Orleans, Bernardo de Gálvez y Madrid, led an expedition of 1,400 Spanish soldiers, American volunteers, and others to capture the fort during the American Revolution. The Battle of Baton Rouge on September 21, 1779, has sometimes been called the only battle of the Revolution fought outside the legal boundaries of the 13 colonies. This claim is somewhat misleading, as Galvez's forces also fought the British in minor actions at Manchac and Natchez on the same campaign in 1779, and laid siege to the British garrison at Pensacola in 1781.

The Spanish were more serious about taking charge of their possessions than their British predecessors had been and were determined that West Florida would be a strong bulwark against the new American republic. Fort New Richmond was renamed Fort San Carlos and armed with 30 cannon. Don Carlos Louis Boucher de Gran Pre, the governor of the new Spanish territory of West Florida, took a personal interest in the settlement at Baton Rouge. In 1805, one of his most far-reaching actions was to grant lands to the east of Fort San Carlos to Spanish settlers who had been displaced when Spanish lands near Bayou Manchac were ceded to the United States as part of the Louisiana Purchase in 1803. Those settlers had no interest in becoming American citizens, and their new home near the fort would be called Spanish Town.

After American insurgents seized Fort San Carlos from the Spanish in 1810 and Louisiana was granted statehood in 1812, a portion of what is now Capitol Park was appropriated by the federal government and designated the Baton Rouge Armory and Ordnance Depot. Until the eve of the Civil War, the garrison was the center of military activity in what was then the American Southwest. From here, troops were dispatched to fight the Battle of New Orleans in the War of 1812, the Mexican-American War in 1845, and the Seminole Wars throughout the first half of the century.

Although Baton Rouge was designated Louisiana's state capital in 1847, it remained a relatively sleepy outpost until the advent of the Civil War. When war was declared, Baton Rouge became the first Southern state capital to be captured by the Union army in early 1862. In response, Confederate general John C. Breckinridge marched his army overland from Camp Moore in Tangipahoa Parish to reclaim it. The Battle of Baton Rouge was fought on August 5, 1862, to little effect. The commander of the Union army, Gen. Thomas Williams, was killed during the battle, and the garrison was soon renamed Fort Williams in his honor. In the aftermath of the battle, Gen. Benjamin Butler, who would earn the nickname "Beast" in New Orleans in the years ahead, ordered most of the houses of Spanish Town demolished so that they could not be used as cover should the rebels return. During the last three years of the war, the Baton Rouge garrison was a staging point for Union forces in the Battle of Port Hudson in 1863 and later skirmishes in western Louisiana and Texas.

After the war, most of the homes in Spanish Town still lay in ashes, and Fort Williams was reduced and eventually shut down altogether in 1869. Newly-freed slaves from surrounding areas of Louisiana and Mississippi poured into the area and began to build new communities in the ruins. Many of the small homes built in Spanish Town in the years immediately following the war that still stand today were built by African Americans who had been born slaves and were tasting freedom for the first time.

Also in 1869, the Seminary of Learning of the State of Louisiana was burned out of its campus near Pineville and was "temporarily" moved to Baton Rouge until the Rapides Parish campus could be rebuilt. Over the next 17 years, the school would struggle and change names several times before it became the Louisiana State University and Agricultural and Mechanical College and petitioned to take over the old buildings of the garrison. With the strong support of Gen. William T. Sherman, who had been president of the school in its earliest days and was a strong supporter of the state's petition to take over the garrison, LSU held classes at its new campus for the first time in 1886.

The university flourished, and its growth transformed the grounds of the garrison as well as nearby Spanish Town, where apartments, fraternity houses, and homes for faculty and students sprouted and provided the neighborhood its unique character.

When LSU moved to its new campus in 1925, many of its old buildings were taken over by the state government. Workers and their families moved into many of the small homes of Spanish Town, and the character of the neighborhood was poised to change once again. In 1928, public service commissioner Huey P. Long was elected Louisiana's 40th governor and immediately proposed a radical expansion of the services provided by the state. To accommodate the new employees and the ego of the new governor, a monument would be required.

Ground was broken for a new state capitol building in December 1930. The 34-floor Beaux Arts masterpiece would be the tallest building in the South and was completed in an incredible 16 months. The capitol featured 26 different kinds of marble from around the world, incorporated the works of dozens of artists from around the United States, and was set amid 10 miles of walks and drives in lush gardens.

New state office buildings came and went on the lands surrounding the capitol after World War II, and Spanish Town would wax, wane, and be reborn again as the neighborhood struggled to form an identity. Homes, apartment buildings, and rooming houses fell into disrepair as Baton Rougeans sought newer and larger homes in the suburbs, but there still remained a small core of urban pioneers in the neighborhood who treasured the opportunity to make a home in the center of the city. In the early 1970s, these residents banded together to form the Historic Spanish Town Civic Association and began to work toward recognition as a National Historic District. The economic incentives and increased security that resulted from this effort assured that Spanish Town, Baton Rouge's first neighborhood, would also be one of its most diverse.

One

Early Baton Rougeans

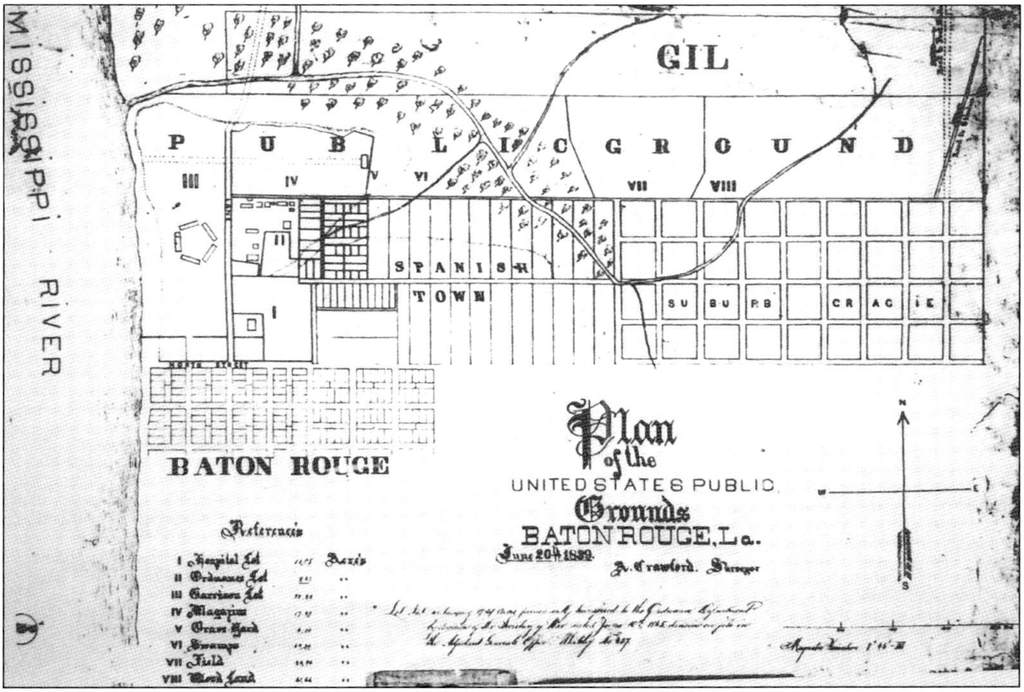

Visitors to Capitol Park and Spanish Town have to look hard for evidence of its earliest settlers, but the signs are there to be seen. Native Americans who may have inhabited the area almost 10,000 years ago built the oldest man-made object remaining here, a ceremonial mound in Capitol Park near the Arsenal Museum. The French, who arrived in 1699, gave the city its name. The English improved the old French fort that would fall to the Spanish in 1779 and to the Americans in 1810. This map of the Baton Rouge Arsenal and Ordnance Depot from 1839 shows the Pentagon Barracks and arsenal near the river and the Spanish Town neighborhood stretching to the east. (Courtesy of the Foundation for Historical Louisiana.)

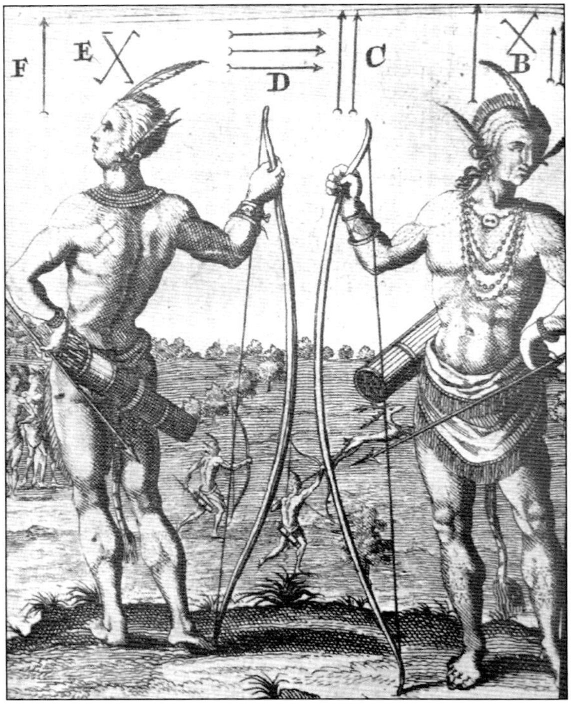

By the late 1600s, the hunting lands of the Bayougoula and Houma tribes allegedly intersected at the red pole on the bank of the river at a place they called Isse Trouma. There are very few contemporary representations of how the members of the tribes might have looked or dressed. This drawing of members of the Bayougoula tribe appeared in France in the early 1700s. (Courtesy of the Foundation for Historical Louisiana.)

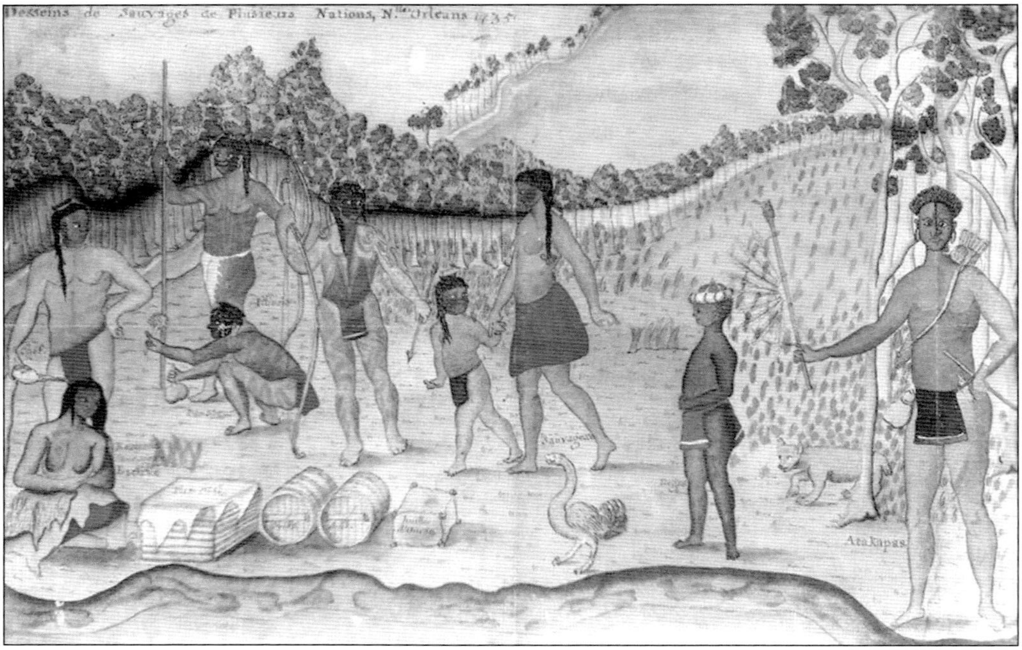

Historians estimate that there were no more than 2,500 Bayougoulas and fewer than 4,500 Houmas in 1699, most living on the west side of the river. The Bayougoulas were absorbed into neighboring tribes in the 1700s and later almost wiped out by wars and disease. This print of Louisiana, *Savages of Several Nations*, was published in France in 1735. (Courtesy of the Louisiana Collection of the State Library of Louisiana.)

Pierre LeMoyne, Sieur d'Iberville, led a French expedition in search of a suitable site for settlement and fortification along the Mississippi River. He first encountered high ground at the Bayougoula village of Isse Trouma on March 17, 1699. D'Iberville is recognized as the founder of the French colony of Louisiana in New France. (Courtesy of the Louisiana Collection of the State Library of Louisiana.)

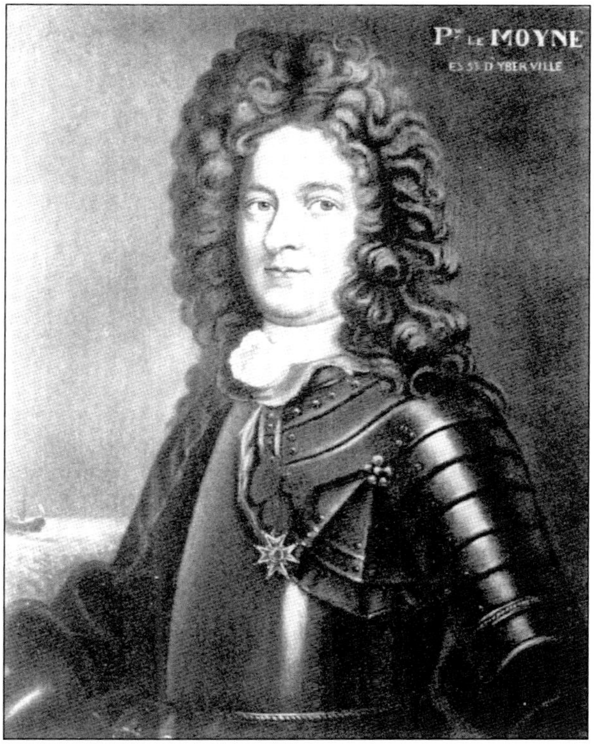

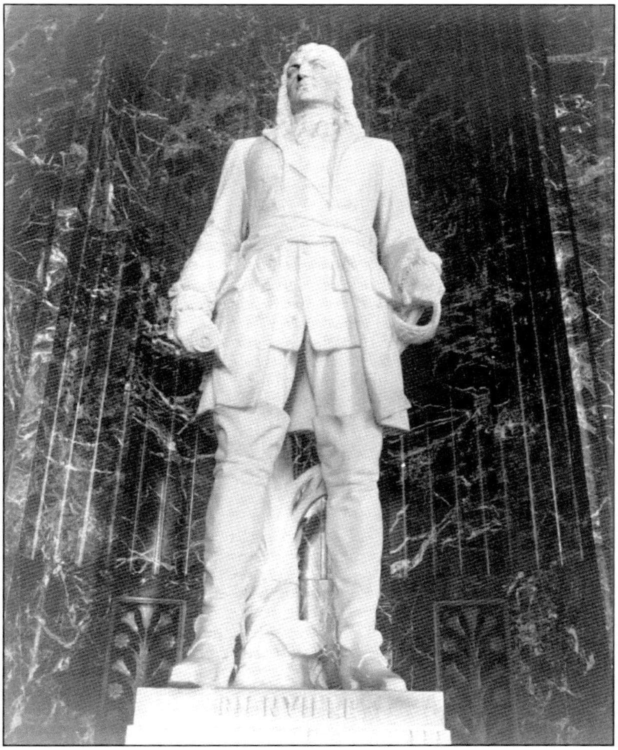

D'Iberville's brother, Jean-Baptiste LeMoyne de Bienville, depicted here in a statue in the Memorial Hall of the State Capitol, was with his brother when they came ashore in what would become Baton Rouge. Between 1701 and 1743, he was appointed governor of the French colony of Louisiana on four occasions. (Author photograph.)

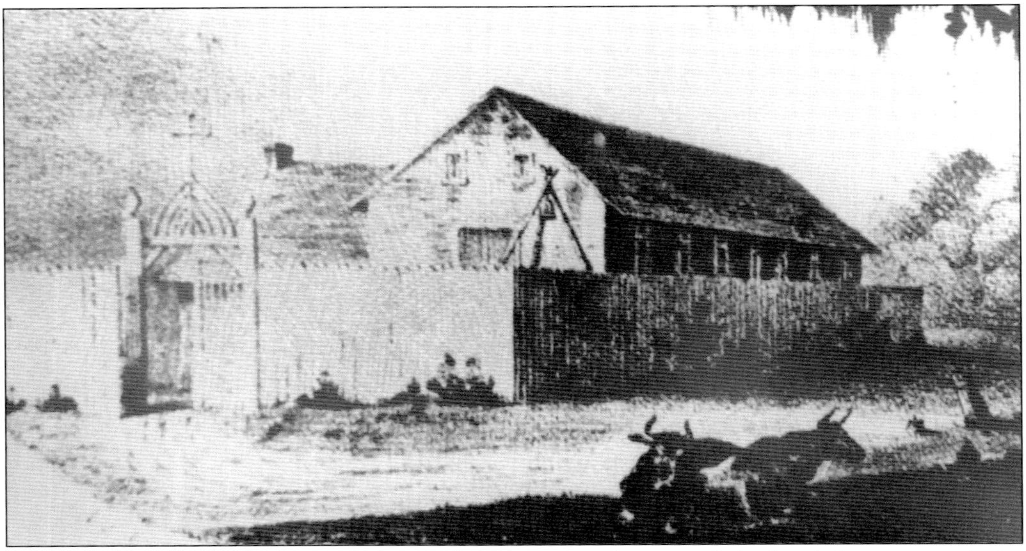

One early French landowner was Diron d'Artaguette, who owned the land that now includes much of Capitol Park. D'Artaguette had wanted to call the settlement around his plantation Dironbourg. He built this chapel, the first religious structure built by Europeans in what would become Baton Rouge. The site of d'Artaguette's home and chapel lies in the middle of what is now Capitol Lake. (Courtesy of the Foundation for Historical Louisiana.)

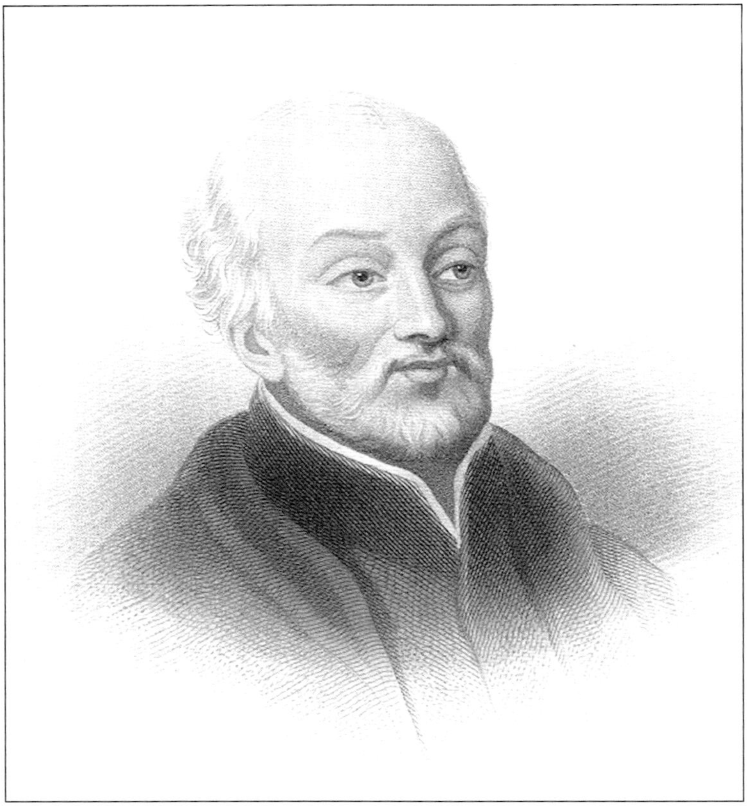

The first church service to be held in what is now Baton Rouge was at the d'Artaguette chapel on January 1, 1722. Pierre François Xavier de Charlevoix, a Jesuit father traveling from Canada to New Orleans and ultimately Haiti, said the mass. Charlevoix is best known as the author of the authoritative *History of New France* in 1744. (Courtesy of the Foundation for Historical Louisiana.)

When France ceded the area around Baton Rouge as part of the Treaty of San Ildefonso in 1763, one of the earliest Scottish settlers was planter and slave owner William Dunbar. He is credited with the invention of the screw press, introduced the square baling of cotton, and was the first to suggest the manufacture of cottonseed oil. (Courtesy of the Foundation for Historical Louisiana.)

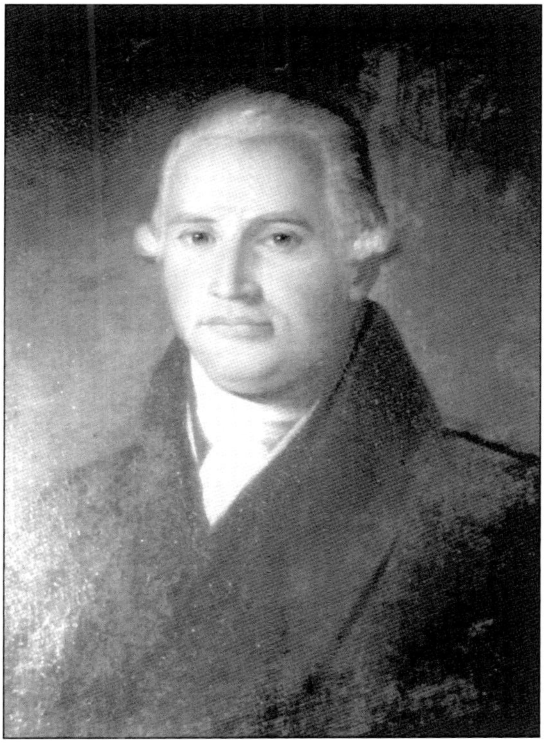

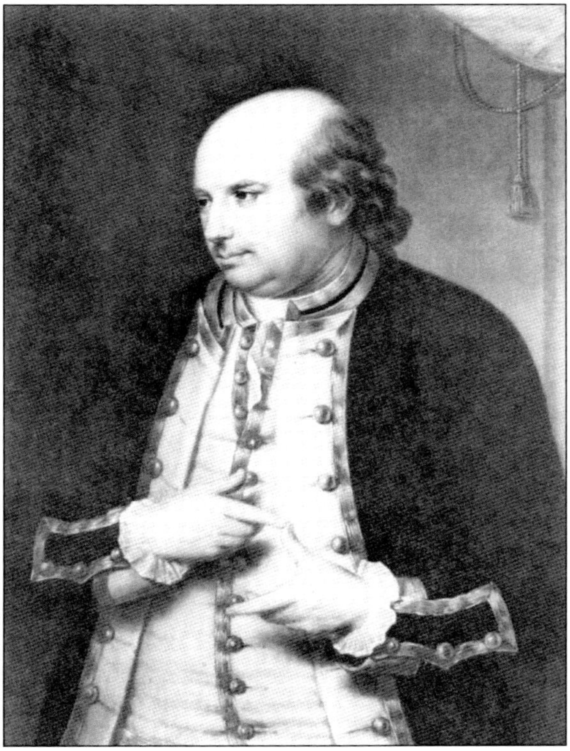

George Johnstone (1730–1787) served as the British governor of the Province of West Florida from 1764 until 1767. Optimistic that West Florida could become a productive colony for the British crown, he encouraged American immigration into the Baton Rouge area. He carried out skillful negotiations with the local Indians and established the basics of civil government in the region. (Courtesy of the Archives of Florida.)

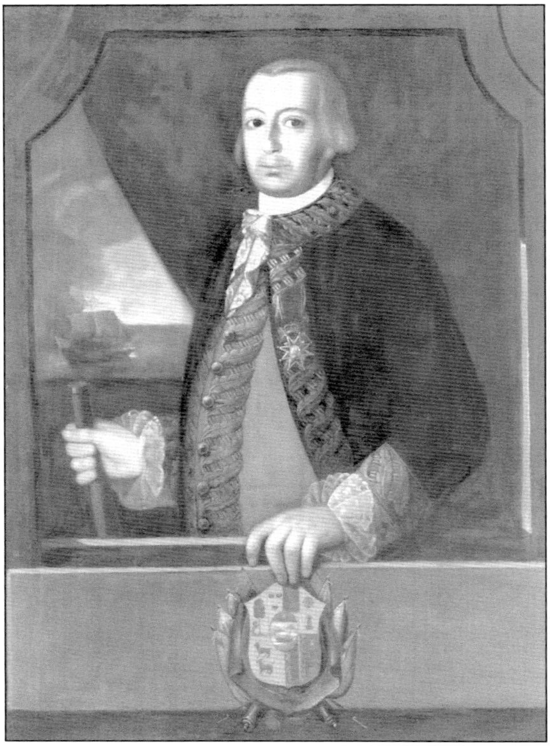

Bernardo Vicente Apolinar de Gálvez y Gallardo, the Spanish governor at New Orleans, provided assistance to American rebels in the Revolutionary War. When it was discovered that the British intended to seize New Orleans, he was ordered to recover territories lost by treaty. Gálvez defeated the British colonial forces at Baton Rouge on September 21, 1779. (Courtesy of the Collections of the Louisiana State Museum.)

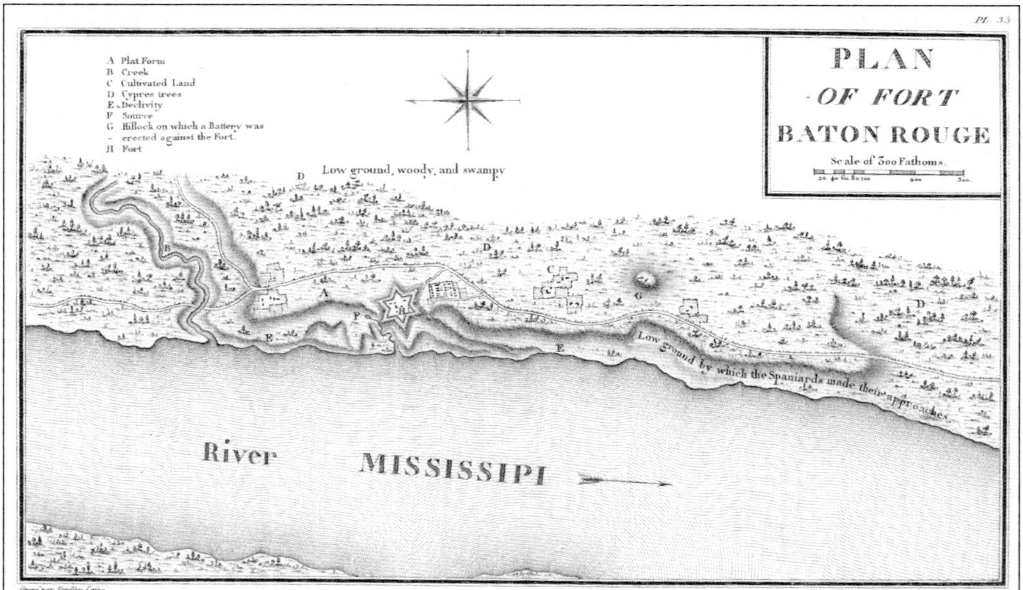

This map from 1779 shows Fort New Richmond at the time of the Battle of Baton Rouge. British commander Alexander Dickson held the fort with 500 troops and 14 cannon. While the British directed their fire at troops in the wooded areas to the north and east of the fort, Gálvez concentrated his cannon on an Indian burial mound to the south. (Courtesy of the Collections of the Louisiana State Museum.)

Approximately 400 Spanish soldiers from the New Orleans District were accompanied by over 1,000 French, American, Native, and African American volunteers who were determined to remove the British from Baton Rouge and West Florida. During the battle on September 21, 1779, Gálvez lost only one soldier. (Courtesy of the Foundation for Historical Louisiana.)

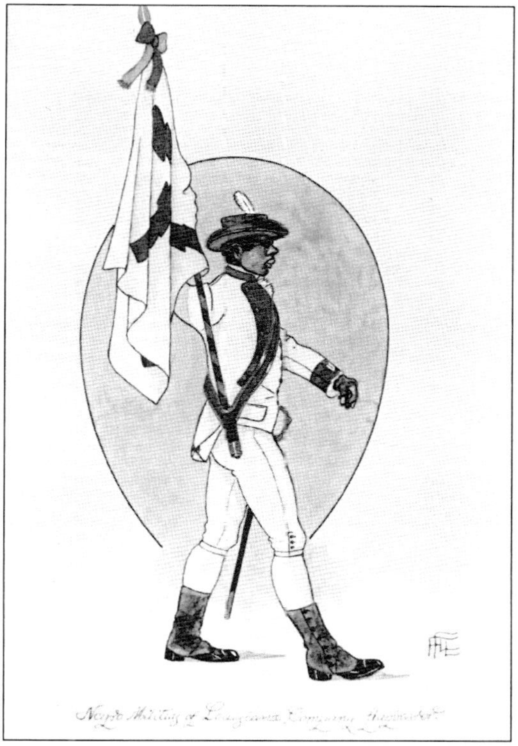

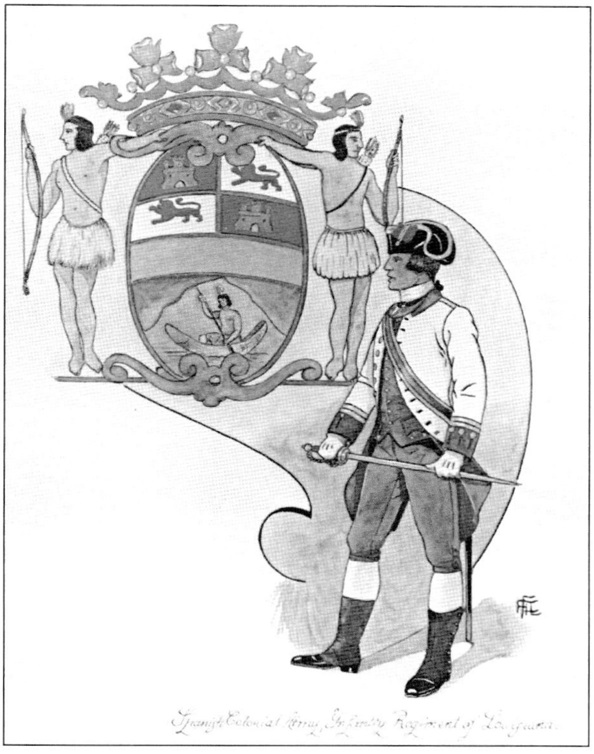

The battle of 1779 is sometimes referred to—erroneously—as the only battle of the American Revolution fought outside the 13 original colonies. This drawing of Gálvez's Spanish and American soldiers is from *Marcha da Gálvez* by Dr. Jack D.L. Holmes for the Baton Rouge Bicentennial Corporation in 1976. (Courtesy of the Foundation for Historical Louisiana.)

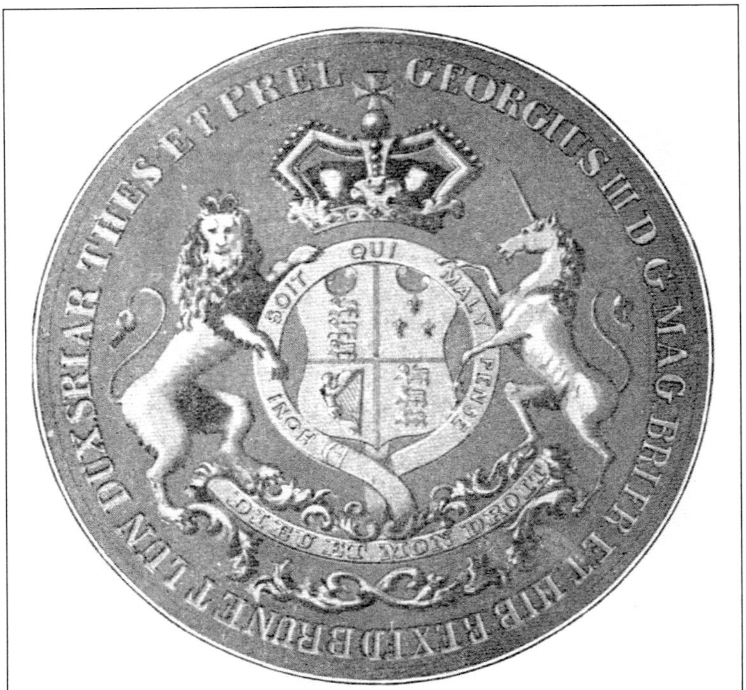

SEAL OF THE PROVINCE OF WEST FLORIDA.

The Spanish made a concerted effort to get along with their new American neighbors, but friction increased as more American settlers flooded into the Baton Rouge area. A key point of dispute was whether the Spanish province of West Florida, whose seal is shown here, was part of French possessions sold to the United States in the Louisiana Purchase of 1803. (Courtesy of the Archives of Florida.)

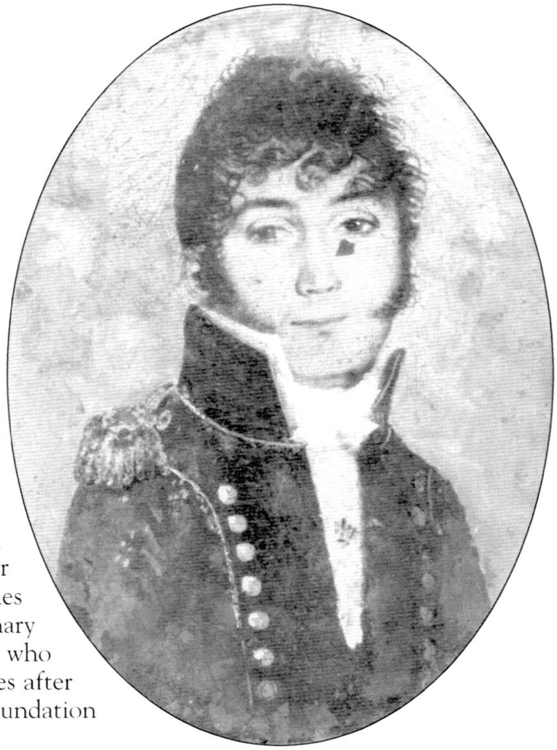

Charles Louis Boucher de Grand Pre served in a number of administrative positions in Spanish Louisiana, the last being governor of West Florida. In 1805, he granted properties along what is now Spanish Town Road to Canary Islanders from the vicinity of Pass Manchac who had no wish to be part of the United States after the Louisiana Purchase. (Courtesy of the Foundation for Historical Louisiana.)

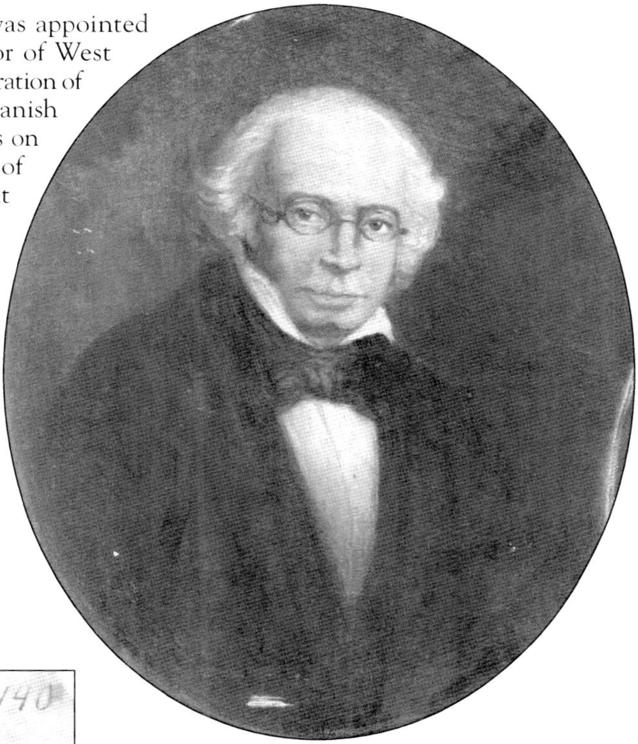

Don Carlos de Hault de Lassus was appointed military commander and governor of West Florida in 1804. His corrupt administration of the province hastened the end of Spanish rule and the fall of Fort San Carlos on September 23, 1810. For the loss of West Florida, De Lassus was tried at court martial and sentenced to death. The penalty was never carried out. (Courtesy of the Foundation for Historical Louisiana.)

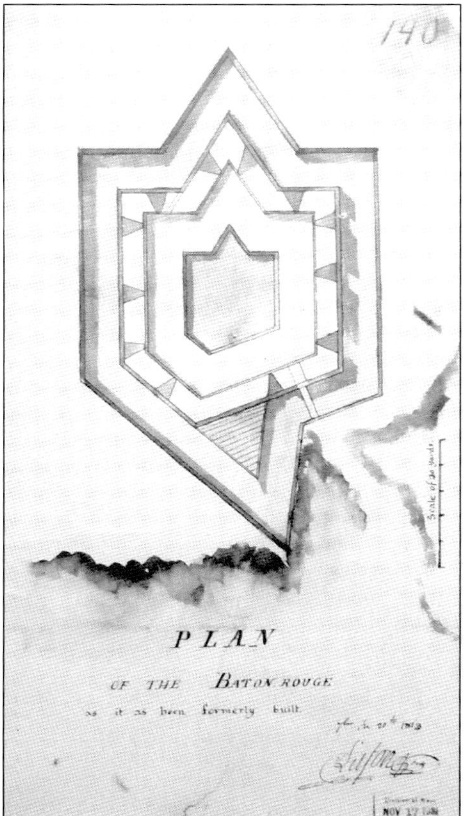

Early on a Sunday morning, 65 Americans made their way into the garrison along a path used by the fort's herd of dairy cattle. Louis de Granpre, commander of the fort and son of the former governor, was one of only two casualties of the attack, shot down when he refused to lower the Spanish flag. (Courtesy of the Foundation for Historical Louisiana.)

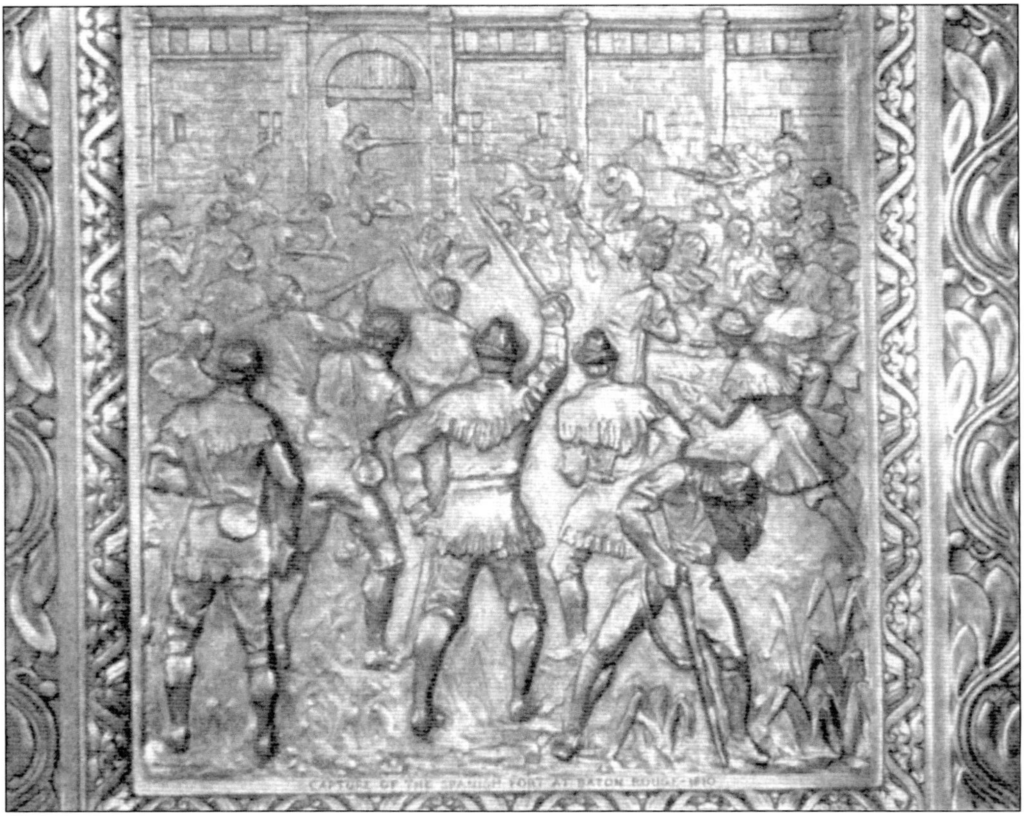

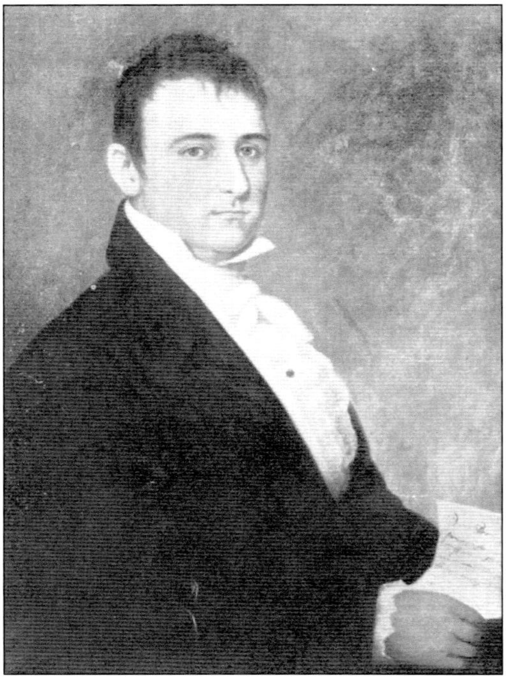

The fortifications at Fort San Carlos had been built up under the administration of the Spanish dons. They did not, however, resemble in any way the impressive massive stone battlements in this depiction of the battle in the bronze work of the doors to the Senate chamber of the State Capitol by sculptor Attilio Piccirilli and his brothers in New York. (Author photograph.)

W.C.C. Claiborne served as the American governor of the Territory of Orleans from 1804 until Louisiana became a state in 1812. Three months after Fort San Carlos was seized by the Americans, Claiborne announced that the Republic of West Florida had been annexed to the United States. The Stars and Stripes were raised over Baton Rouge for the first time on December 10, 1810. (Courtesy of the Foundation for Historical Louisiana.)

Two

The Garrison

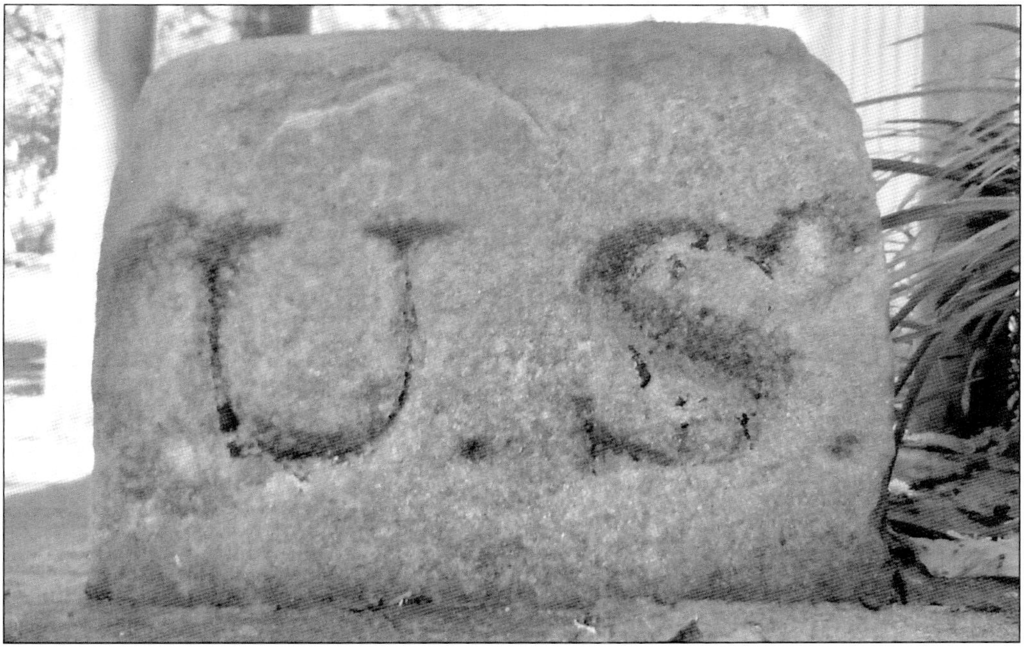

Baton Rouge, the first high ground along the Mississippi that d'Iberville had found in 1699, was the last river outpost to fall into American hands. The Americans, eager to incorporate Baton Rouge and Louisiana into the United States, were quick to establish a military garrison around old Fort San Carlos and the French, British, and Spanish buildings around it. The Baton Rouge Arsenal and Ordnance Depot was commissioned by the US Army in 1817. From here, the Army would prosecute its activities in the old Southwest, first against Native American tribes and ultimately against Mexico. This marker at the intersection of Fifth Street and Spanish Town Road marks the boundary line of the garrison, which would also be known for a brief time as Cantonment Robertson and during the Civil War as Fort Williams. The first structures to be built were the Pentagon Barracks, which still stand. Prominent buildings to be built later included two powder magazines (one of which, the Arsenal Museum, still stands), a large armory, and a barracks called the Colony. The famous warriors and statesmen who found their way to the garrison included Lafayette, Zachary Taylor, Abraham Lincoln, William T. Sherman, Jefferson Davis, and Robert E. Lee. Meanwhile, a few blocks to the east, the area known as Spanish Town began to grow and prosper. (Author photograph.)

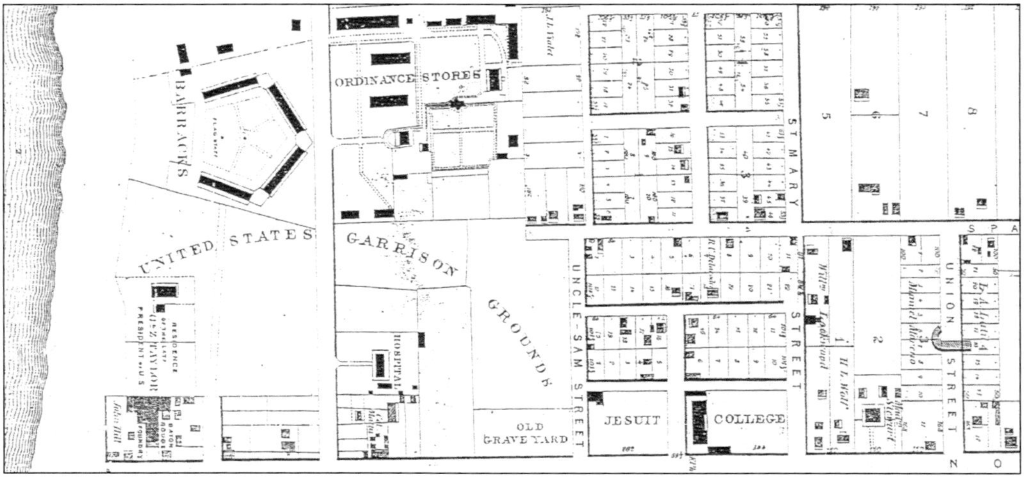

The ordnance depot established by the Army soon grew to become the largest Army installation in the South. It served as a main supply depot during the Second Florida Seminole War (1835–1842), the Mexican-American War (1846–1848), and various other actions. This map of the Second Ward of Baton Rouge from the 1850s shows the military facility and the Spanish Town neighborhood adjoining it. (Courtesy of the Foundation for Historical Louisiana.)

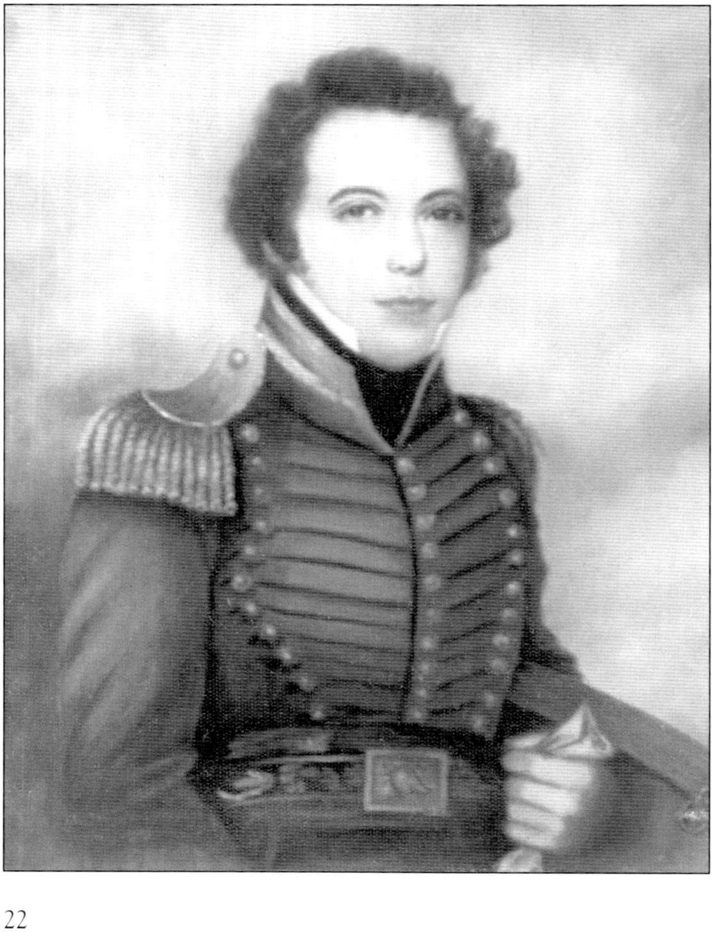

Construction of the barracks at the Arsenal began in 1819 from designs by Lt. James Gadsden, who later became famous as the author of the Gadsden Purchase. The original design included four barracks buildings and a single quartermaster building arranged in a pentagon. Construction was completed in 1821. The quartermaster building was determined to be defective and was torn down the same year. (Courtesy of the Archives of Florida.)

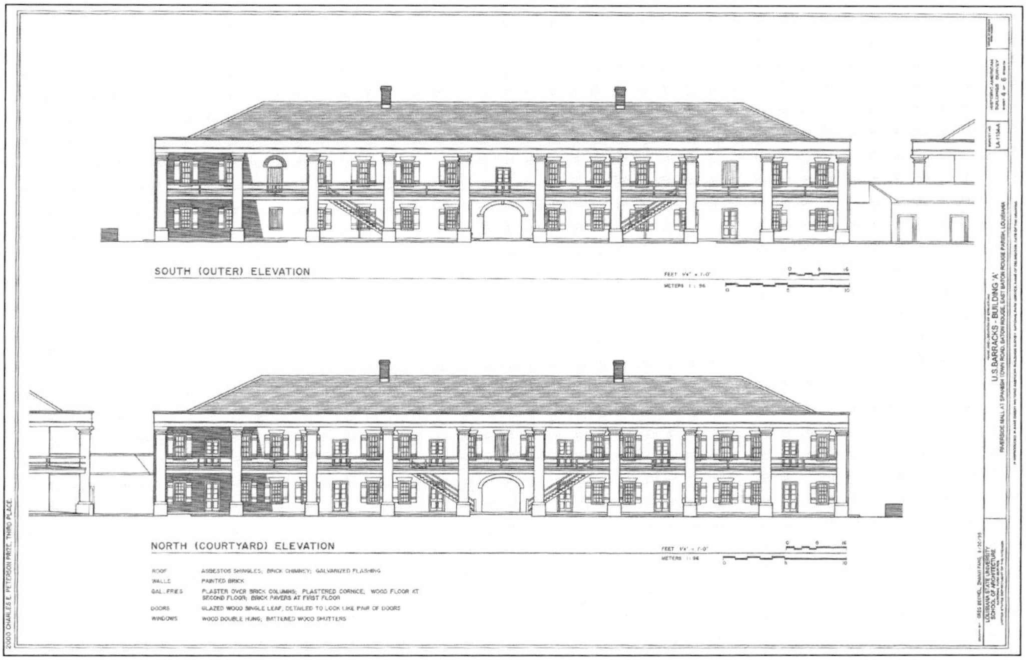

The four remaining barracks buildings were constructed of brick and designed to quarter 1,000 troops. Each featured wide verandas on the interior side. Verandas on the outward-facing sides were added later. (Courtesy of the Library of Congress.)

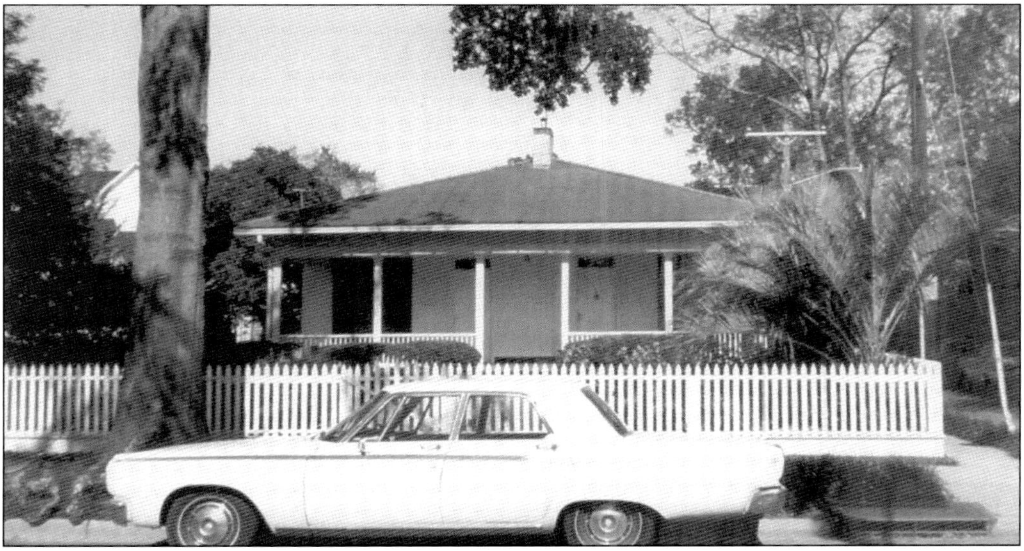

Spanish Town's oldest remaining residence was built in the 1820s at 721 North Street. Now referred to as the Pino-Wolfe House, it was built by Etienne de Gran Pre and later owned by Canary Islander Antonio Pino, and is one of the few to survive the destruction during the Civil War.

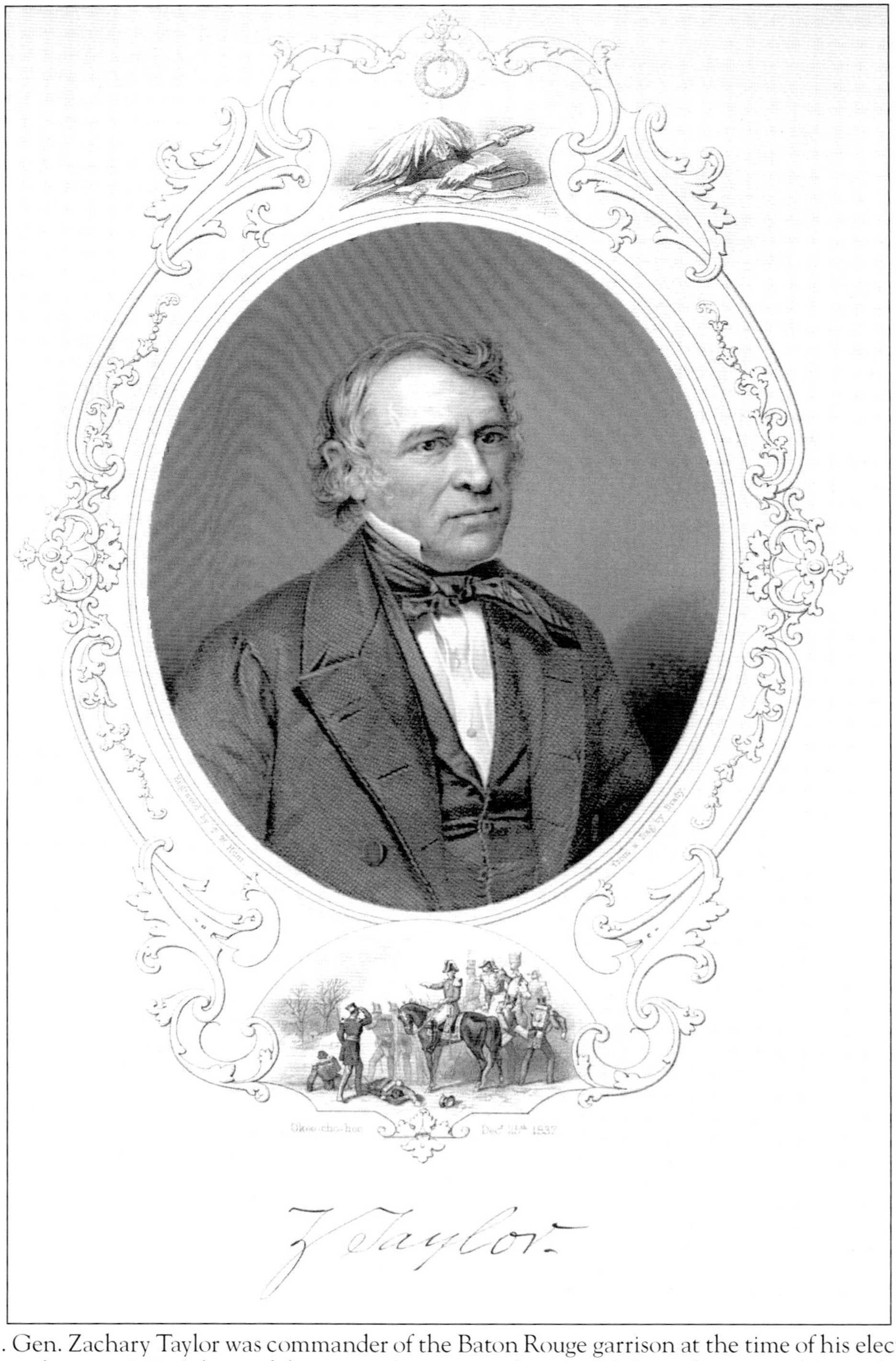

Maj. Gen. Zachary Taylor was commander of the Baton Rouge garrison at the time of his election as president in 1848. A hero of the war with Mexico who earned the nickname "Old Rough and Ready," Taylor acquired a plantation near Baton Rouge in the early 1820s and considered it his home until his death in 1850. (Courtesy of the Archives of Florida.)

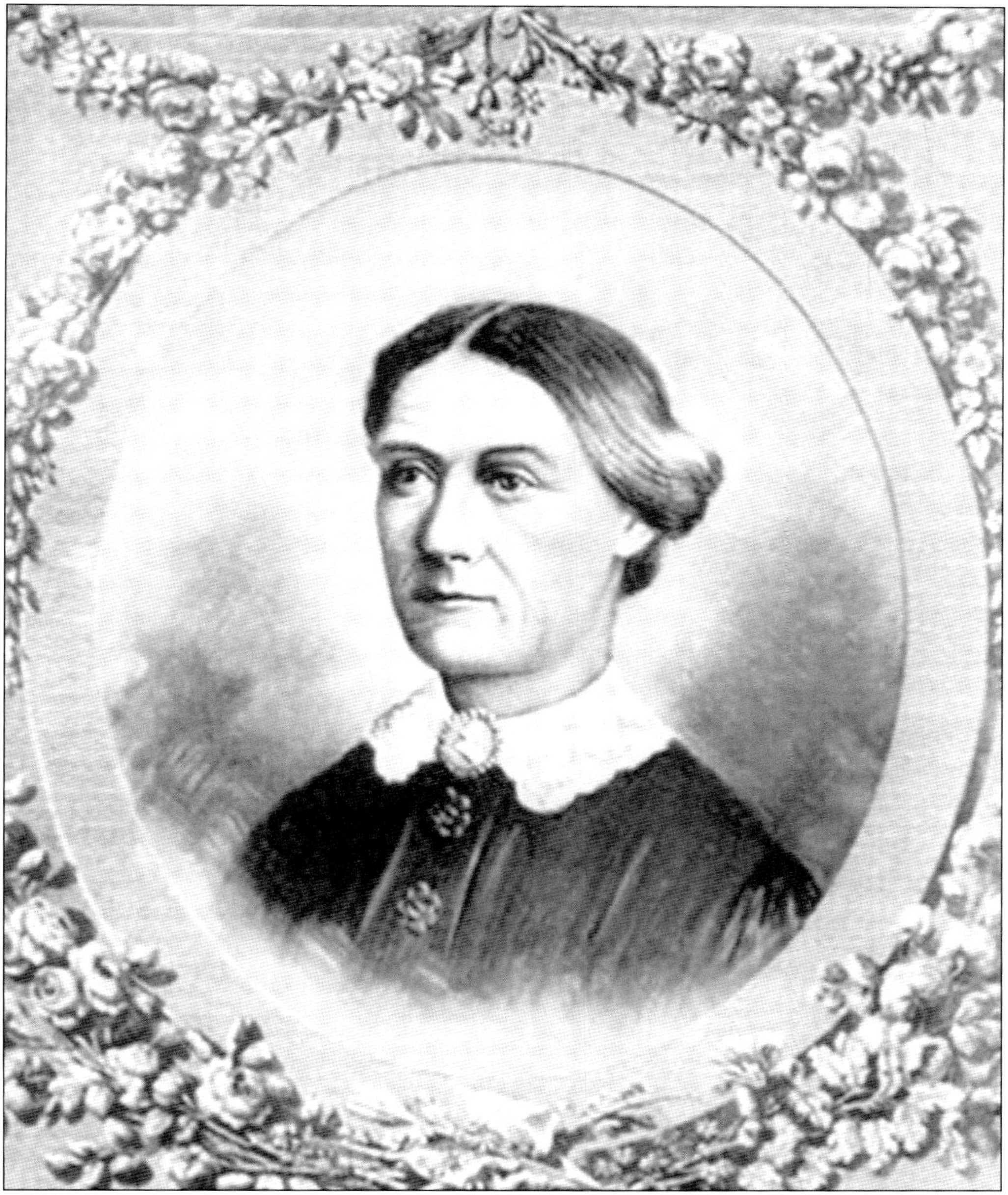

Taylor and his wife, Margaret "Peggy" Mackall Smith, had six children. Peggy was very comfortable in Baton Rouge and chose to remain there whenever her husband was called to duty. She eschewed more modern quarters and chose to live in the old house just south of the Pentagon Barracks that had been built by Alexander Dickson for the British commander of Fort New Richmond. (Courtesy of the Foundation for Historical Louisiana.)

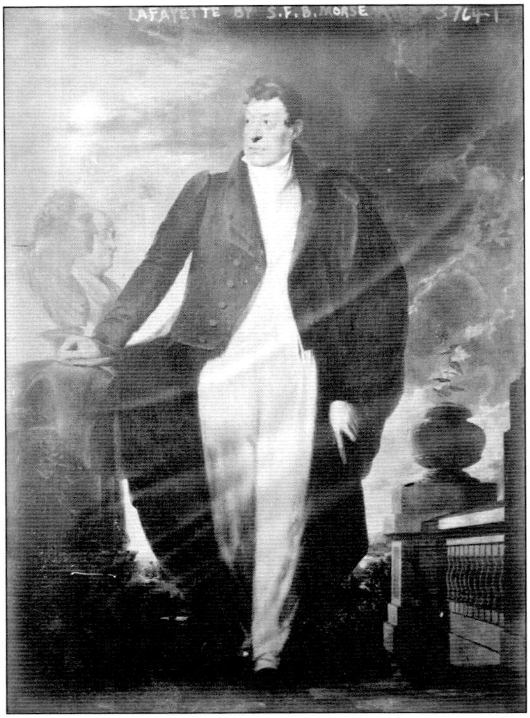

In 1824–1825, the Marquis de Lafayette traveled to all 24 American states on his last visit to his adopted country. On April 16, 1825, he arrived in the city of Baton Rouge by steamboat and marched at the head of a parade up Second Street to the newly completed Pentagon Barracks to review the troops of the garrison. Second Street was renamed Lafayette Street in his honor. (Courtesy of the Foundation for Historical Louisiana.)

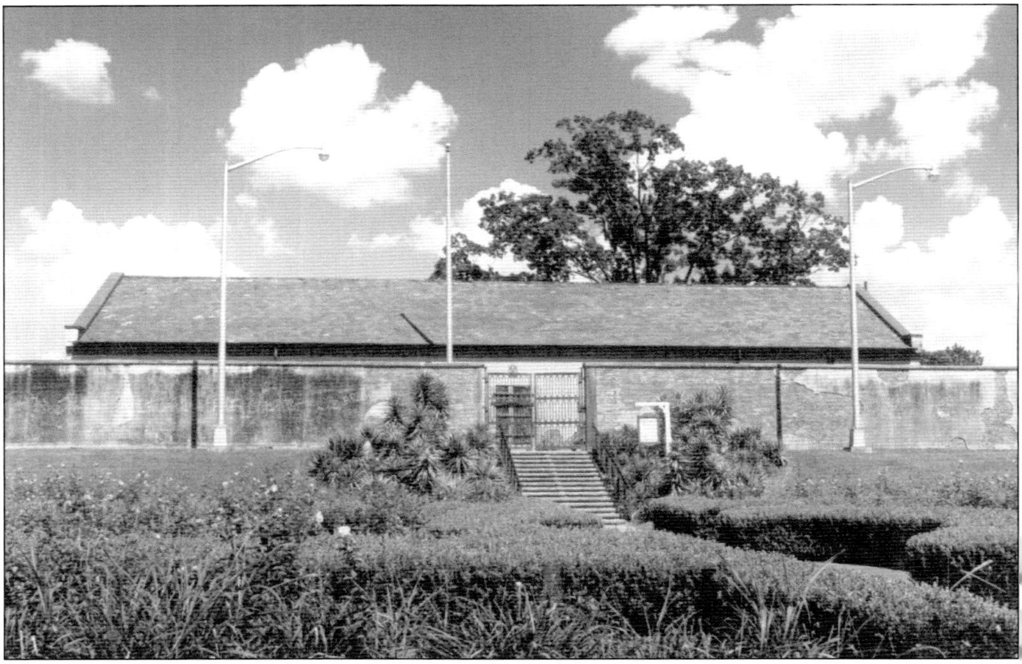

The garrison's powder magazine, now the Arsenal Museum, was completed in 1832. Although the magazine was built on flat land at the garrison, this photograph from the 1970s shows that soil from around the magazine was removed to shore up the land around the new State Capitol in the 1930s. (Courtesy of the Louisiana Collection of the State Library of Louisiana.)

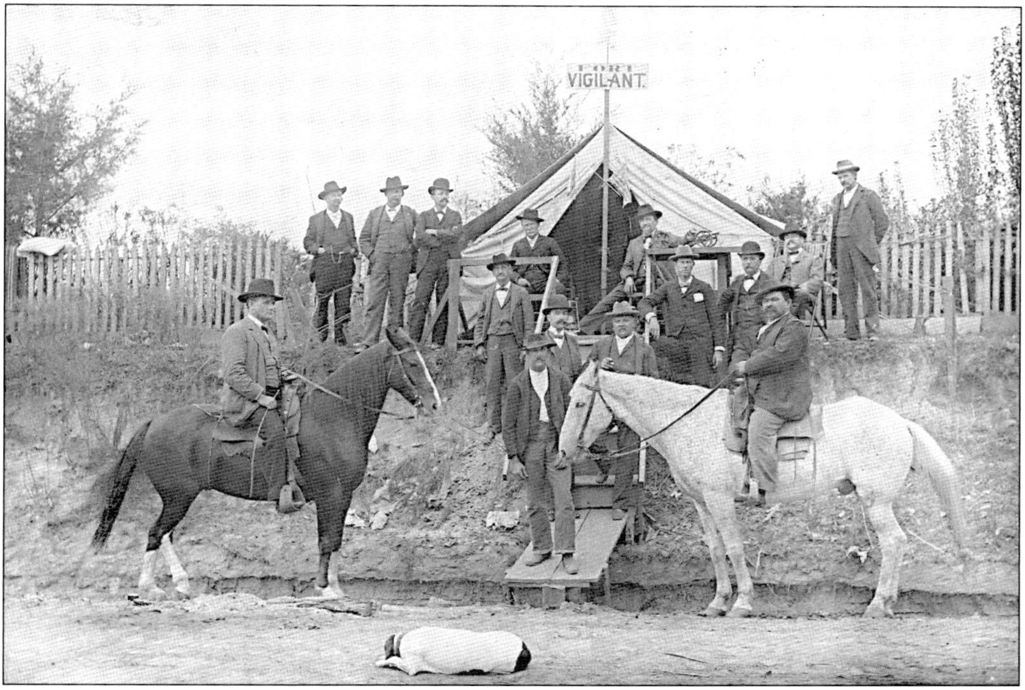

Throughout the 19th century, yellow fever and Asiatic cholera ravaged the garrison and Spanish Town community so frequently that the Baton Rouge military post was spoken of as the "graveyard of the regiment." This photograph from 1897 shows a yellow fever quarantine station on the edge of the community. (Courtesy of the Joseph St. Clair Favrot Family Papers, Mss. 3317, Louisiana and Lower Mississippi Valley Collections, LSU Libraries.)

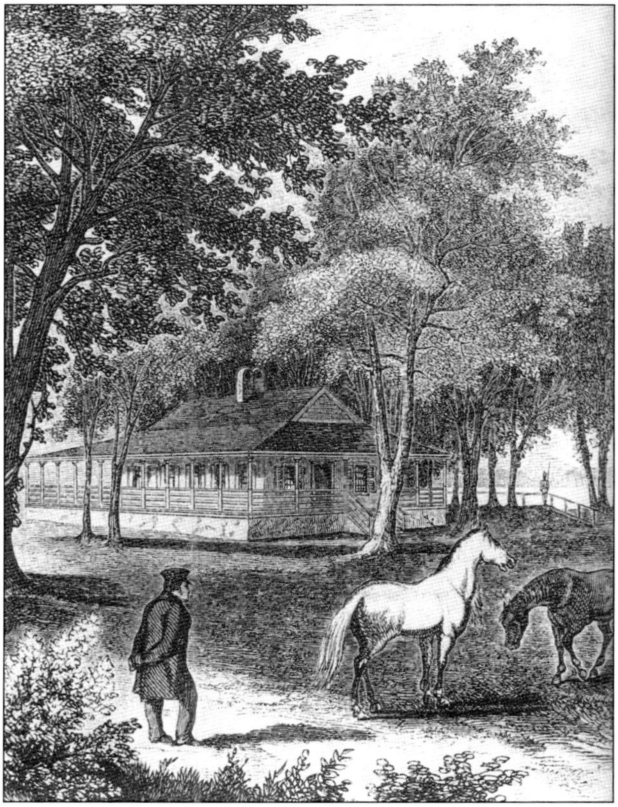

Old Rough and Ready's house on the bluff was a popular attraction for steamboat captains passing on the river. They knew that when they blew their whistles, Taylor's horse, Whitey, who was almost as well-known as the general himself, would rush to the fence and rear his head in greeting. A marker in the State Capitol garden notes that the Taylor home was nearby. (Courtesy of the Foundation for Historical Louisiana.)

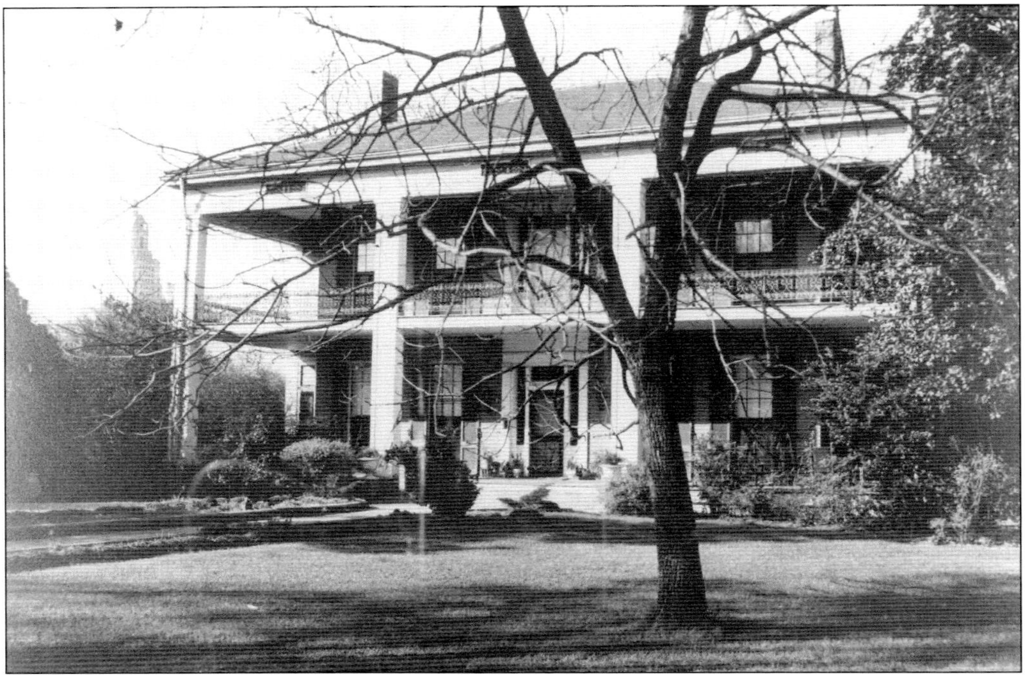

The grandest house in Spanish Town was built in 1850 at 741 North Street as a home for widow Elvira McCalop Stewart. After Elvira's death, the house passed to her granddaughter Nellie Dougherty, who was married to Arthur T. Prescott, first president of Louisiana Tech University. During the Civil War, the house was used as a hospital for Union soldiers. (Courtesy of the Baton Rouge Room of East Baton Rouge Public Library.)

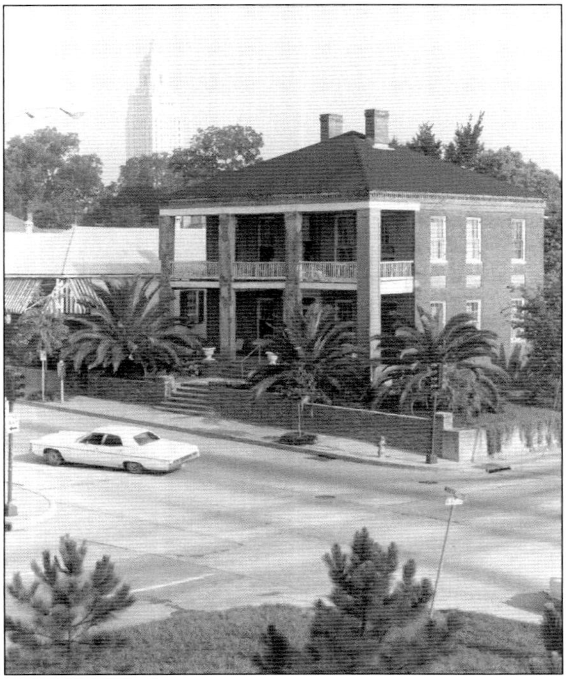

One of Spanish Town's most impressive homes was built in the 1850s by Nelson Potts. A New Jersey native, Potts was a brick maker who came to Baton Rouge to ply his trade. The home he built at 829 North Street featured four rooms and a central hall on each floor. Potts also built the Stewart-Dougherty House on North Street. (Courtesy of the Baton Rouge Room of East Baton Rouge Public Library.)

Three

Civil War

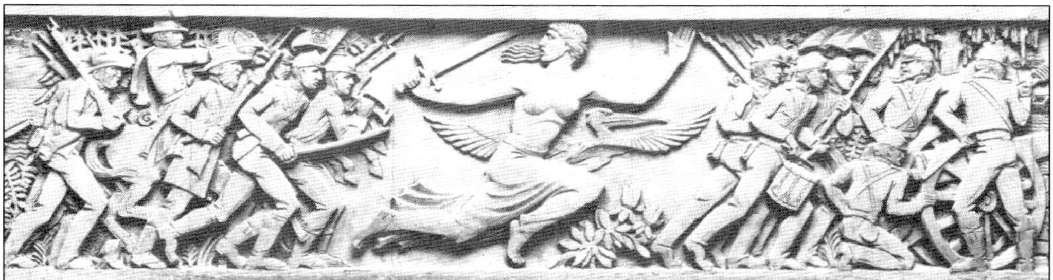

In mid-April 1862, Union forces captured New Orleans and directed their attention to Baton Rouge. The state legislature, understanding that the Confederate army had neither the means nor ability to defend the city, fled to Opelousas at the end of the month. By the end of May, Baton Rouge would earn the distinction of becoming the first capital of a seceding state to be captured by Union forces. On August 5, 1862, approximately 5,000 Confederate troops under Maj. Gen. John C. Breckinridge engaged a similar number of Union troops in the Battle of Baton Rouge in an unsuccessful effort to recapture the city. The battle was fought on the outskirts of town, in what is now the area around the National Cemetery between Nineteenth and Twenty-Second Streets. In the weeks that followed, Union general Benjamin Butler gave the order to destroy houses around the garrison in Spanish Town, giving Baton Rouge the additional distinction of becoming the first Confederate state capital to be burned by Union troops. (Courtesy of the Foundation for Historical Louisiana.)

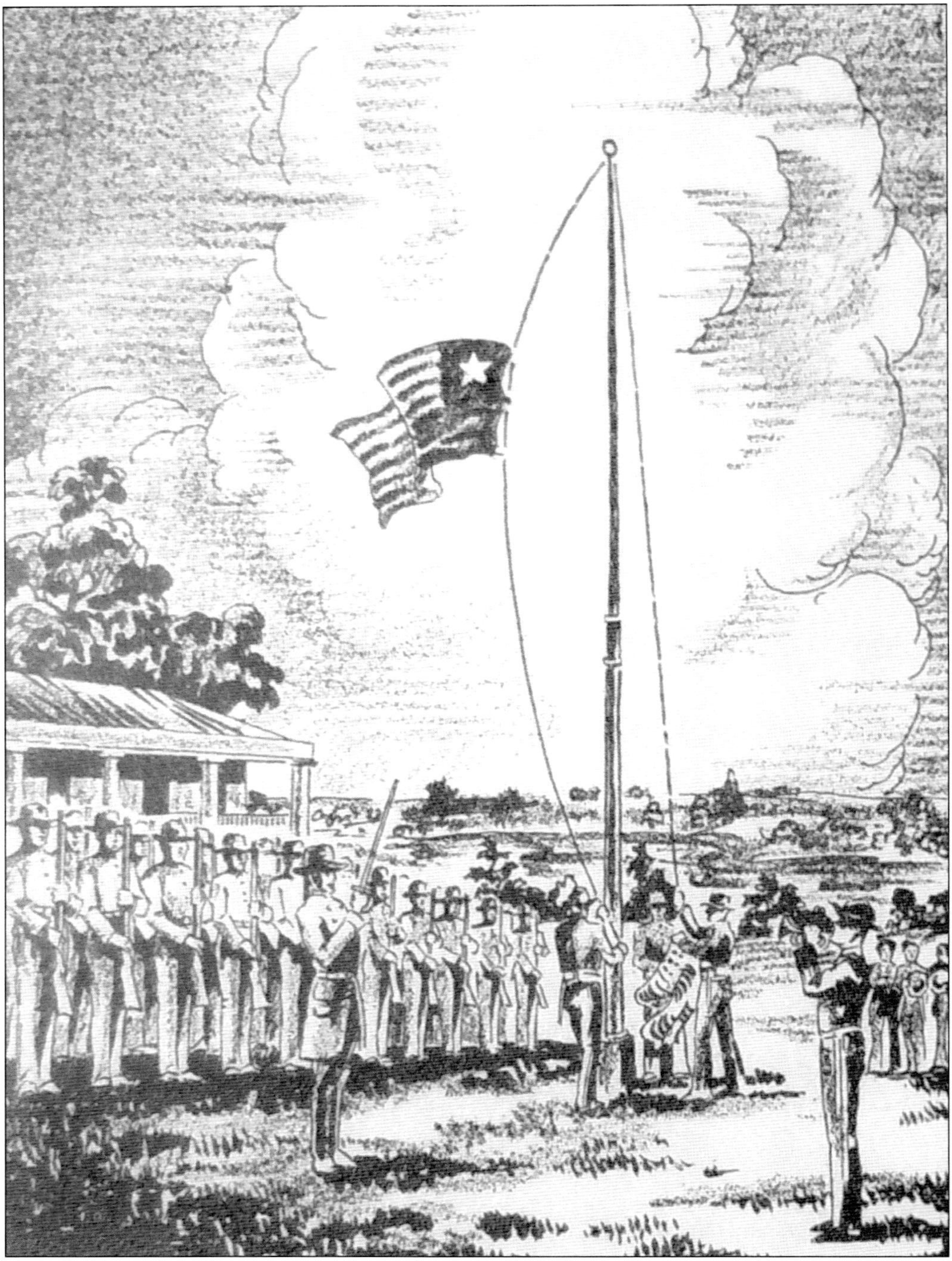

Seventeen days prior to Louisiana's declaration of secession on January 26, 1861, Gov. Thomas O. Moore ordered the state militia to seize the Baton Rouge garrison. His order arrived too late, as the garrison commander had already ordered munitions and arms to be removed. This drawing from the 1930 LSU *Gumbo* shows the lowering of the flag at the Pentagon Barracks. (Courtesy of the Special Collections of the LSU Libraries.)

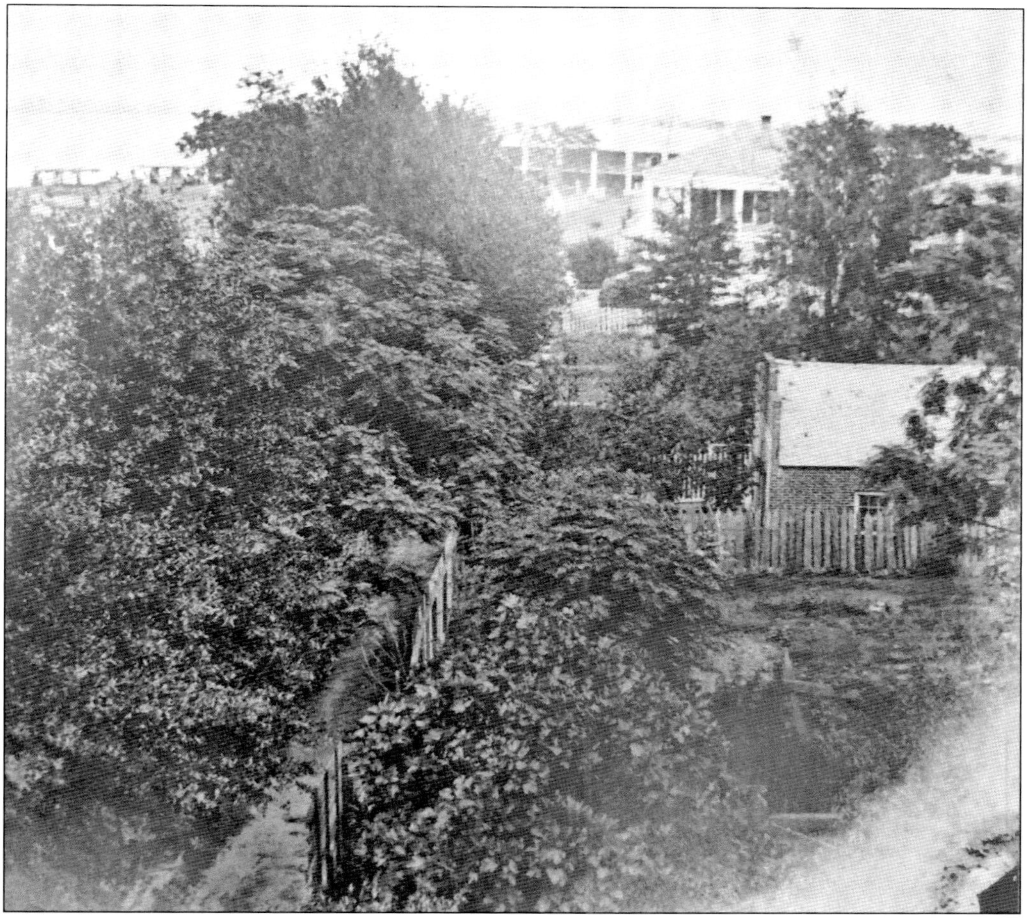

Andrew D. Lytle moved to Baton Rouge in 1857 and began a career in photography that would continue to the end of the century. This bucolic photograph of the Pentagon Barracks from 1861 was taken from the upper story of a building on Main Street. In the following year, several of these buildings were burned and the garrison was dotted with the tents of occupying troops. (Courtesy of the Foundation for Historical Louisiana.)

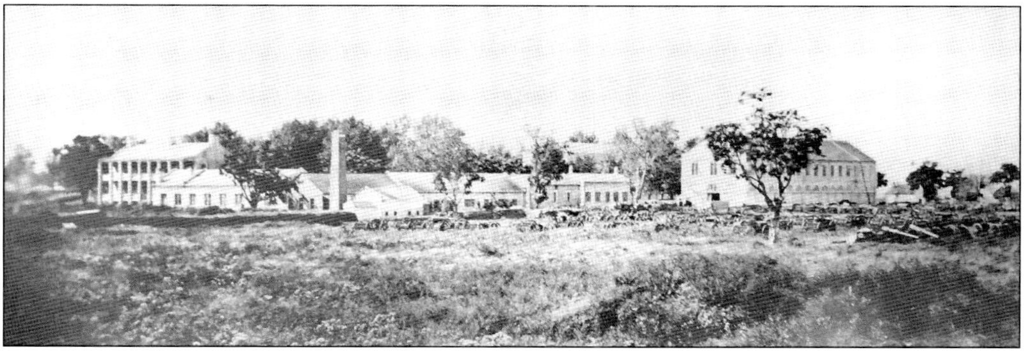

This photograph of the garrison from the 1850s shows the Colony Barracks at far left and the main arsenal building at far right. The smaller buildings in between contain machine shops, storehouses, and offices. (Courtesy of the Foundation for Historical Louisiana.)

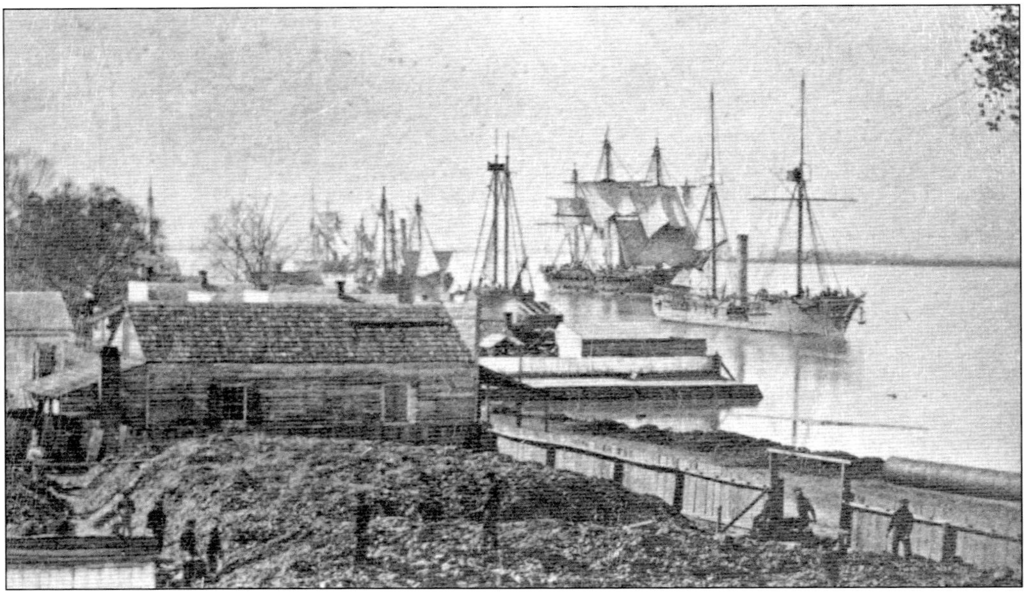

On May 28, 1862, James B. Kimball, chief engineer of the USS *Hartford*, seen here at Baton Rouge in 1863, was ambushed and killed. In retaliation, Adm. David Farragut shelled the city, destroying several homes and killing four women. In the 1970s, a renovation of the Stewart-Dougherty House on North Street revealed a cannonball that had lodged in the attic during the attack. (Courtesy of the Library of Congress.)

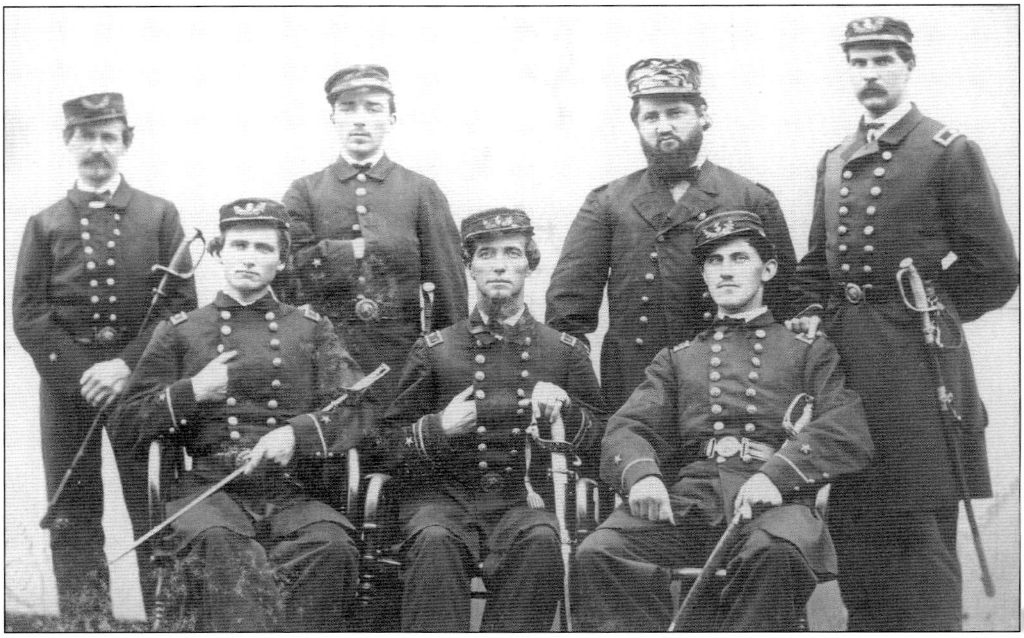

Other Union soldiers and sailors were more courteously received in the city. This photograph from 1862 shows Union sailors posing for a group photograph at the studio of Baton Rouge photographer Andrew D. Lytle. (Courtesy of Andrew D. Lytle Collection, Mss. 893, 1254, Louisiana and Lower Mississippi Valley Collections, LSU Libraries.)

The Union commander in Baton Rouge was Brig. Gen. Thomas Williams, a native of Albany, New York. On May 29, 1862, General Williams led six regiments of infantry, two artillery batteries, and a troop of cavalry into the city and began the occupation of Baton Rouge. (Courtesy of the Library of Congress.)

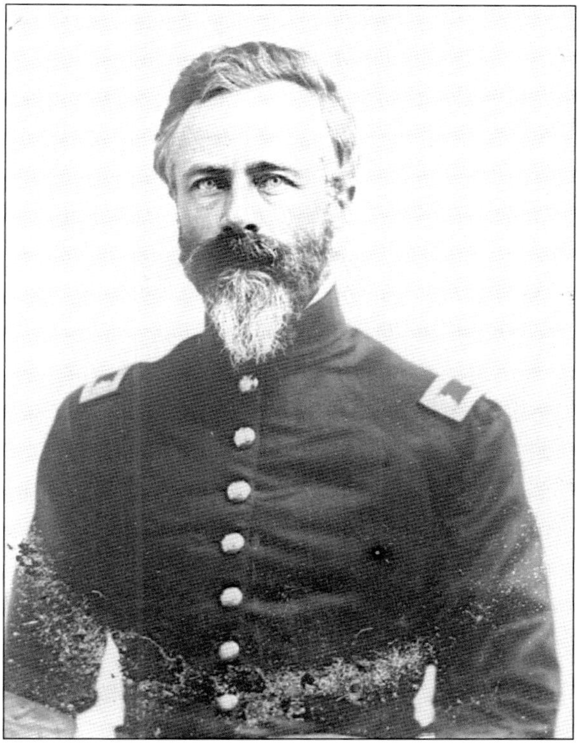

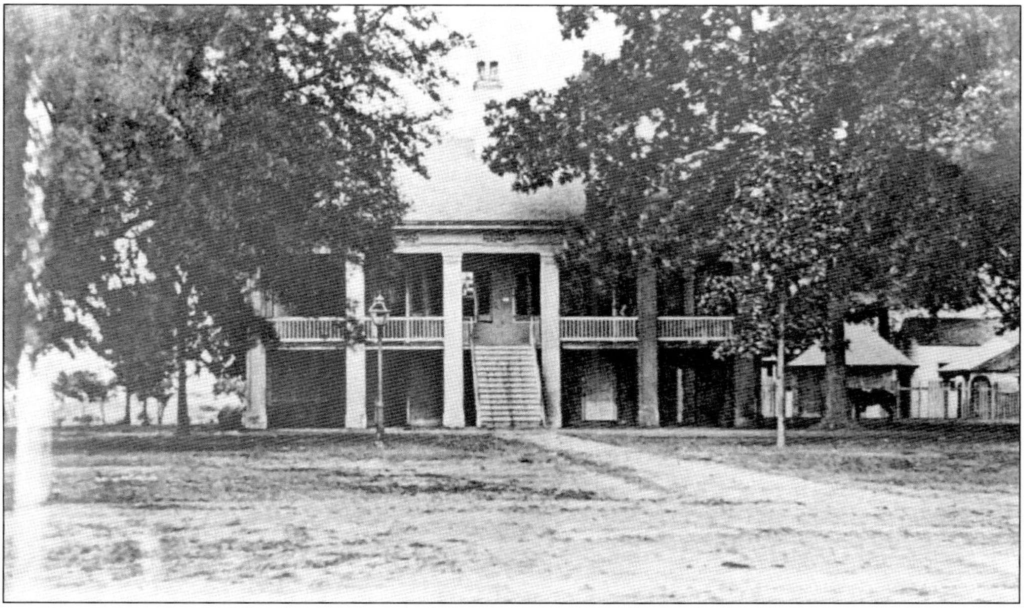

On August 5, 1862, Williams led approximately 2,500 Union troops against a similar number of Confederates. Never a popular commander, he was killed in the fighting, rumored by some to be the work of his own men. After the battle, the garrison was renamed Fort Williams in his honor. The Commandant's House is shown here in 1863. (Courtesy of the Louisiana Collection of the State Library of Louisiana.)

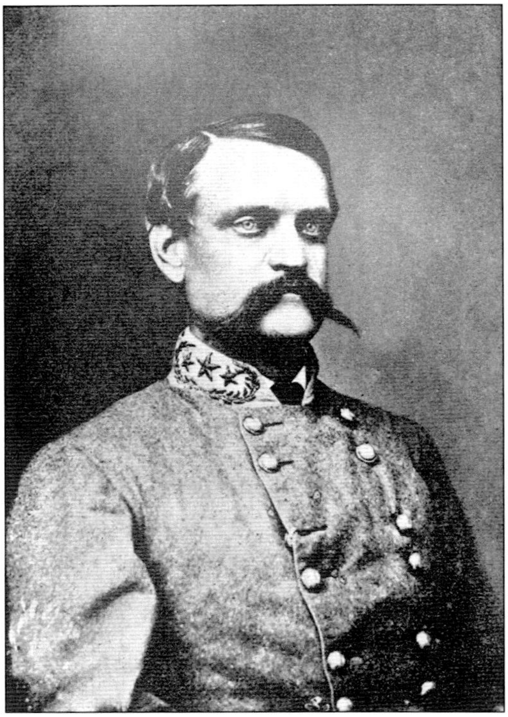

The man who failed to retake Baton Rouge for the Confederacy was Maj. Gen. John C. Breckinridge. A native of Kentucky, Breckinridge had finished second in the Presidential election of 1860. In 1864, Jefferson Davis promoted him to secretary of war, where he quickly determined that the war could not be won and urged Davis to arrange a national surrender. (Courtesy of the Archives of Florida.)

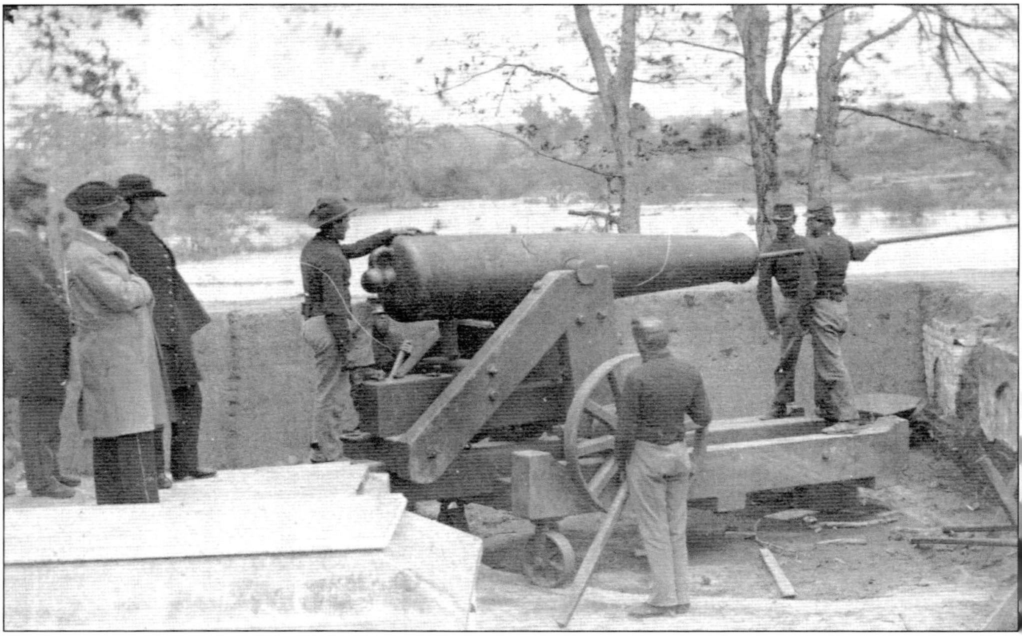

This photograph was taken during the war on the Indian Mound near the Arsenal in Capitol Park. As the tombstones suggest, the mound had been used since the 1830s as a burial site for US military officers. The tombs were moved to the Baton Rouge National Cemetery in 1867. (Courtesy of G.H. Suydam Collection, Mss. 1394, Louisiana and Lower Mississippi Valley Collections, LSU Libraries.)

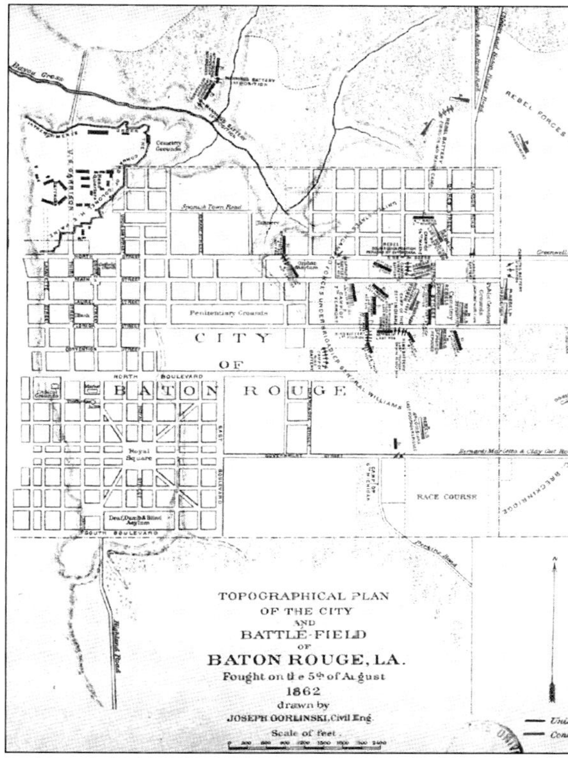

Most of the Battle of Baton Rouge was fought to the east of the city, around Florida Avenue and Nineteenth Street. The site is now the US National Cemetery, where many of those who died in the battle are buried. This map shows that there were Union soldiers placed between North Street and Spanish Town Road to protect the garrison. (Courtesy of the Foundation for Historical Louisiana.)

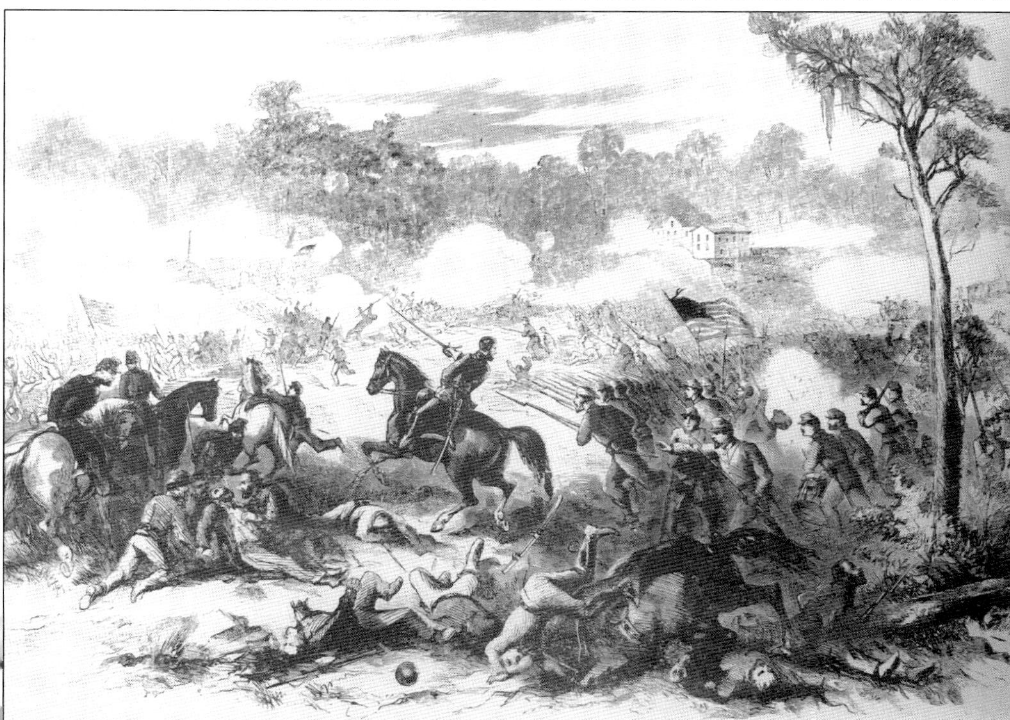

While many historians suggest the Battle of Baton Rouge was a minor skirmish, this lithograph from *Harper's Weekly* magazine in 1862 shows that it meant life or death to those who participated in it. Perhaps the only suggestion that this scene was in Baton Rouge and not another scene of carnage in the brutal war is the Spanish moss hanging in the trees. (Courtesy of the Foundation for Historical Louisiana.)

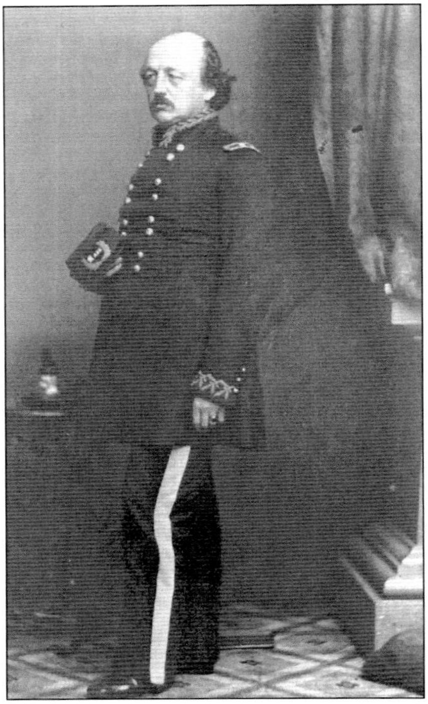

One week after the battle, Williams's successor, Maj. Gen. Benjamin Butler, ordered a number of houses around the garrison destroyed so that Confederate guerillas could not use them as shelter in a surprise attack. Butler also helped to establish the legal precedent of effectively freeing fugitive slaves as contraband in service of military objectives. (Courtesy of the Foundation for Historical Louisiana.)

Butler's orders doomed almost all of the buildings in Spanish Town except for a few homes along North Street that were being used by the Union army as hospitals and housing for officers, troops, and nurses. This photograph from shortly after the battle shows houses that had been deliberately destroyed. (Courtesy of the Andrew D. Lytle Collection, Mss. 893, 1254, Louisiana and Lower Mississippi Valley Collections, LSU Libraries.)

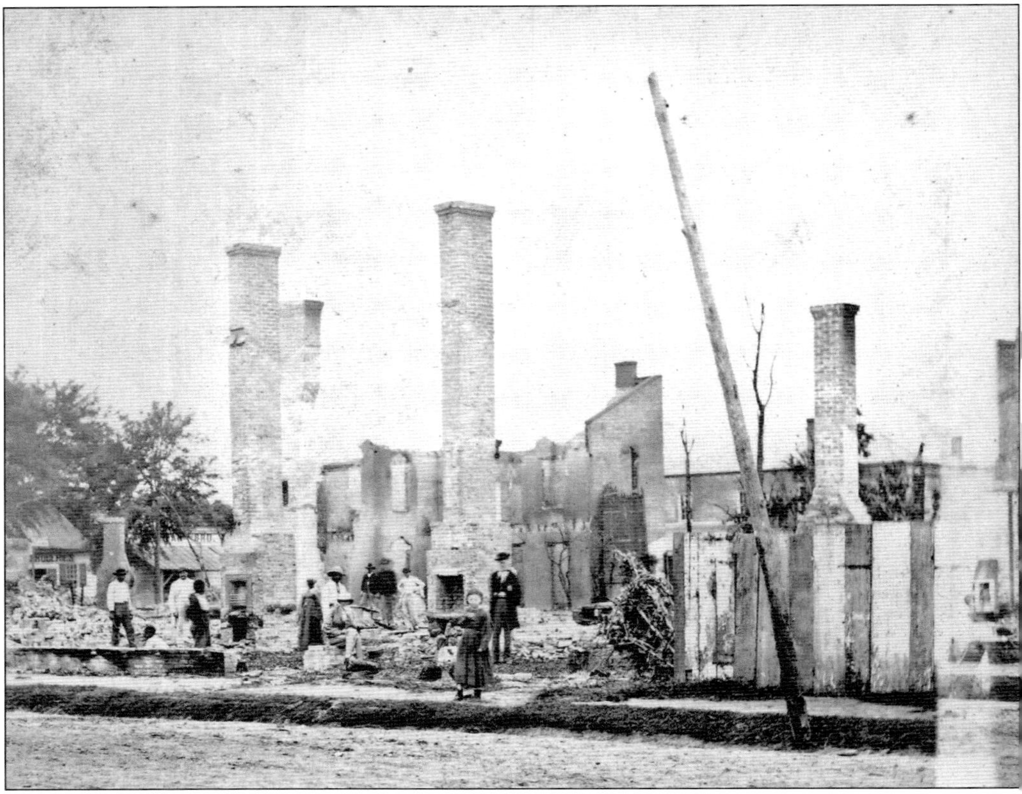

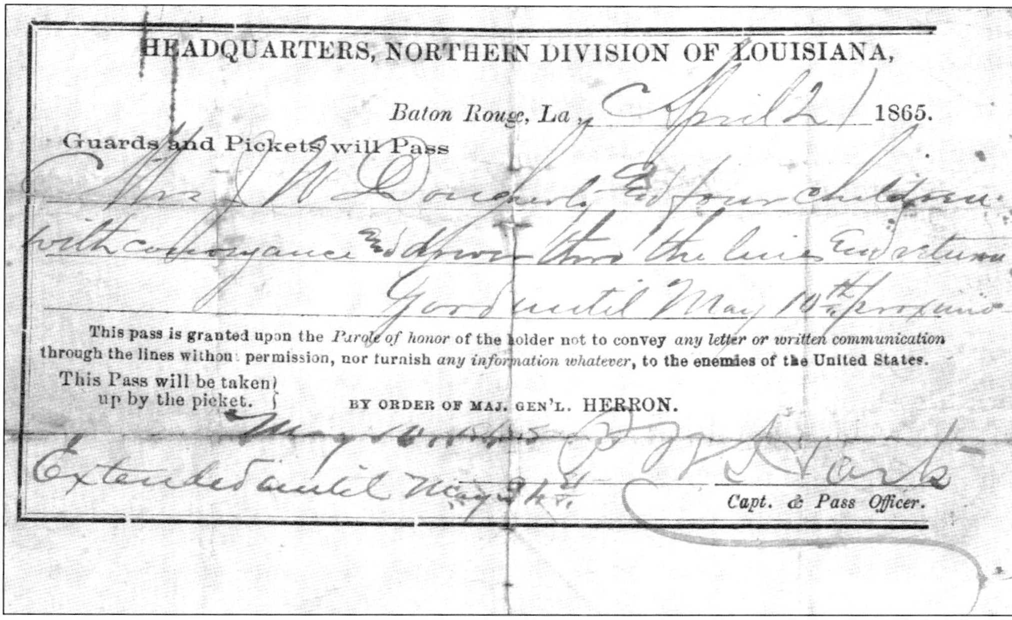

HEADQUARTERS, NORTHERN DIVISION OF LOUISIANA,

Baton Rouge, La., April 21 1865.

Guards and Pickets will Pass

Mrs J W Dougherty and four children with conveyance and driver thro the lines and return

Good until May 10th proximo

This pass is granted upon the *Parole of honor* of the holder not to convey *any letter or written communication* through the lines without permission, nor furnish *any information whatever*, to the enemies of the United States.

This Pass will be taken up by the picket.

BY ORDER OF MAJ. GEN'L. HERRON.

Capt. & Pass Officer.

Even after burning many of the homes around the garrison, Union occupiers remained suspicious of the residents who remained. As the Stewart-Dougherty House on North Street was being used as a Union hospital, its owner, Nellie Dougherty was issued this pass to come and go on the base. (Courtesy of Mrs. J.W. Dougherty Pass, Mss. 893, Louisiana and Lower Mississippi Valley Collections, LSU Libraries.)

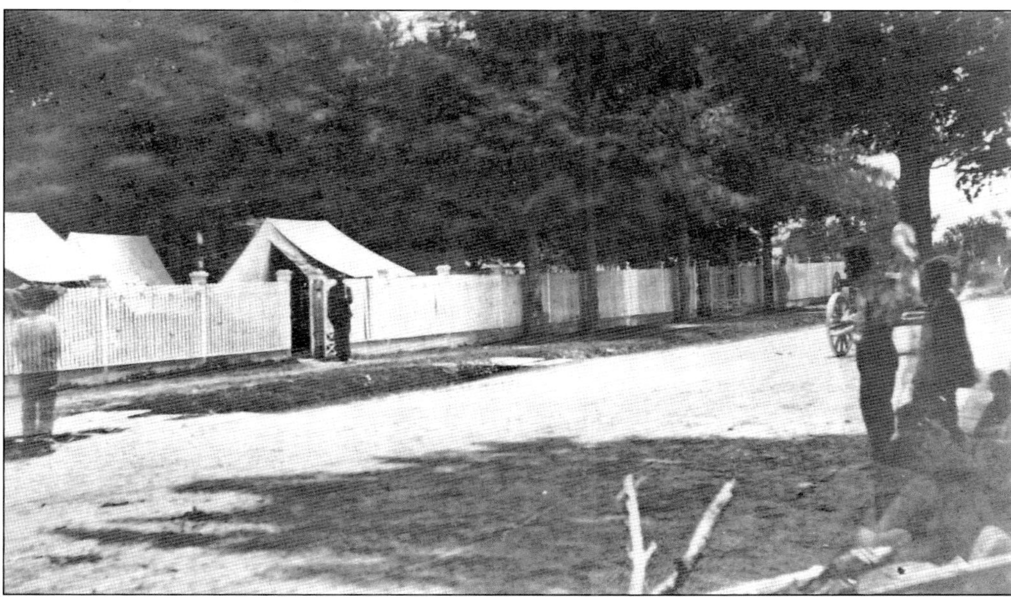

During the course of the war, the camps of Union troops stationed at Fort Williams spilled out into the areas surrounding the garrison. This photograph from 1864 shows tents along North Street near the site of the Catholic-Presbyterian Apartments between Sixth and Seventh Streets. (Courtesy of Marshall Dunham Photograph Album, Mss. 3241, Louisiana and Lower Mississippi Valley Collections, LSU Libraries.)

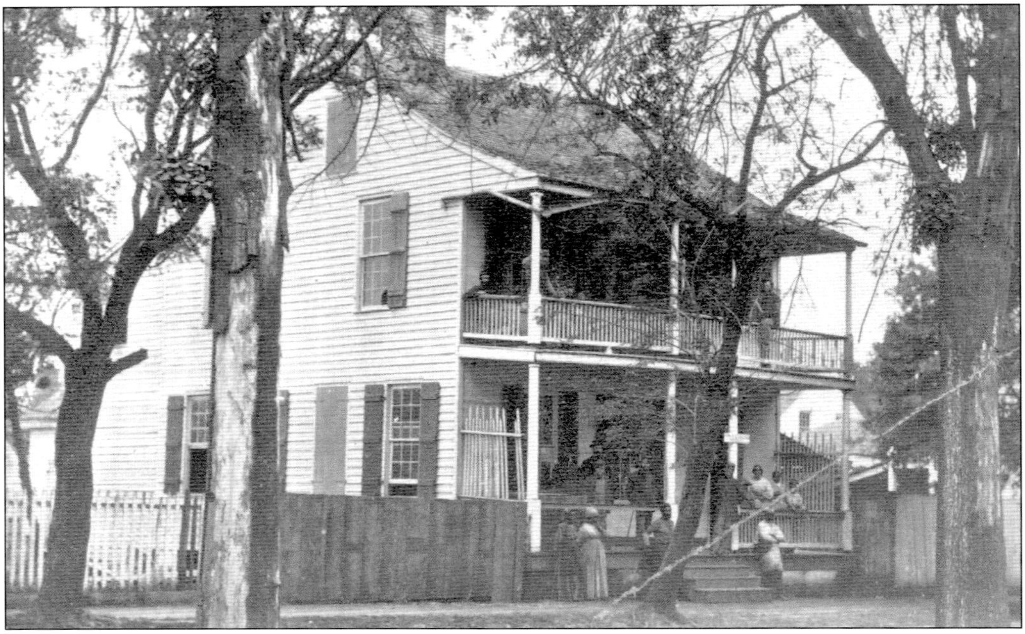

The first contraband camp in Baton Rouge was established on North Street at the site of the former Catholic schools between Fourth and Sixth Streets. After many of the newly freed slaves were released from the camps, they began to take up residence in burned out or abandoned homes in Spanish Town. (Courtesy of G.H. Suydam Collection, Mss. 1394, Louisiana and Lower Mississippi Valley Collections, LSU Libraries.)

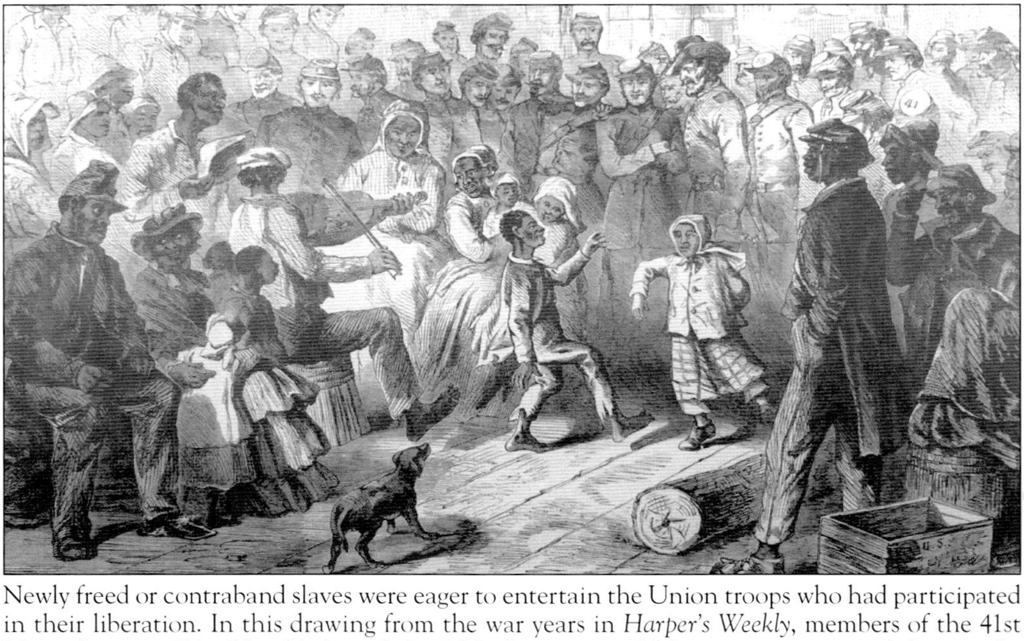

Newly freed or contraband slaves were eager to entertain the Union troops who had participated in their liberation. In this drawing from the war years in *Harper's Weekly*, members of the 41st Massachusetts, 131st New York, and the 25th Connecticut Volunteers enjoy an exhibition of a dance called the breakdown at the armory building at the garrison. (Courtesy of the Louisiana Collection of the State Library of Louisiana.)

Four

Reconstruction and the Ole War Skule

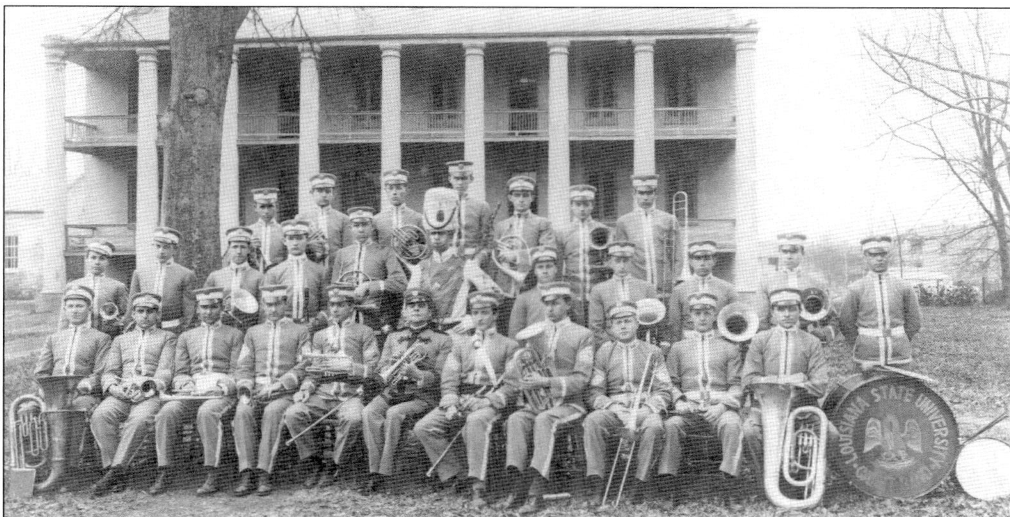

At the end of the Civil War, the garrison known as Fort Williams stretched across the northern end of what is now Capitol Park. Principal buildings included an armory, two powder magazines, a hospital, and barracks at the Pentagon and Colony. These buildings would soon find new purpose. Downtown Baton Rouge was not the first home of Louisiana State University, nor would it be the last. The university was originally established near Pineville in 1853 by the legislature as the Seminary of Learning for the State of Louisiana. The school's first superintendent was an army general named William T. Sherman, who would leave less than a year later when Louisiana seceded from the Union. The school shut down during the war but reopened in 1865. Fire destroyed the campus in 1869, and the seminary was forced to move "temporarily" to Baton Rouge. The school shared a campus in Beauregard Town with the State Institute for the Deaf, Mute, and Blind. More than a decade later, the university was finally given the grounds of the Baton Rouge Garrison. Former military buildings like the Pentagon and Colony Barracks were part of the campus until the university moved to its present home in South Baton Rouge in the mid-1920s. The LSU Cadet Band is pictured here at the Colony in 1912. (Courtesy of Louisiana State University Photograph Collection, A5000, Louisiana State University Archives, LSU Libraries.)

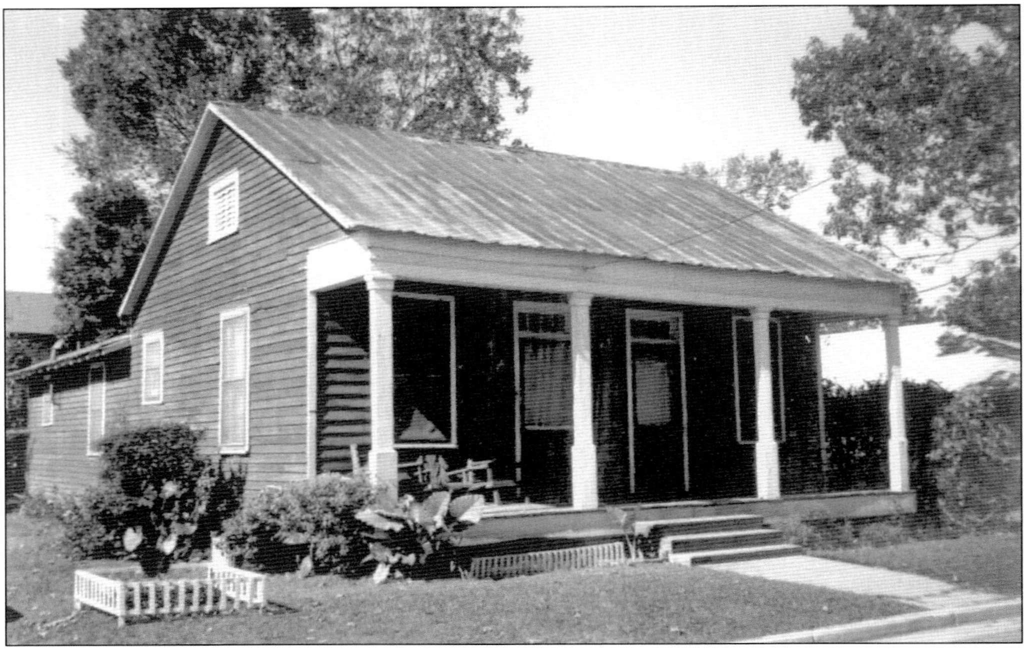

This Victorian cottage at 835 North Seventh Street is one of the first new homes built in Spanish Town after the Civil War. George Thompson, an African American sawmill owner, built the house for his family in the early 1870s. Thompson was one of many African Americans who gravitated to Spanish Town in the years after the Civil War to build a new life. (Courtesy of the Baton Rouge Room of East Baton Rouge Public Library.)

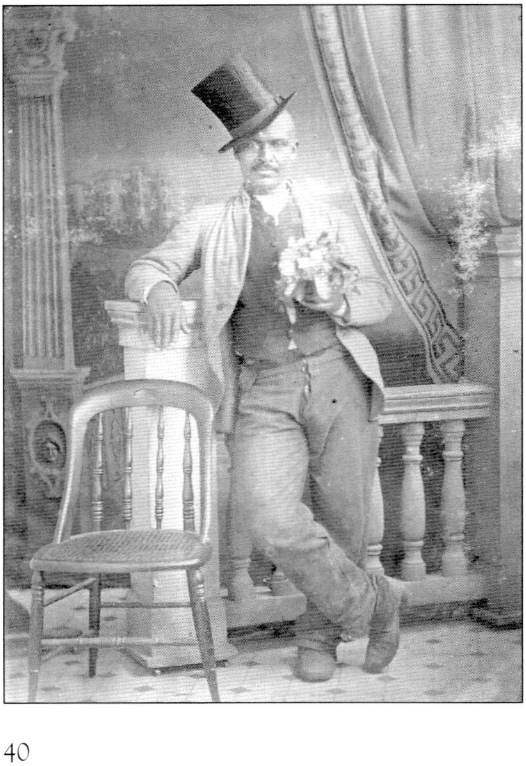

Little is known of this dapper gent except that his name was Scot Gordon and he lived on North Street near the ferry landing. It is believed that he worked at a nearby sawmill. He was one of many African Americans who gravitated to Spanish Town in the aftermath of the Civil War. (Courtesy of Andrew D. Lytle Collection, Mss. 893, 1254, Louisiana and Lower Mississippi Valley Collections, LSU Libraries.)

In 1872, the first known church in Spanish Town was established when Rev. George Byrd from Virginia and his congregation laid the cornerstone for the first Shiloh Missionary Baptist Church. The church grew and prospered in Spanish Town before moving to a larger home on Fourteenth Street, now Eddie Robinson Sr. Drive. (Courtesy of Shiloh Missionary Baptist Church.)

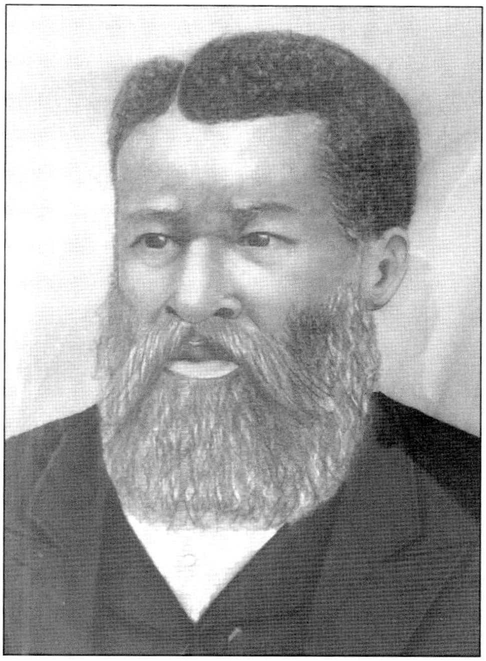

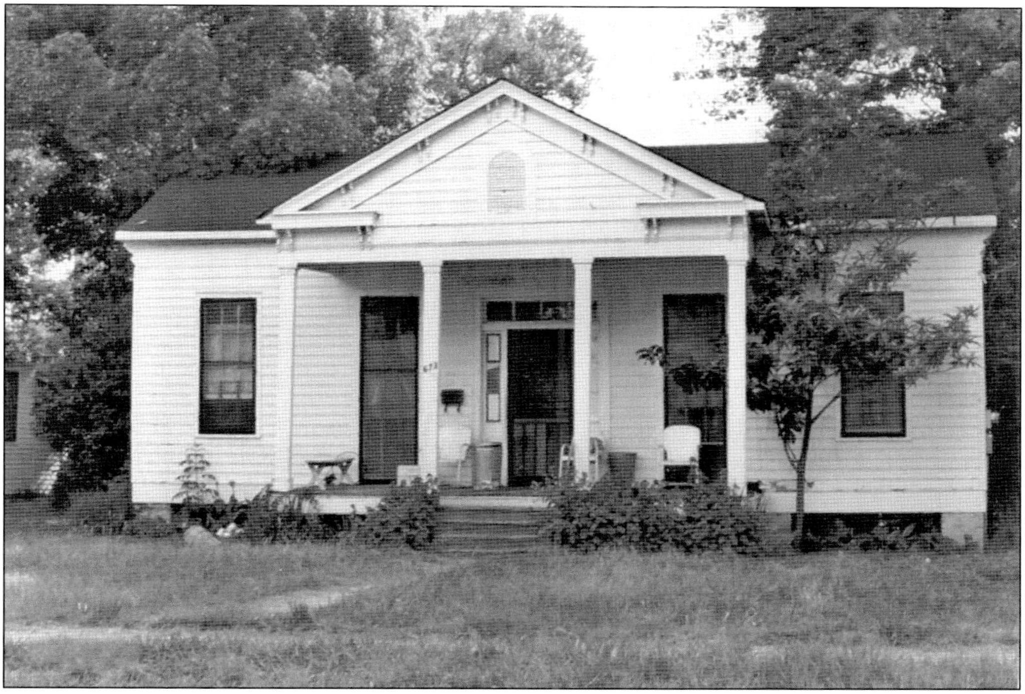

Like many homes built in Spanish Town in the 1800s, this cottage at 673 North Seventh Street was constructed from raft timbers floated down the Mississippi River and broken up for sale. The house was built shortly before or after the Civil War by Abraham Byrd for the minister of the First Presbyterian Church and is still referred to as the Presbyterian Minister's House. (Courtesy of the Baton Rouge Room of East Baton Rouge Public Library.)

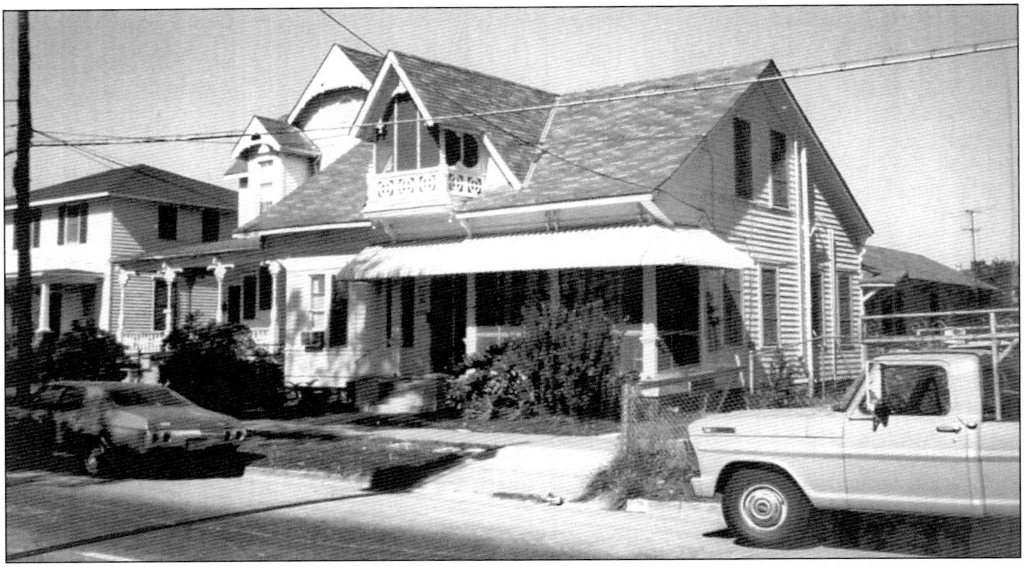

This stick-style home was built by Confederate veteran Henry Gentles around 1875 at 547 North Street. Gentles was active in postwar politics in the city and owned and operated the Mississippi River ferry at the foot of North Street. (Courtesy of the Baton Rouge Room of East Baton Rouge Public Library.)

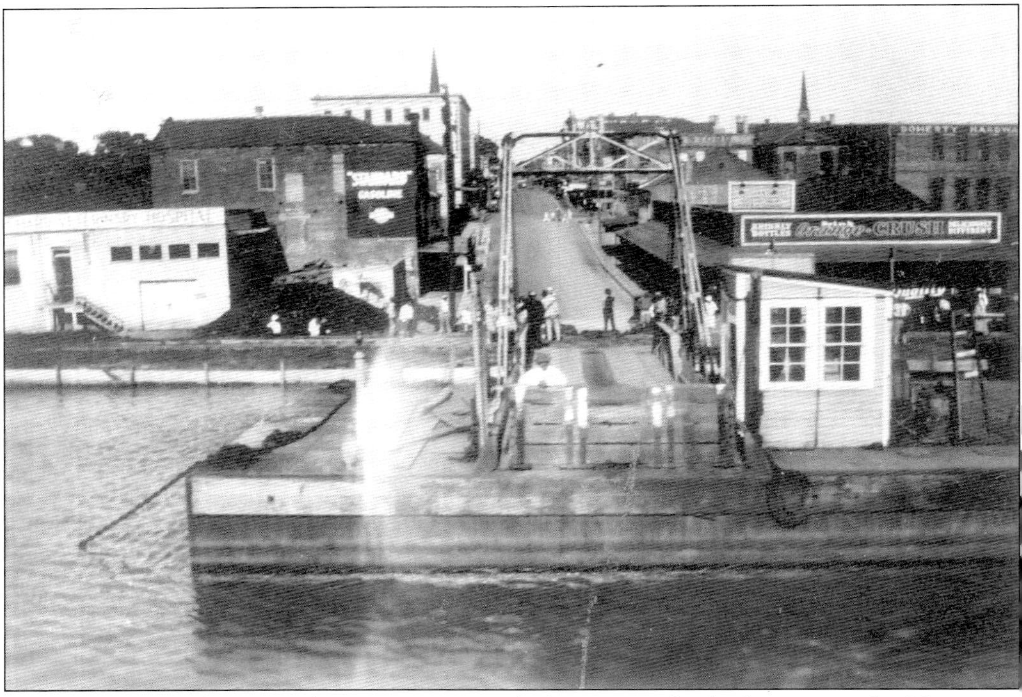

The North Street ferry was the primary means for humans and vehicles to cross the Mississippi River until the Huey P. Long–O.K. Allen Bridge was completed in 1940. The ferry landing, shown here in 1917, continued in operation until the Horace Wilkinson Bridge opened in downtown Baton Rouge in 1968. (Courtesy of the Foundation for Historical Louisiana.)

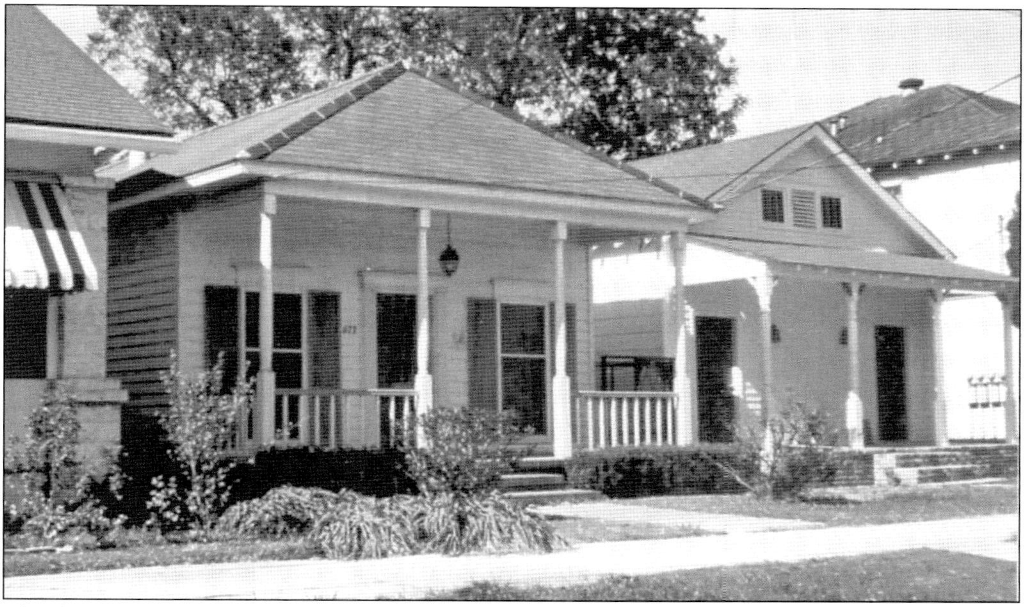

This home at 673 North Eighth Street has been called both the Bonnecaze House and the J. Clifford Yaun House over the years. It was built in 1881 by Joseph Brooks and divided into two shotgun-style cottages after 1908. In the early 1900s, it was home to Daniel Webster Lusk, captain of Henry Gentles's Baton Rouge ferry. (Courtesy of the Baton Rouge Room of East Baton Rouge Public Library.)

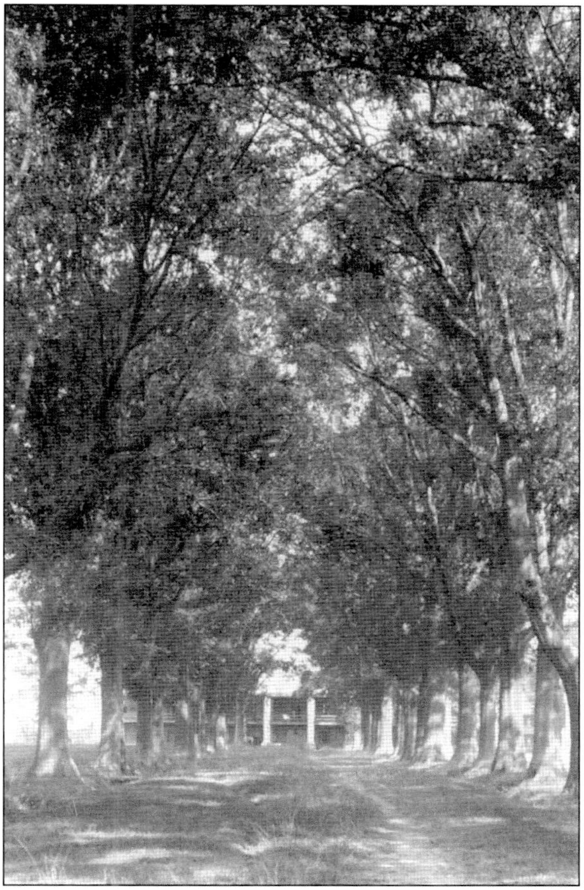

The main entrance to the campus from downtown Baton Rouge was along this avenue of oaks along Lafayette Street. (Courtesy of Louisiana State University Photograph Collection, A5000, Louisiana State University Archives, LSU Libraries.)

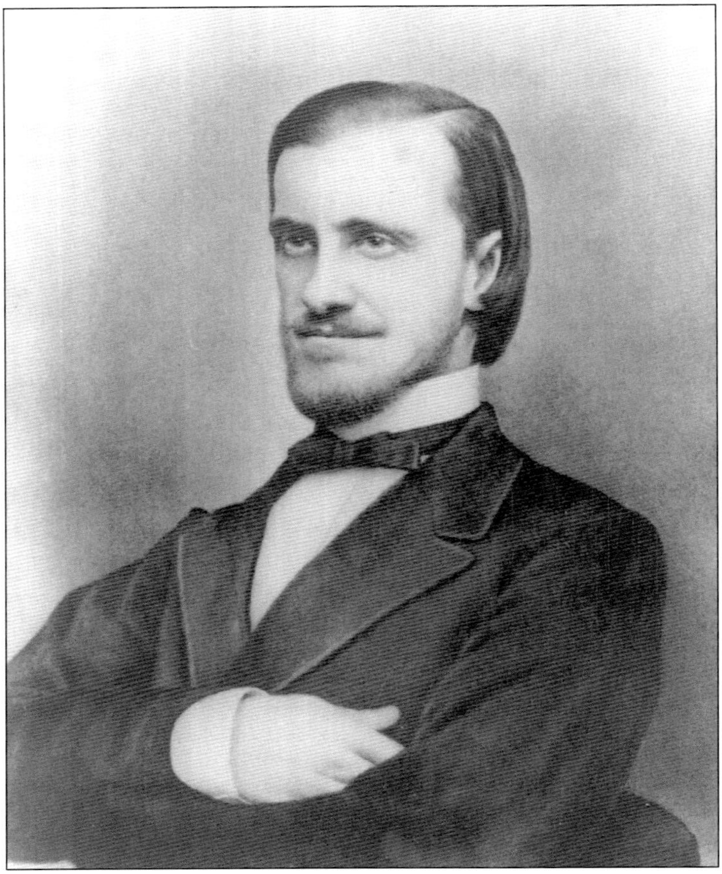

A member of the original faculty of the Seminary of Learning of the State of Louisiana, David French Boyd moved to Baton Rouge with the school after fire destroyed the Rapides Parish campus. He served as superintendent of the seminary from 1865 until 1880 and as LSU president from 1884 until 1886, when he was succeeded by his brother, Thomas Duckett Boyd. (Courtesy of the Foundation for Historical Louisiana.)

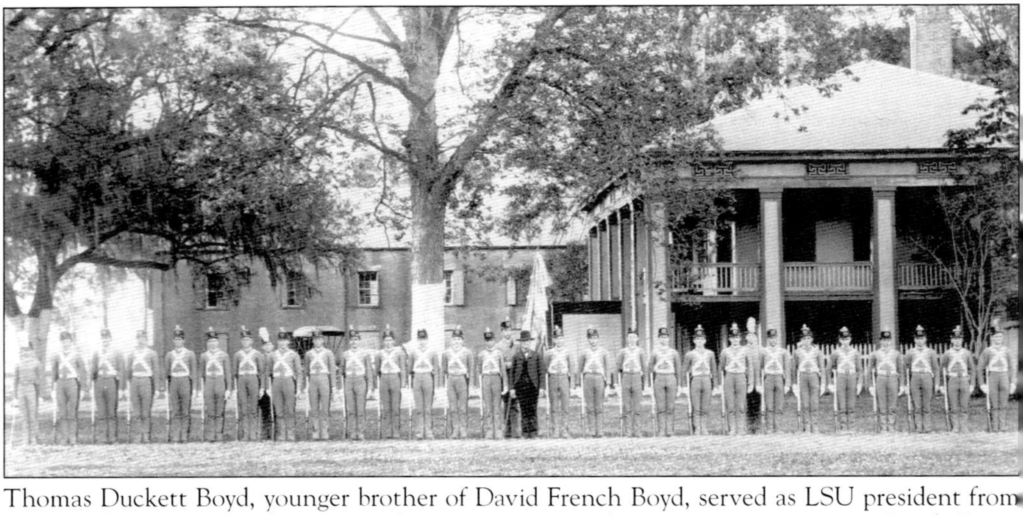

Thomas Duckett Boyd, younger brother of David French Boyd, served as LSU president from 1886 until 1926. During his tenure, the university moved to its present campus in South Baton Rouge. Boyd is seen here in front of the President's House with the company of cadets judged to be the university's best in 1887. (Courtesy of Louisiana State University Photograph Collection, A5000, Louisiana State University Archives, LSU Libraries.)

Almost 20 years after Gen. William T. Sherman served as the first superintendent of the Seminary of Learning of the State of Louisiana, he returned to LSU for a visit in 1879 and agreed to use his influence with the War Department to secure the abandoned garrison as a new LSU campus. (Courtesy of Louisiana State University Photograph Collection, A5000, Louisiana State University Archives, LSU Libraries.)

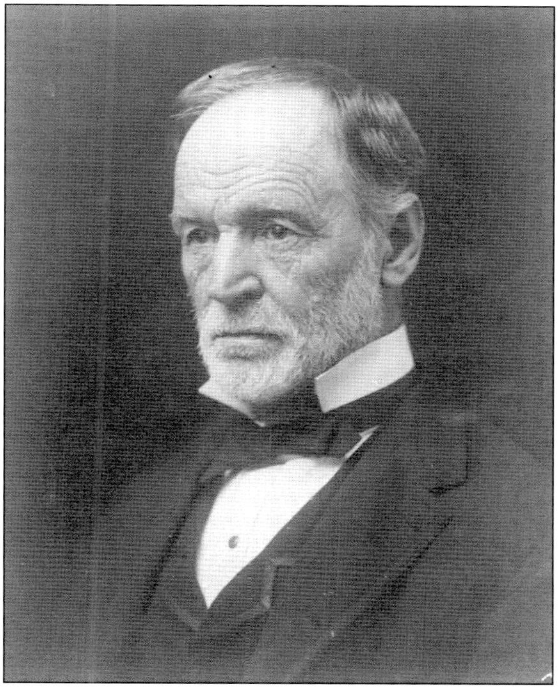

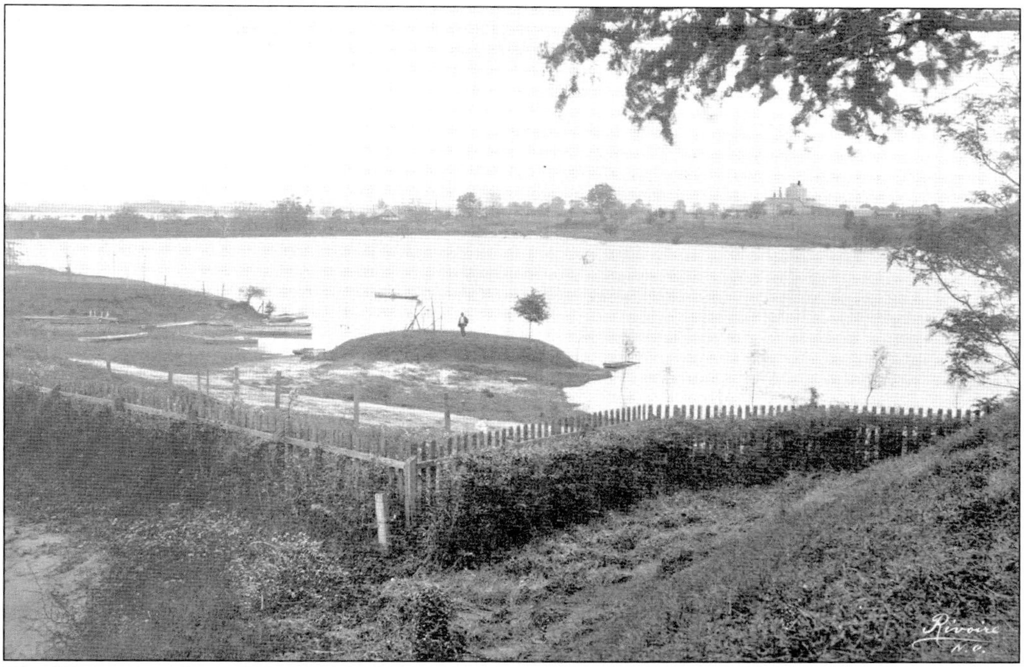

The bayou that flowed into the Mississippi River north of the campus was dammed up and the lake that is now Capitol Lake began to form. During the years that LSU occupied the downtown campus, it was referred to as University Lake. It was renamed when the new State Capitol was built. (Courtesy of Louisiana State University Photograph Collection, A5000, Louisiana State University Archives, LSU Libraries.)

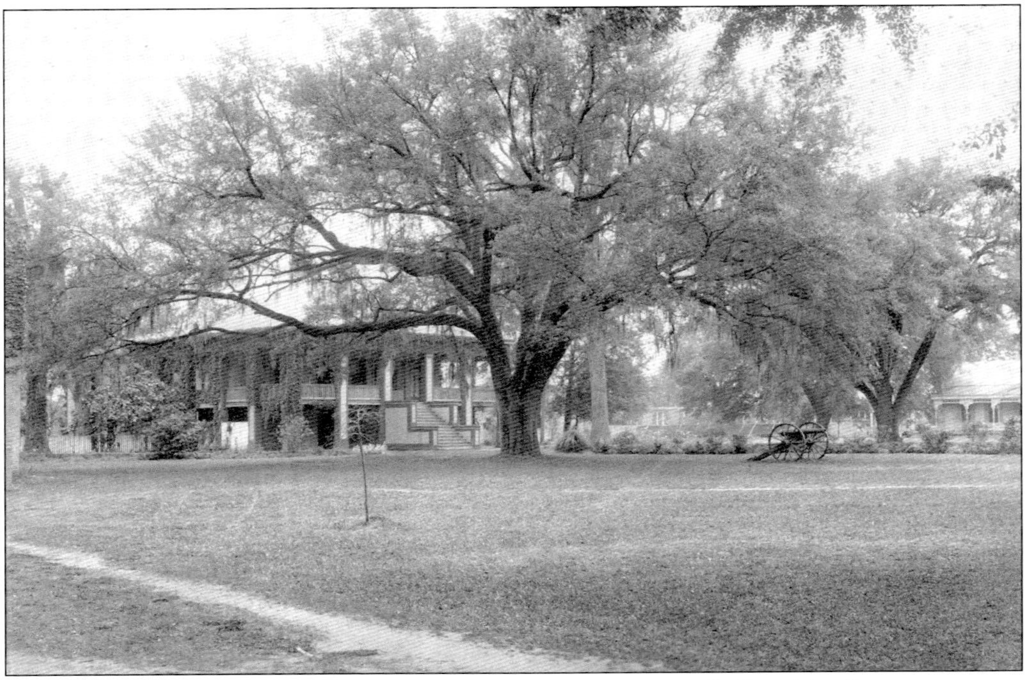

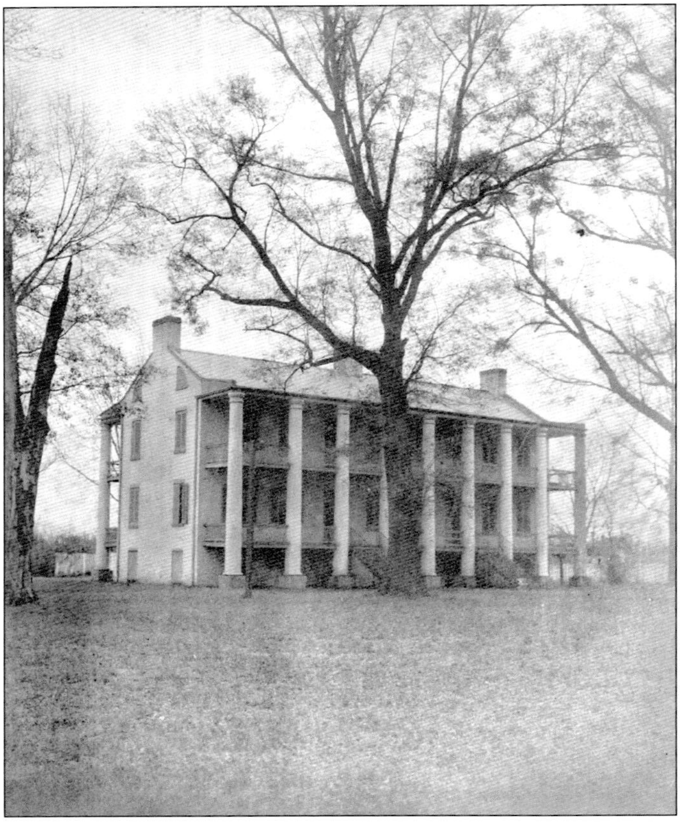

Built originally to serve as the home of the commander of the Baton Rouge garrison, this home later become the President's House at LSU. (Courtesy of the Collections of the Louisiana State Museum.)

Like the Pentagon Barracks, the Colony Barracks at the garrison served as housing for LSU students until the university moved to its new campus in the early 1920s. (Courtesy of the Collections of the Louisiana State Museum.)

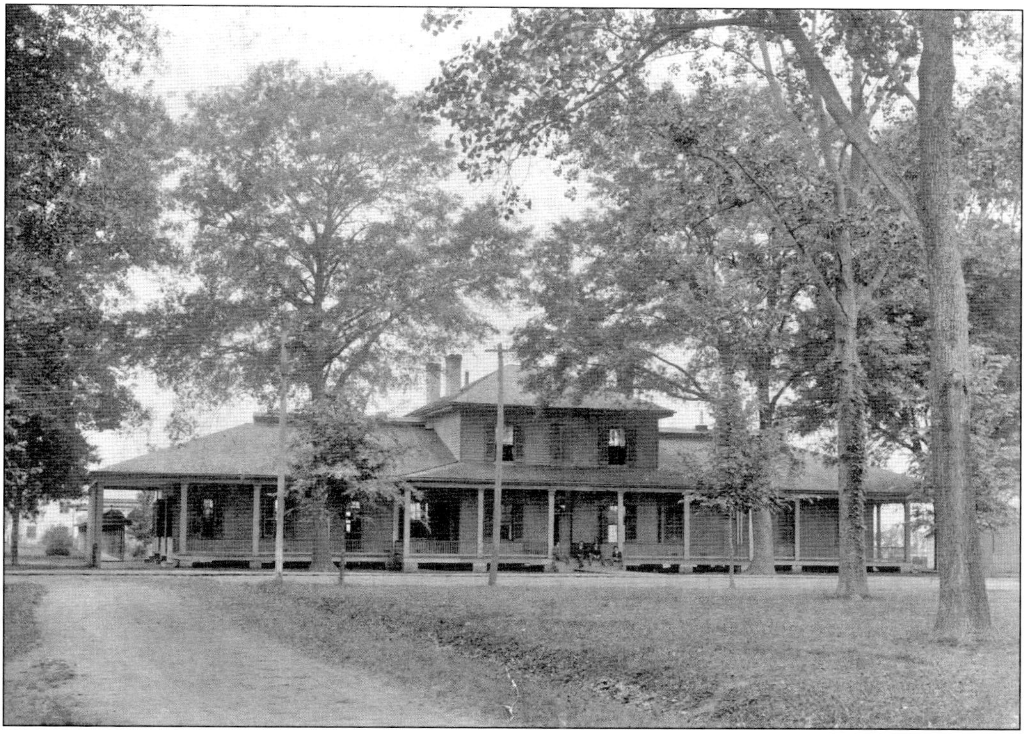

LSU Hospital dates from the US garrison, when it was originally built to be a hospital. It served as the mess for cadets until a new mess facility could be built at Foster Hall. Afterward, the building reverted to its original use as a hospital. (Courtesy of the Collections of the Louisiana State Museum.)

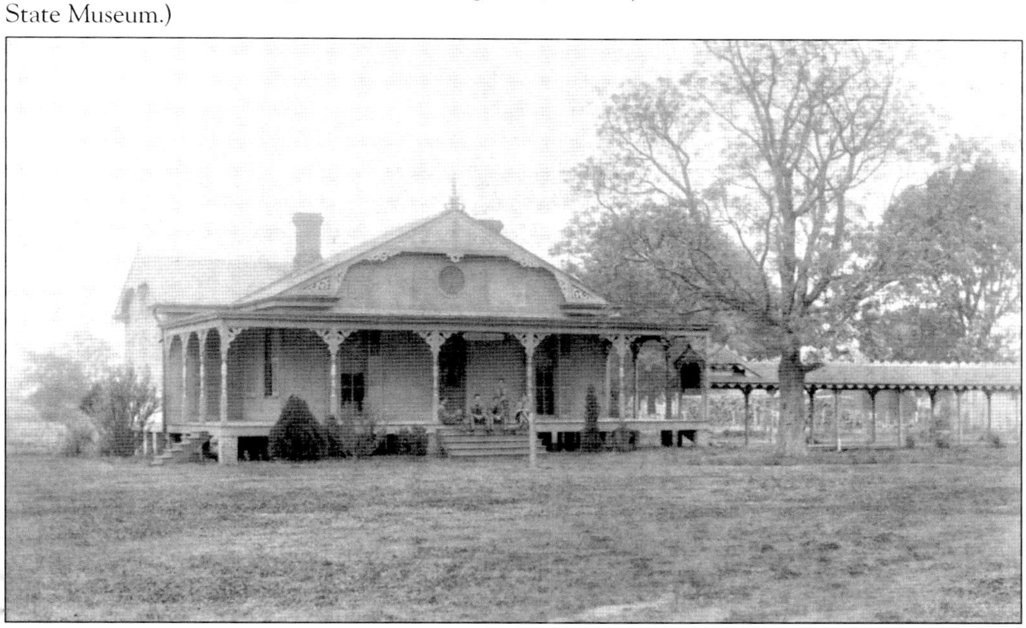

An old arsenal building near the garrison hospital was used as a surgeon's laboratory for the hospital. (Courtesy of the Collections of the Louisiana State Museum.)

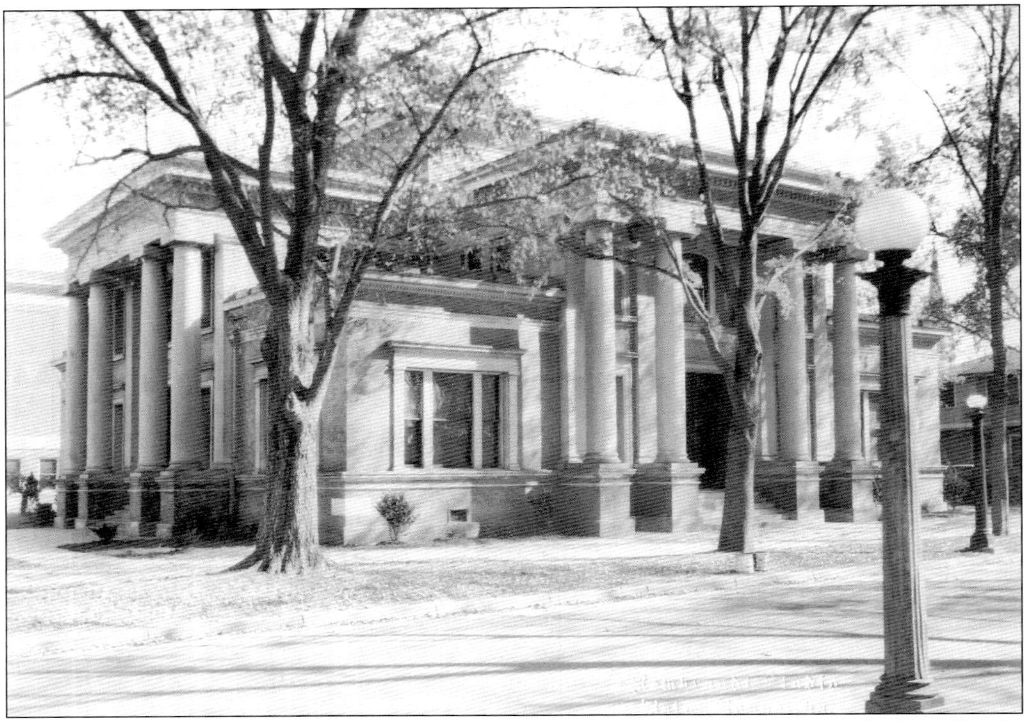

Alumni Hall on the LSU campus served as the office of the university president and other officials. It was built with funds donated by alumni to honor Pres. David French Boyd. (Courtesy of the Louisiana Collection of the State Library of Louisiana.)

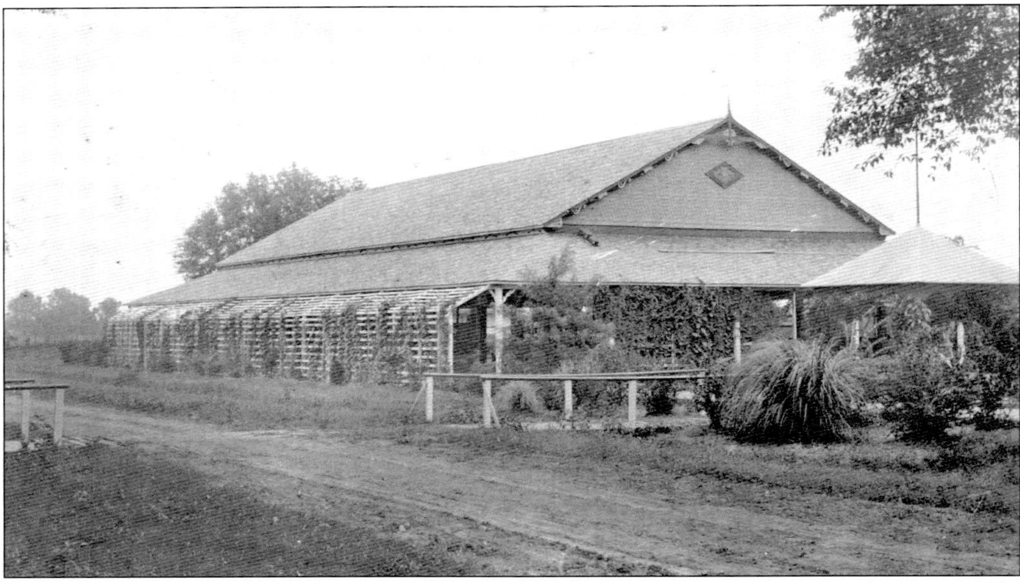

The Pavilion at LSU was a gift of the managers of the Louisiana State Fair in 1887 and 1888. Initially, it was used for social functions, including an address by presidential candidate William Jennings Bryan in 1896. Later, walls were added and the building was used as a lecture hall and finally a women's dormitory. (Courtesy of Louisiana Collection of the State Library of Louisiana.)

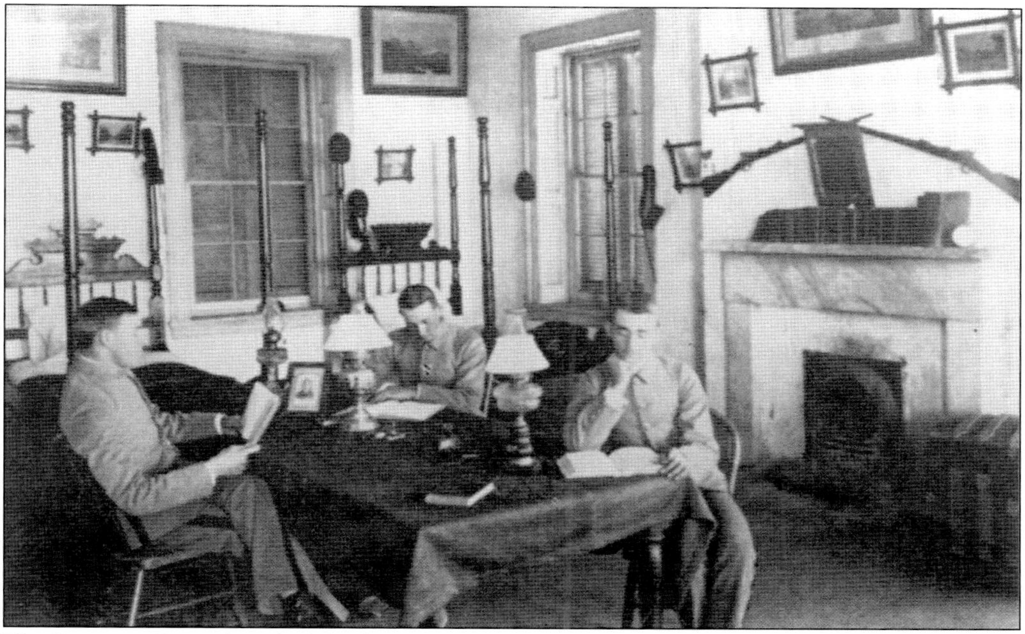

The Pentagon Barracks, which had been constructed to provide housing for 1,000 troops, provided less than half that when it was converted to university housing. This photograph from the early 1900s shows cadets in a Pentagon Barracks dormitory room. (Courtesy of the Louisiana Collection of the State Library of Louisiana.)

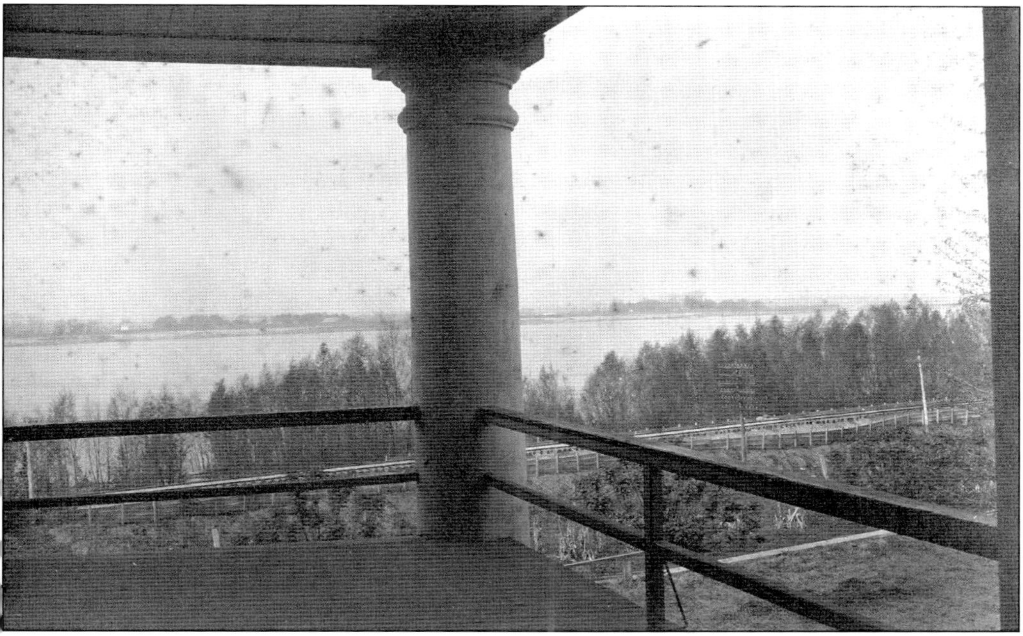

The Pentagon Barracks were originally built without verandas on the outward-facing sides of the building. When these were added, university cadets were provided with a wonderful vantage point for observing the Mississippi River and the sunsets beyond. (Courtesy of the Collections of the Louisiana State Museum.)

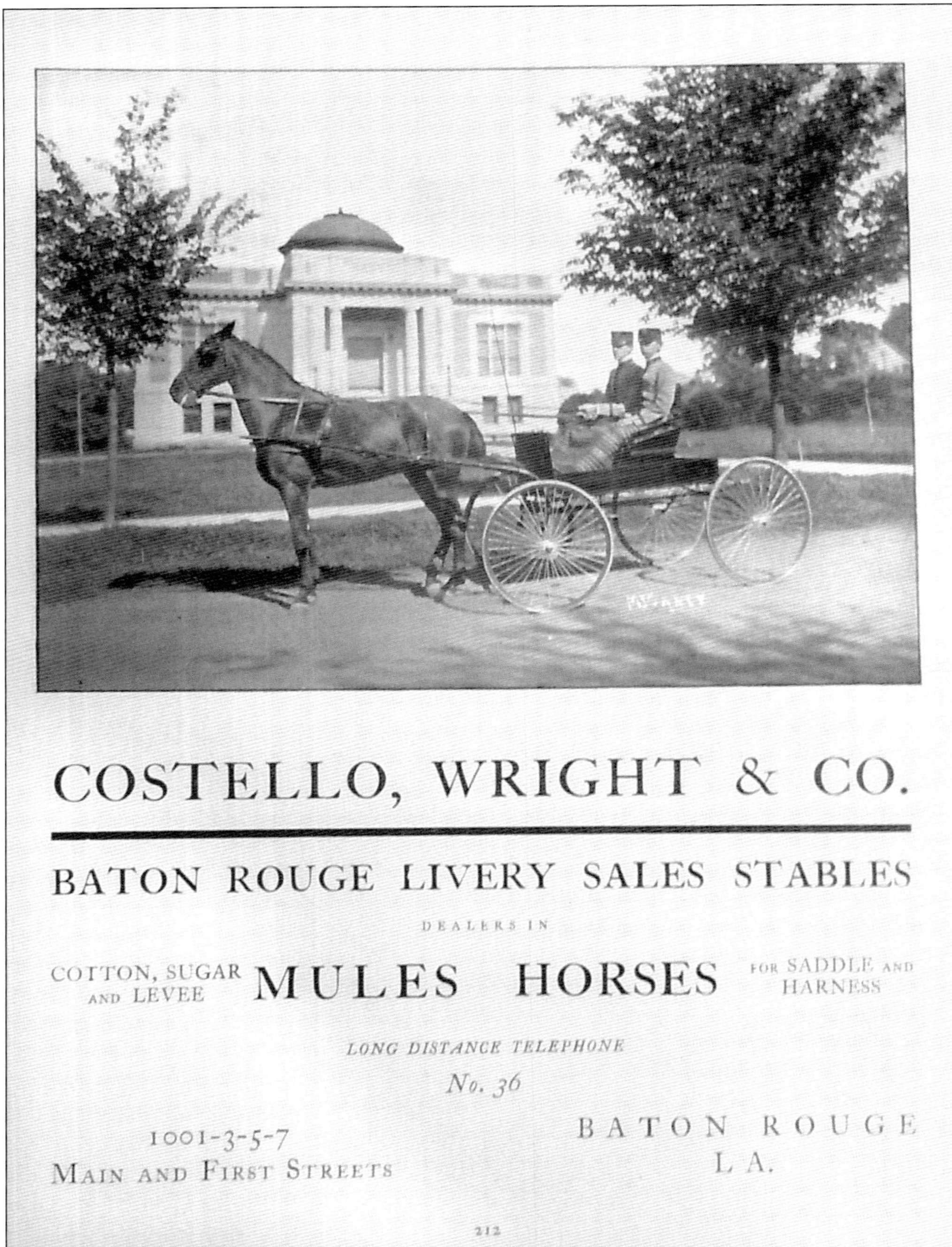

Hill Memorial Library served as the main campus library. It was built partially with funds given by John Hill to honor his son, John Hill Jr., who was an alumnus of the university. (Courtesy of LSU Libraries Special Collections.)

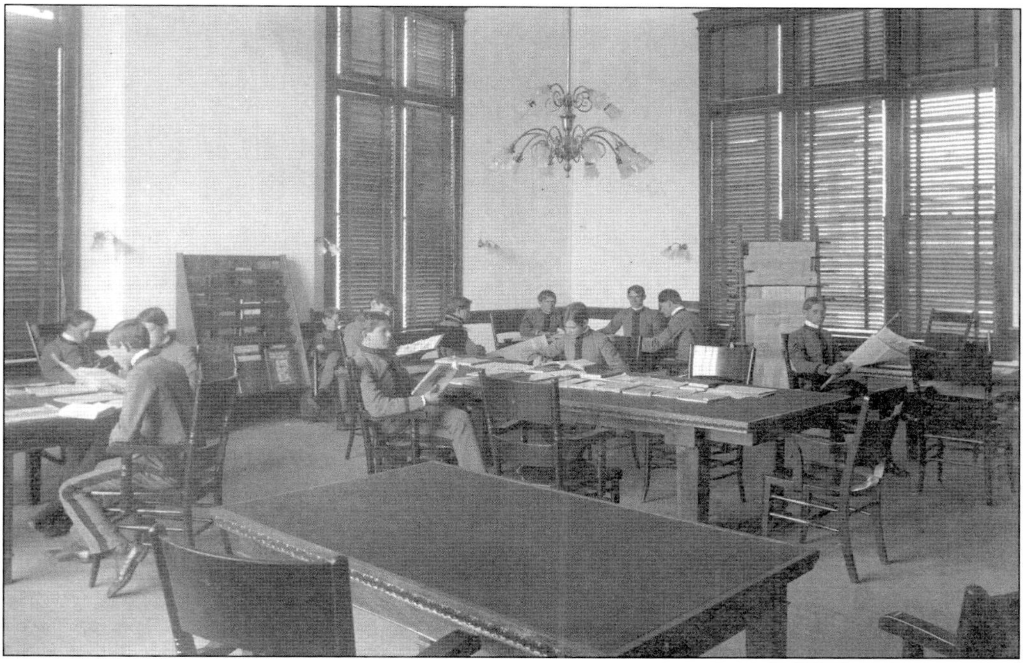

Hill Memorial Library Reading Room is seen in the early 1900s. When the university moved to its new campus in the 1920s, the new campus library continued to use the name Hill Memorial Library. That building is still in use and houses the Special Collections of the LSU Libraries. (Courtesy of the Collections of the Louisiana State Museum.)

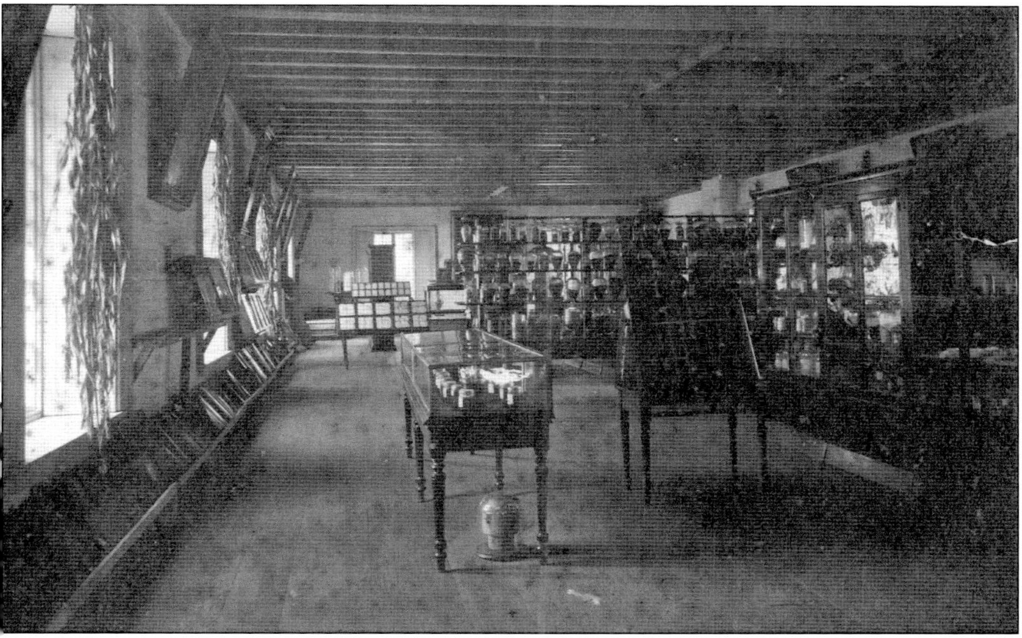

A small campus museum contained specimens, objects, and artifacts documenting the extraordinary natural history of Louisiana. It eventually became the Louisiana Museum of Natural History on the LSU campus. (Courtesy of the Collections of the Louisiana State Museum.)

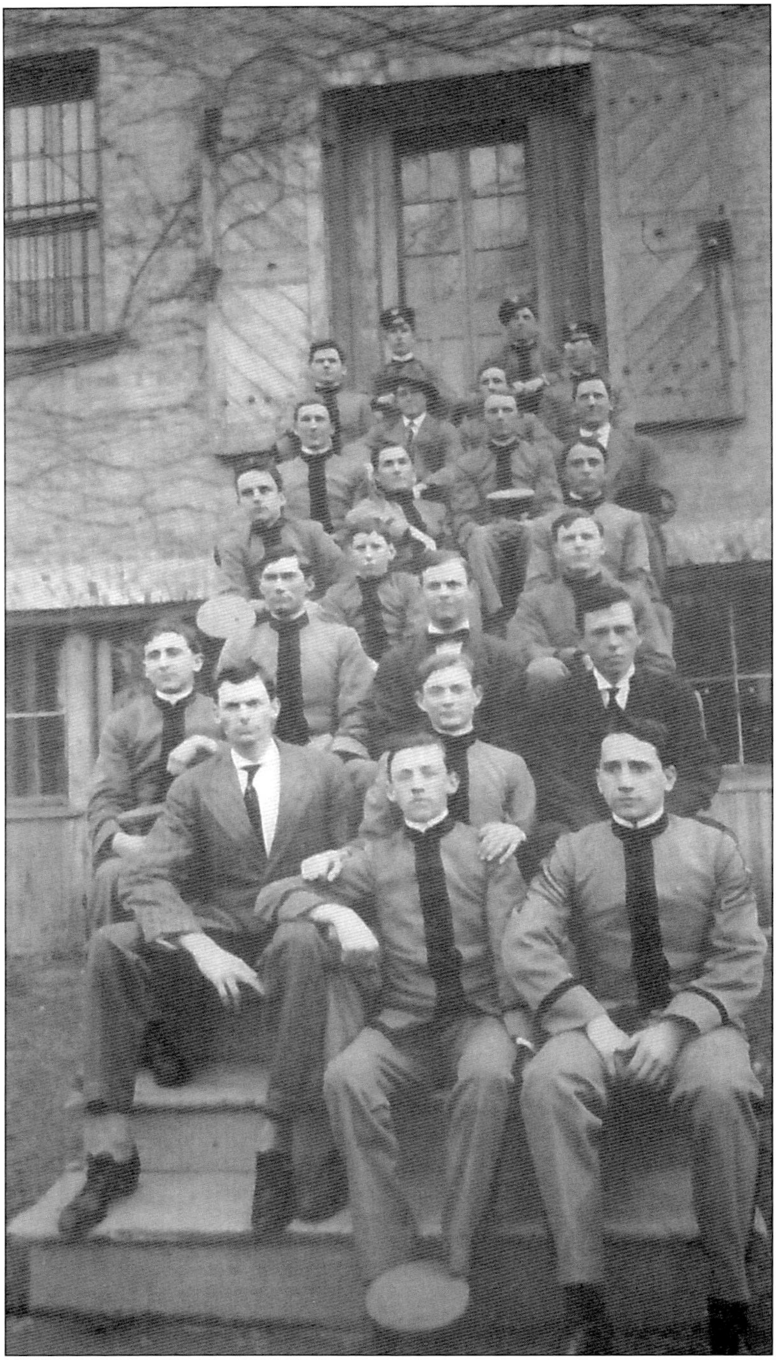

Sugar has been a major component of Louisiana's economy since the earliest days of the colony. Major advances in the growing of sugar were pioneered by LSU at its Audubon Sugar Institute in New Orleans and on the Baton Rouge campus. In this photograph from 1910, members of the Sugar and Agriculture Club pose on the steps of the Agriculture Building. (Courtesy of the Louisiana Collection of the State Library of Louisiana.)

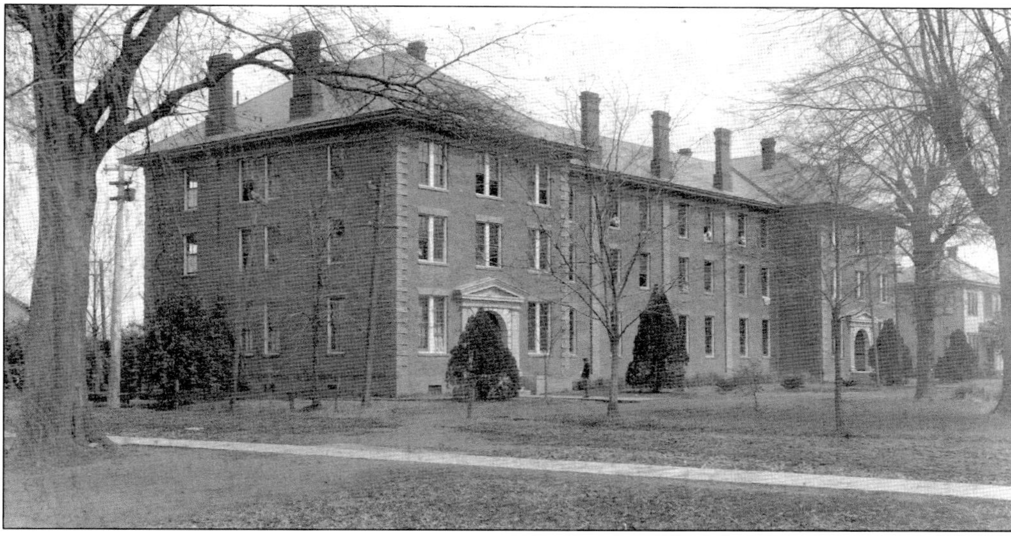

Foster Hall was completed in 1901 and stood between the hospital and the agricultural hall, near the current site of the State Capitol. The three-story building provided a mess for cadets on its first floor and dormitory rooms on upper floors. It was named for Murphy J. Foster, governor of Louisiana from 1892 to 1900, when funding for the building was approved. (Courtesy of the Collections of the Louisiana State Museum.)

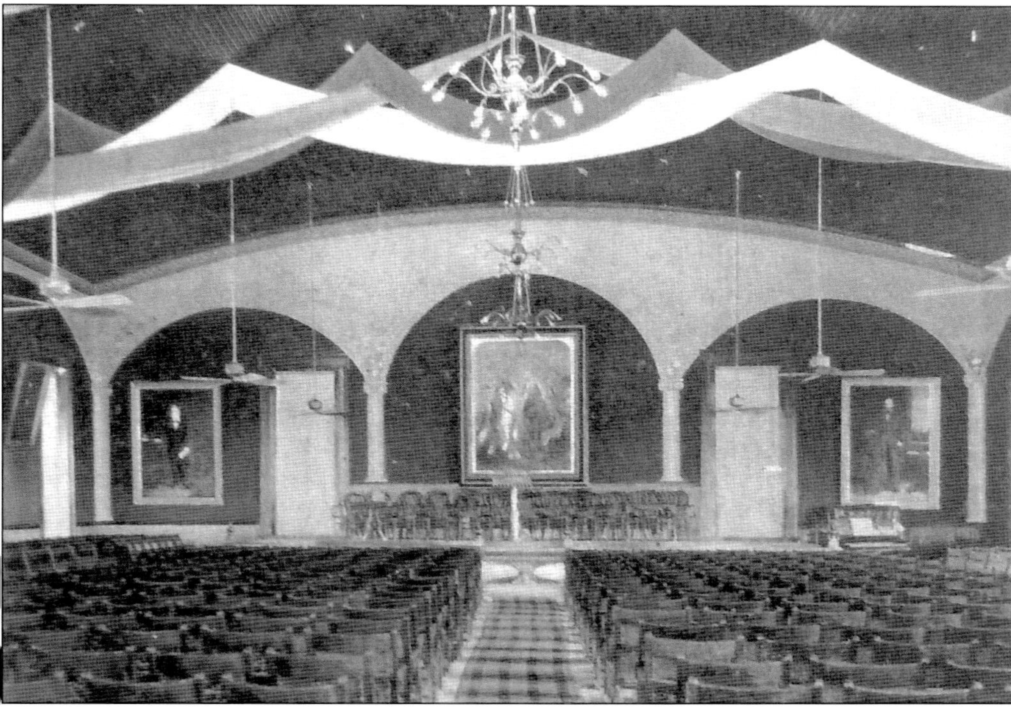

A gift of Baton Rouge businessman William J. Garig, Garig Hall was used as a classroom building for chemistry and other natural sciences. Garig's daughter Louise was among the first seven undergraduate women admitted to the university in 1907. (Courtesy of the Baton Rouge Room of the East Baton Rouge Parish Public Library.)

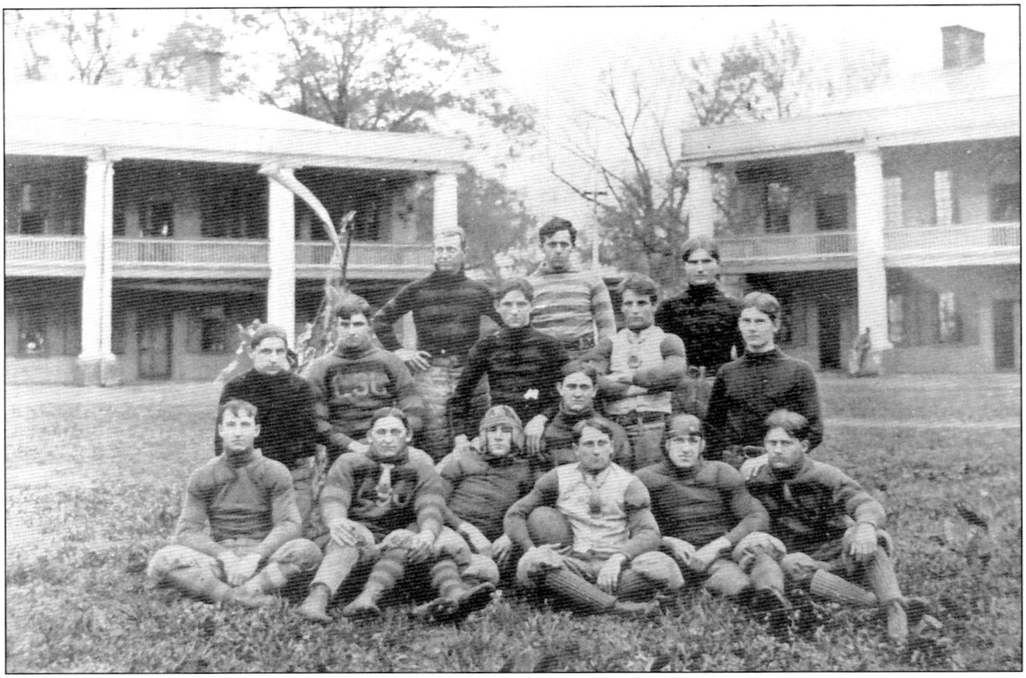

In the 18th century, the area just south of the Pentagon Barracks was the site of French, English, and Spanish forts. In the 19th century, it was home to Zachary Taylor, the only Louisianan elected president of the United States. In the early 20th century, it was the LSU parade ground and athletic field, where the 1900 LSU football team posed for this photograph. (Courtesy of LSU Libraries Special Collections.)

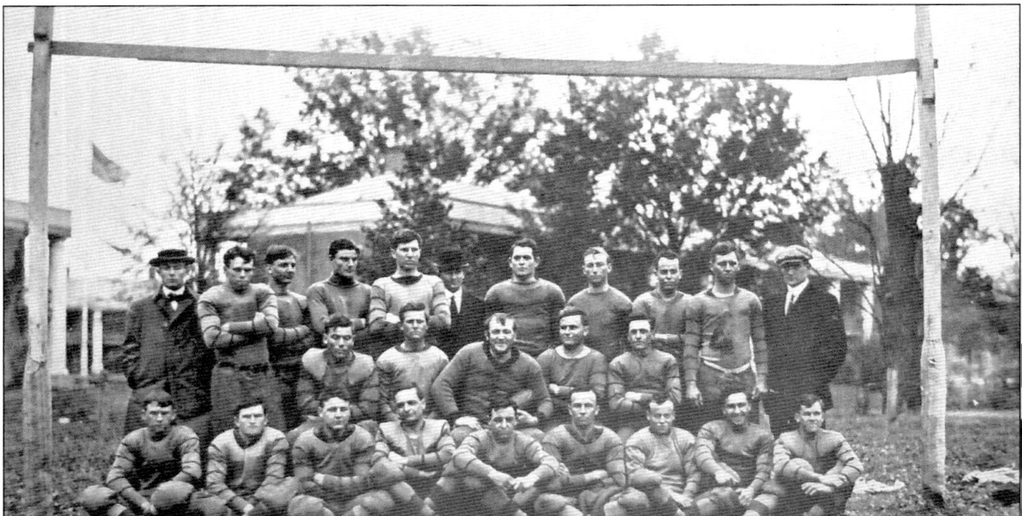

LSU played its first football game on November 23, 1893. The team's first coach was chemistry professor and Spanish Town resident Charles E. Coates. On October 26, 1895, the Tigers won their first game on campus, defeating Tulane 8-4. The 1911 team pictured here finished the season with a record of 6-3. (Courtesy of the Louisiana Collection of the State Library of Louisiana.)

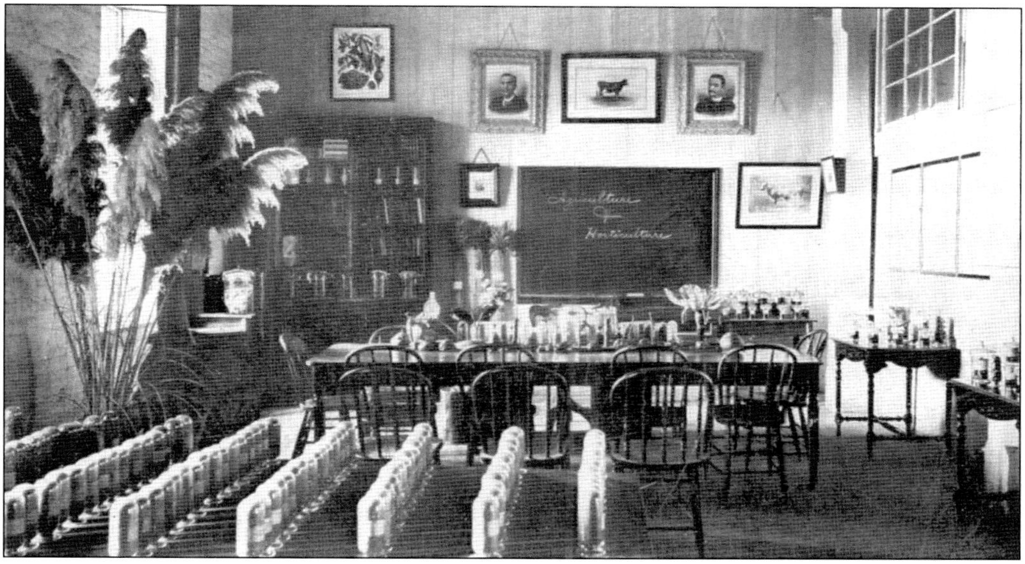

Primitive by current standards, classroom facilities at LSU were state-of-the-art for the early 1900s. This photograph of a classroom in the campus agriculture and horticulture building in the early 1900s features a collection of soil samples ready for examination. (Courtesy of the Louisiana Collection of the State Library of Louisiana.)

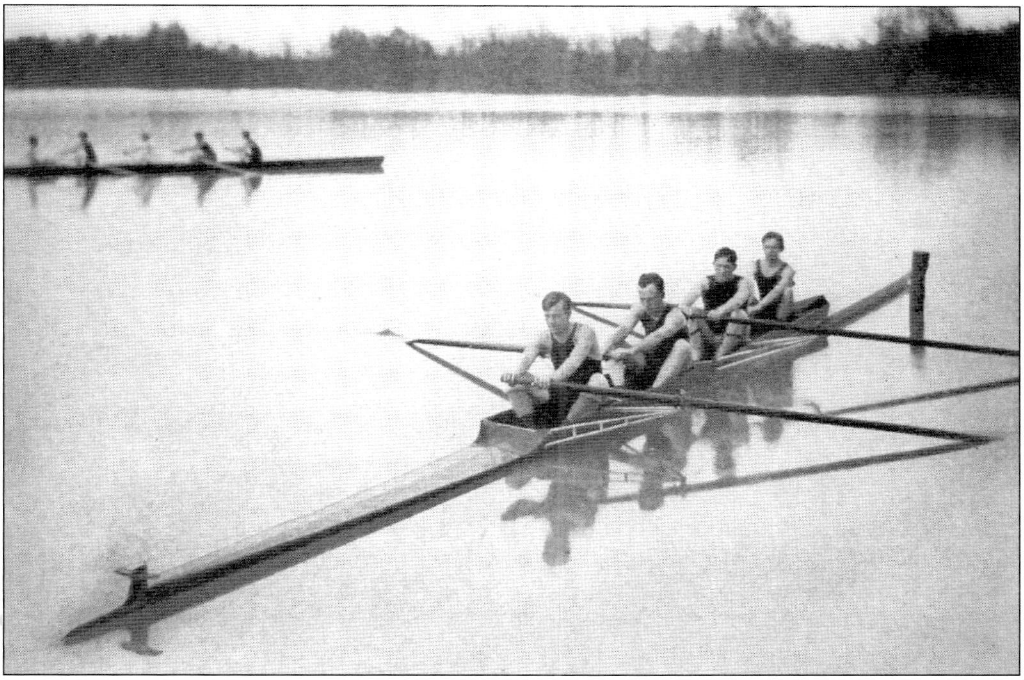

Over the years, the rivulet that emptied into the Mississippi near the spot alleged to have been the Bayougoula settlement of Istrouma bore no less than five different names before being dammed and creating the body of water first known as University Lake, now Capitol Lake. The 1910 LSU rowing team is seen here at practice on the lake. (Courtesy of the Louisiana Collection of the State Library of Louisiana.)

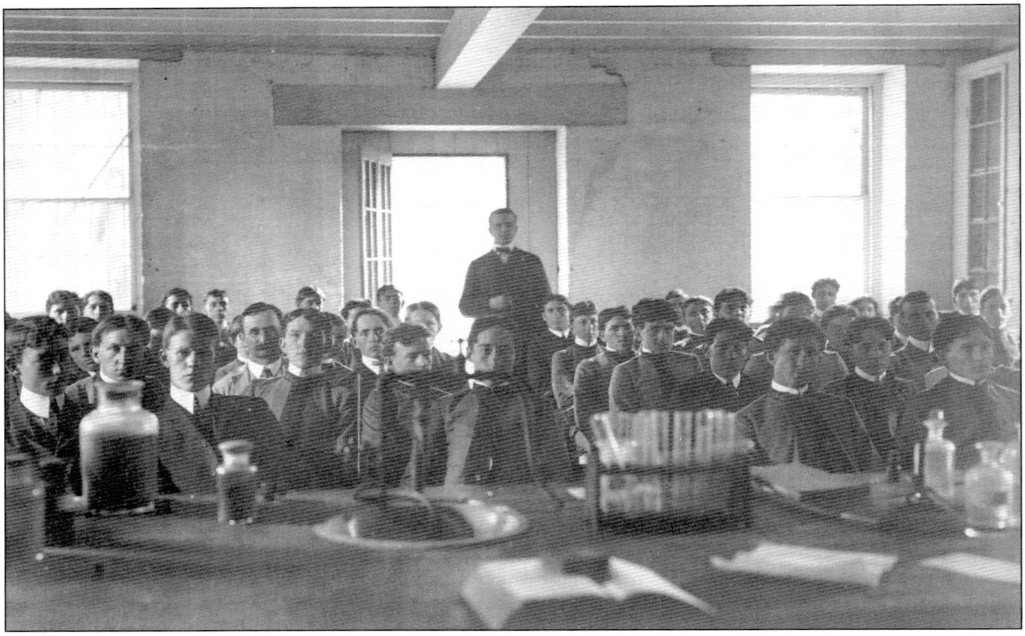

One of the most revered members of the LSU faculty in the early 1900s was chemistry professor Charles E. Coates, seen here in a chemistry class in Garig Hall in the early 1900s. (Courtesy of Louisiana State University Photograph Collection, A5000, Louisiana State University Archives, LSU Libraries.)

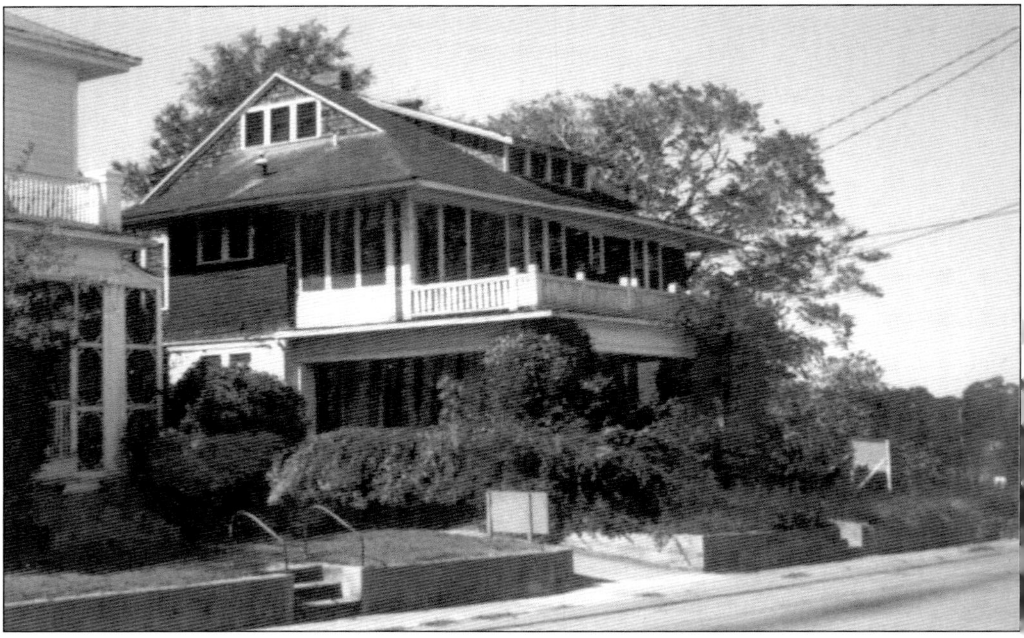

Professor Coates was a Spanish Town resident who lived in this bungalow-style house at 807 North Ninth Street, now demolished. In addition to his academic distinctions, he is remembered as LSU's first football coach. (Courtesy of the Baton Rouge Collection of the East Baton Rouge Public Library.)

Professor Ira S. Flory was a member of the faculty of the LSU School of Law from 1912 until 1917, and from 1919 until 1950. He served as acting dean of the school during the 1920s and 1930s. He lived at 642 North Eighth Street in Spanish Town, in an airplane bungalow built by Edmund Lee Buffington McGavarin in 1913. (Courtesy of LSU Libraries Special Collections.)

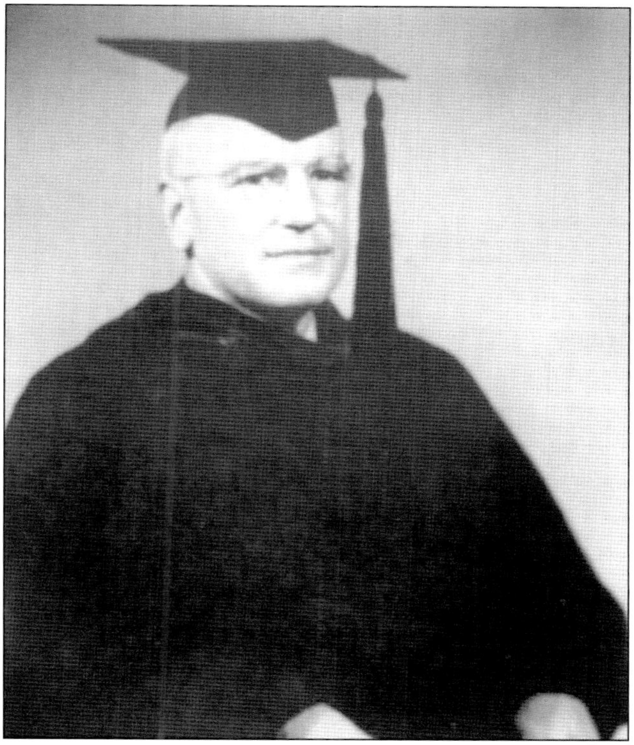

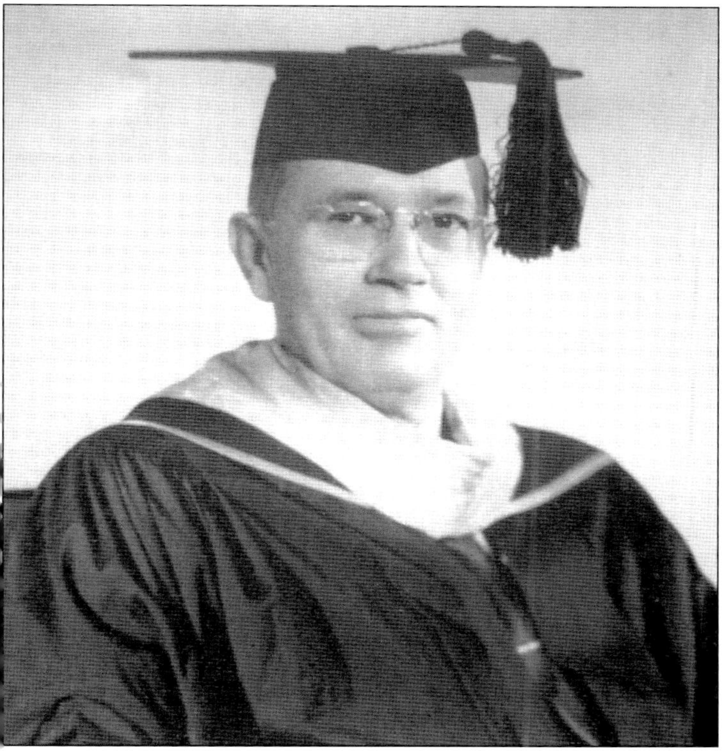

Another prominent LSU professor who called Spanish Town home was Jordan Gray Lee. Lee organized the state's first school of forestry and has been called "the father of forestry in Louisiana." His home at 714 North Fifth Street was built in 1911. (Courtesy of the Foundation for Historical Louisiana.)

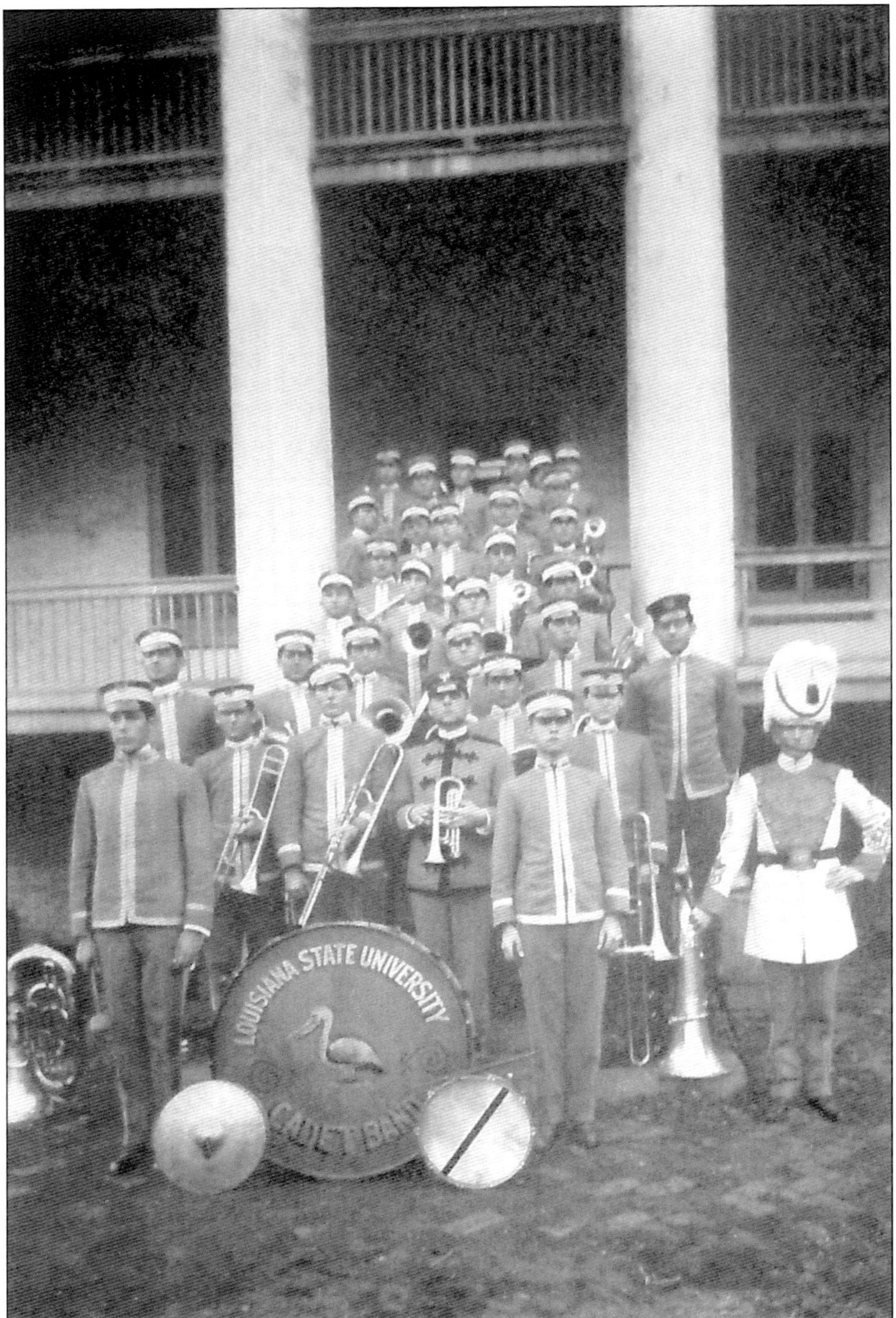

From the university's earliest days in Baton Rouge, the cadet band was an integral part of campus life. By the late 1800s, the band's mission of providing musical accompaniment for cadet parades and drills had expanded to performing in parades and competitions around the South. The 1910 band poses here in front of the Colony dormitory. (Courtesy of the Foundation for Historical Louisiana.)

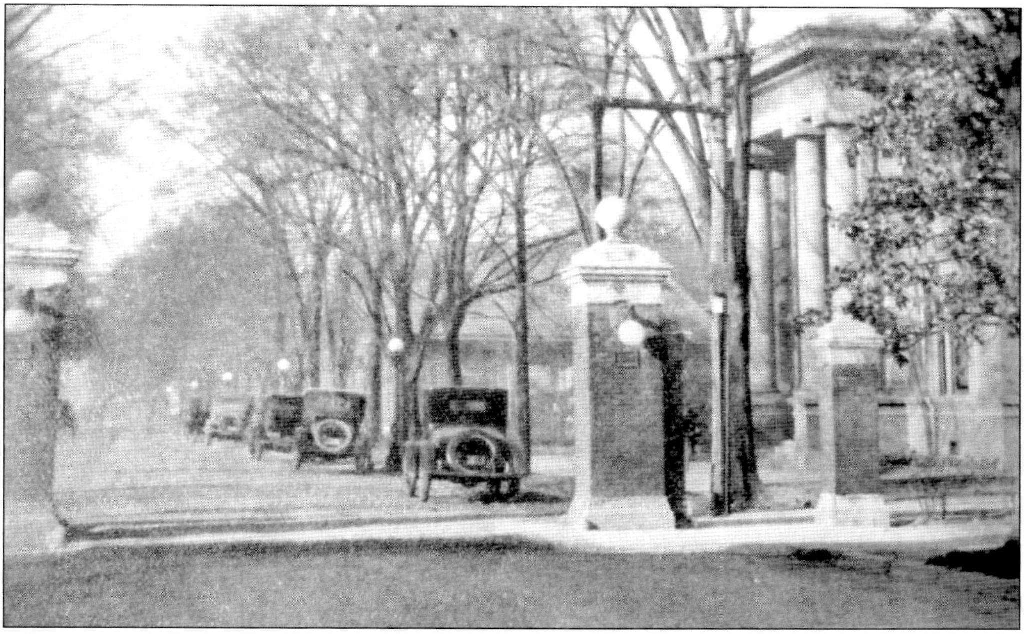

"The Gates of LSU" never really existed, but the Third Street entrance was considered to be the front door to the campus. Alumni Hall, home to university administration, appears at right in this photograph from the 1920s. (Courtesy of the Foundation for Historical Louisiana.)

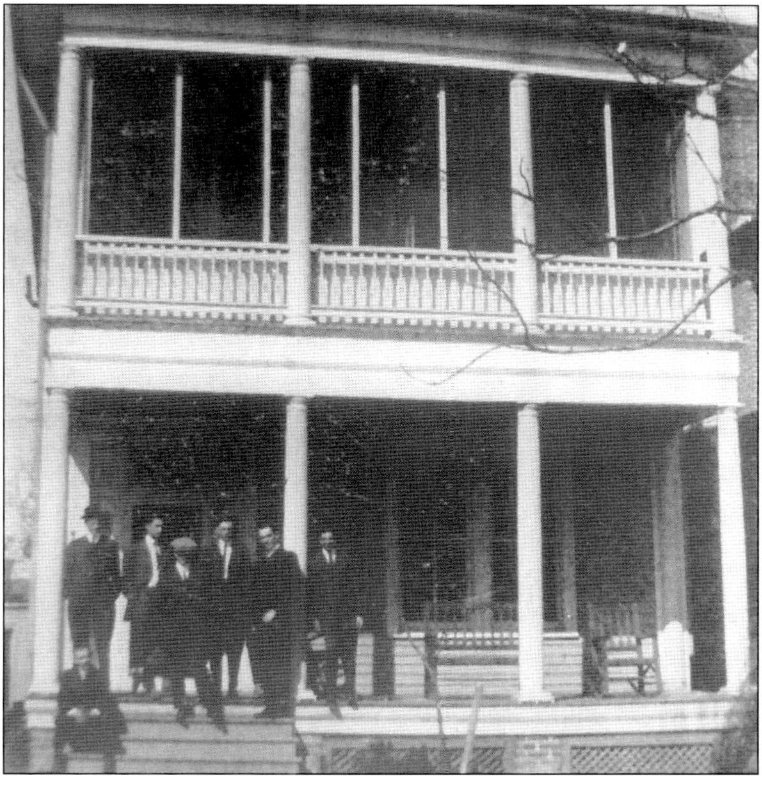

Kappa Alpha fraternity was one of the first social fraternities to make its appearance on the LSU campus in the early 1900s. Seven members of the fraternity are pictured at their house on Spanish Town Road in 1913. Later that year, the fraternity moved to a house at 711 Spanish Town Road that still stands and is referred to as the Lobdell House. (Courtesy of the Foundation for Historical Louisiana.)

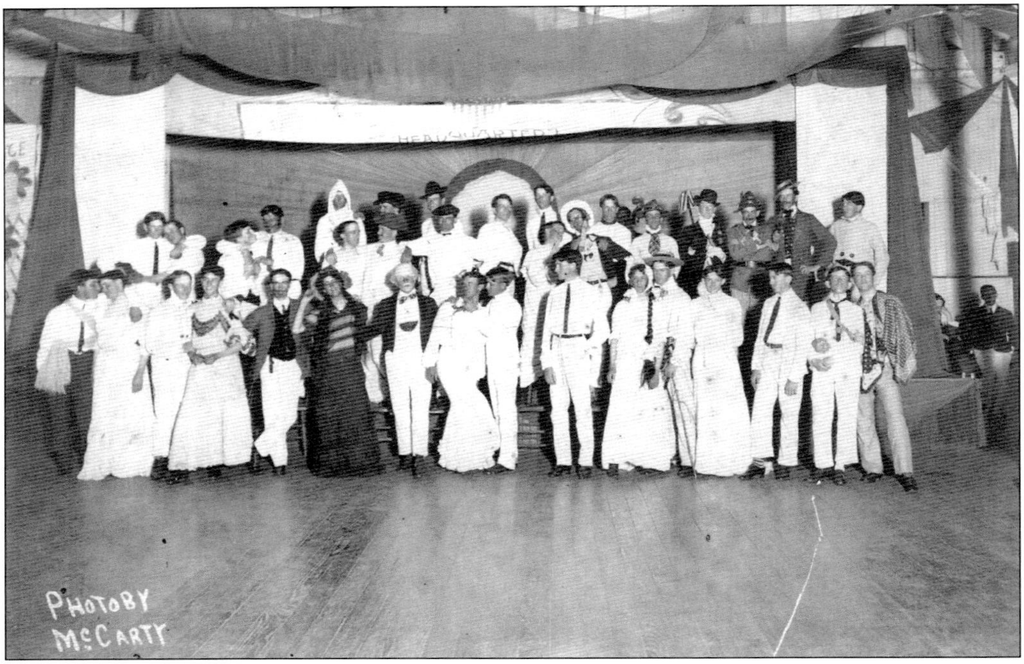

In the early 1900s, Baton Rouge was a small college town where students were expected to generate their own entertainment. One of the highlights of the 1904 school year was the Annual Fancy Dress Up Stag Party. (Courtesy of Louisiana State University Photograph Collection, A5000, Louisiana State University Archives, LSU Libraries.)

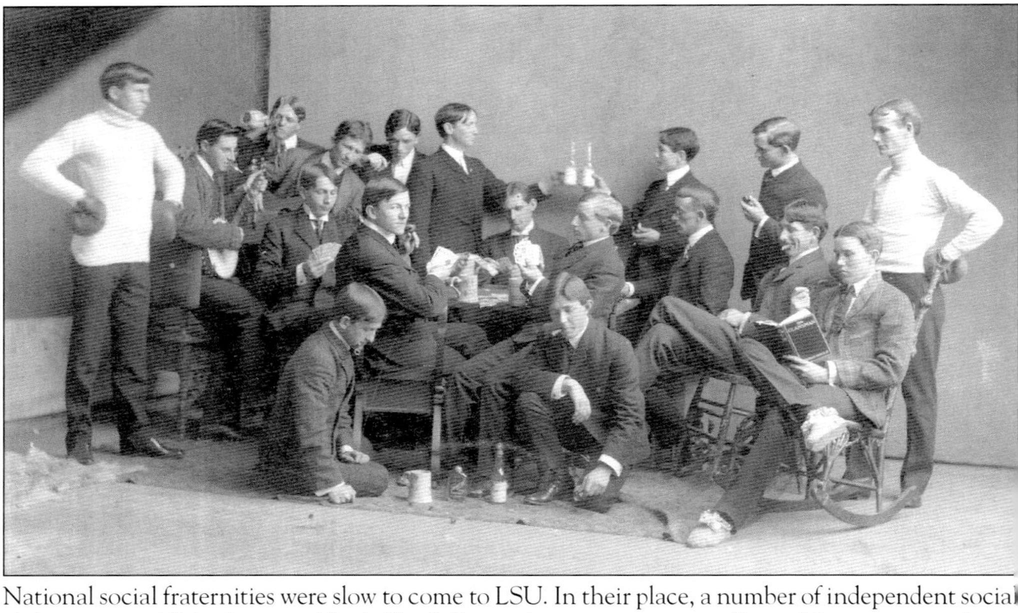

National social fraternities were slow to come to LSU. In their place, a number of independent social clubs were established to provide civilized distractions to young men. One of the more prominent clubs was the Hobo Gang, pictured here in the 1905 LSU yearbook smoking, drinking, rolling dice, and reading illicit books. (Courtesy of Louisiana State University Photograph Collection A5000, Louisiana State University Archives, LSU Libraries.)

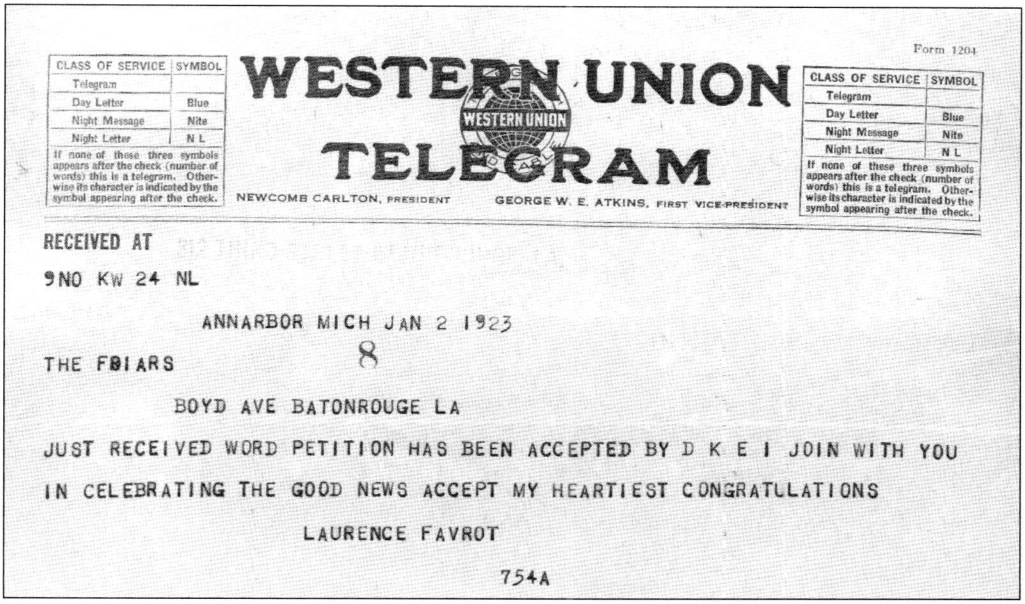

Form 1204

CLASS OF SERVICE	SYMBOL
Telegram	
Day Letter	Blue
Night Message	Nite
Night Letter	N L

If none of these three symbols appears after the check (number of words) this is a telegram. Otherwise its character is indicated by the symbol appearing after the check.

WESTERN UNION TELEGRAM

NEWCOMB CARLTON, PRESIDENT GEORGE W. E. ATKINS, FIRST VICE-PRESIDENT

CLASS OF SERVICE	SYMBOL
Telegram	
Day Letter	Blue
Night Message	Nite
Night Letter	N L

If none of these three symbols appears after the check (number of words) this is a telegram. Otherwise its character is indicated by the symbol appearing after the check.

RECEIVED AT

9NO KW 24 NL

ANNARBOR MICH JAN 2 1923

THE FRIARS 8

BOYD AVE BATONROUGE LA

JUST RECEIVED WORD PETITION HAS BEEN ACCEPTED BY D K E I JOIN WITH YOU IN CELEBRATING THE GOOD NEWS ACCEPT MY HEARTIEST CONGRATULATIONS

LAURENCE FAVROT

754A

One of the independent clubs in the early 1900s was the Friars Club. In 1910, the club built a house for its members at 507 Boyd Avenue, later renamed Spanish Town Road in the 1970s. This 1922 telegram informs the club that it has achieved affiliation with the Delta Kappa Epsilon fraternity. (Courtesy of Delta Kappa Epsilon, Zeta Zeta Chapter Records, A5806, Louisiana State University Archives, LSU Libraries.)

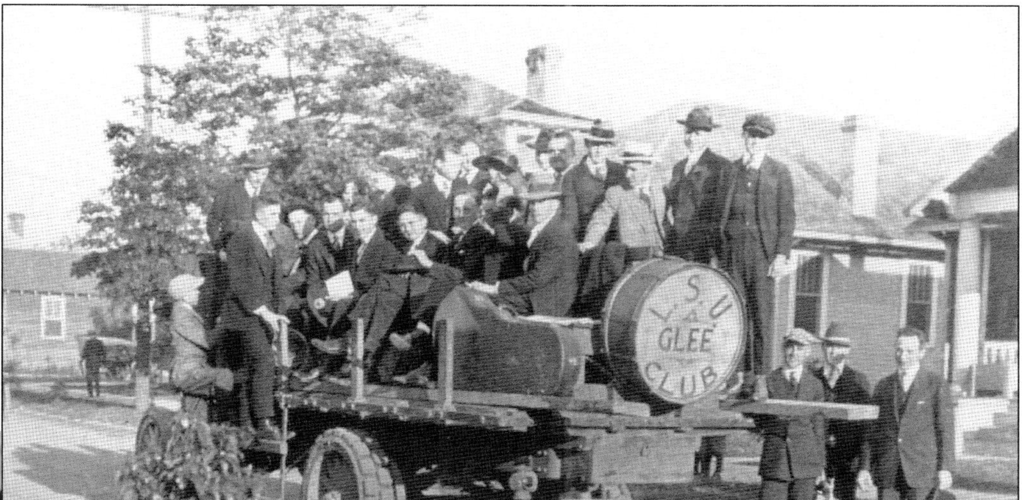

The oldest choral group on the LSU campus is the LSU Tiger Glee Club, founded in 1916. In its early days, the club participated in glee club competitions throughout the South. Today, the club gives regular concerts on campus, performs for civic organizations, and entertains at sporting events. (Courtesy of the Louisiana Collection of the State Library of Louisiana.)

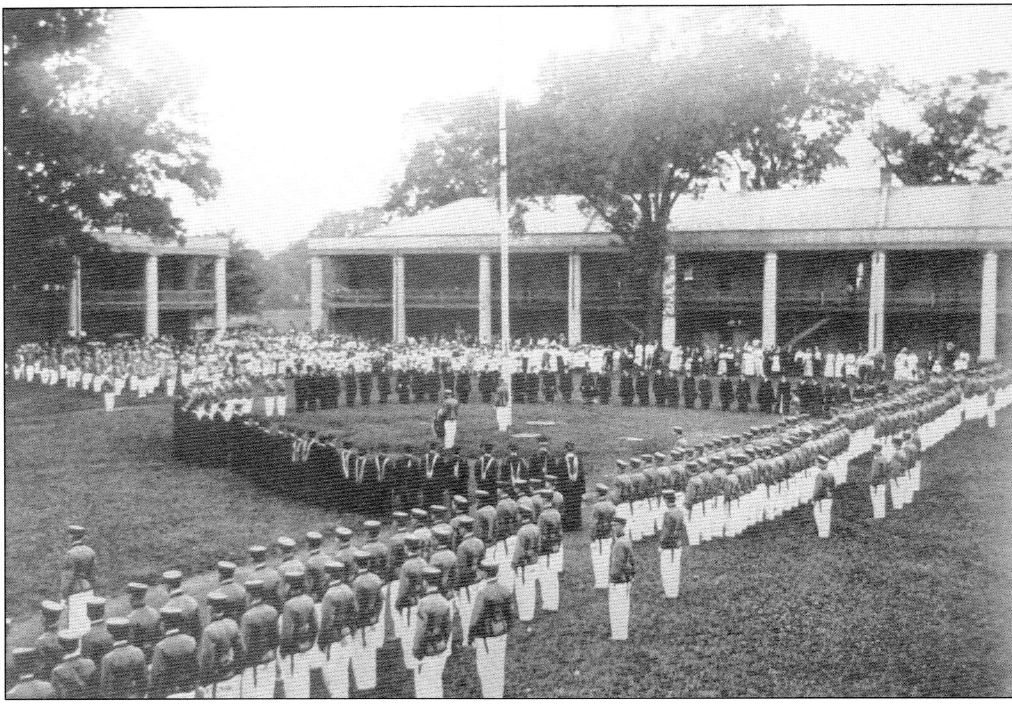

The courtyard of the Pentagon Barracks was used for many university functions, including the 1914 university commencement. This photograph was taken from the northwest, with the Mississippi River behind the cadet corps to the right. (Courtesy of LSU Libraries Special Collections.)

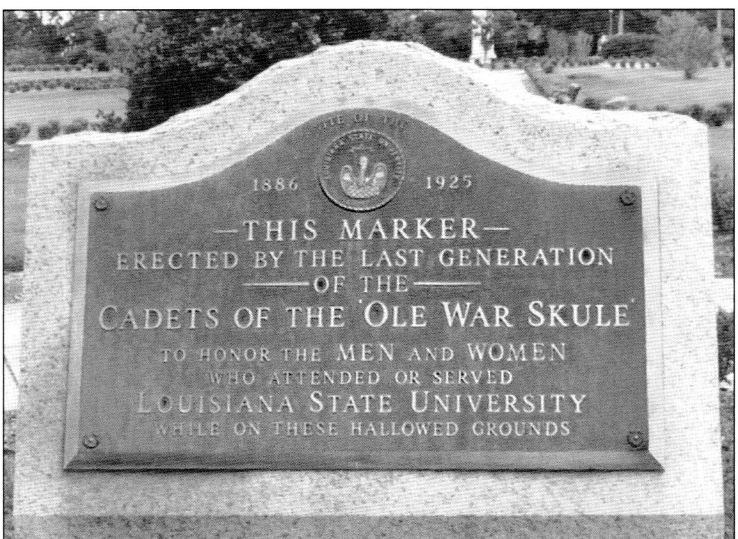

By the early 1920s, enrollment at the university had grown to more than 1,500 students, and the state authorized construction of the new campus in South Baton Rouge. The new campus was dedicated on April 30, 1926, and state government offices moved into most of the vacated buildings. (Author photograph.)

Five

EARLY 20TH CENTURY

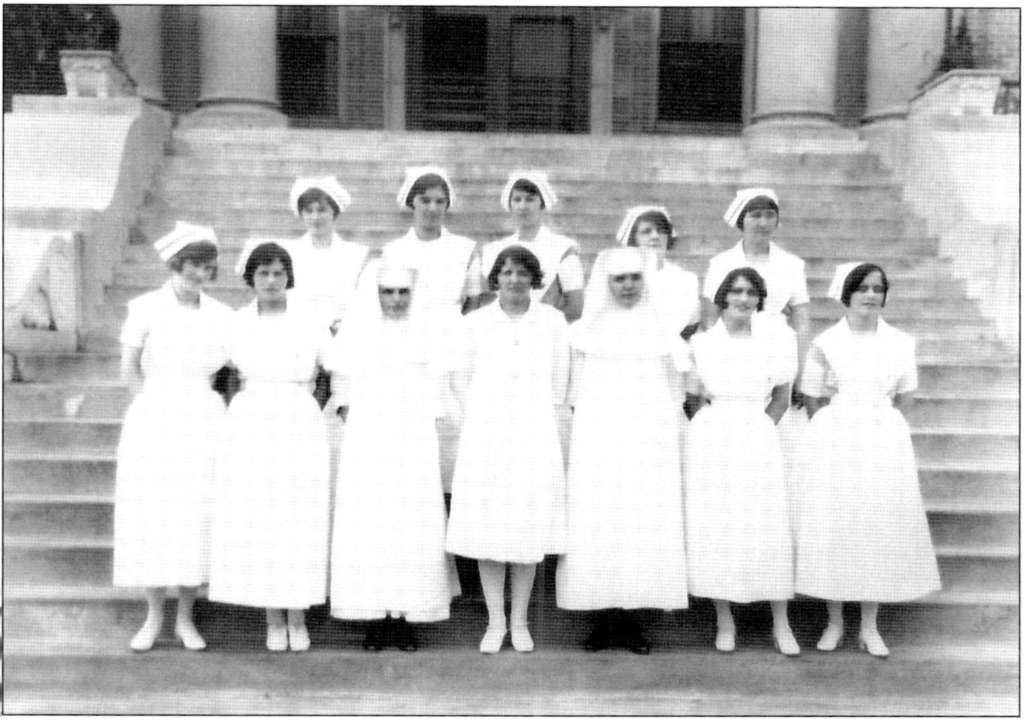

Baton Rouge experienced a radical transformation in the early years of the 20th century. In 1909, John D. Rockefeller's Standard Oil Company established a massive oil refinery in the city, just to the north of what is now Capitol Lake, and many of the men and women who worked there made their homes in Spanish Town. Two years later, the Franciscan Missionaries of Our Lady (several pictured here in the 1930s) selected an undeveloped parcel of land beside the lake to build Our Lady of the Lake Sanitarium, many employees of which also chose to live in Spanish Town. The Louisiana State University continued to grow, and Spanish Town became home to a striking collection of educators and other personalities who gave it a level of diversity unique in the city. Finally, after 40 years of unprecedented growth, LSU left its downtown campus in 1924, setting the stage for the area's most radical transformation of all. (Courtesy of the Franciscan Missionaries of Our Lady.)

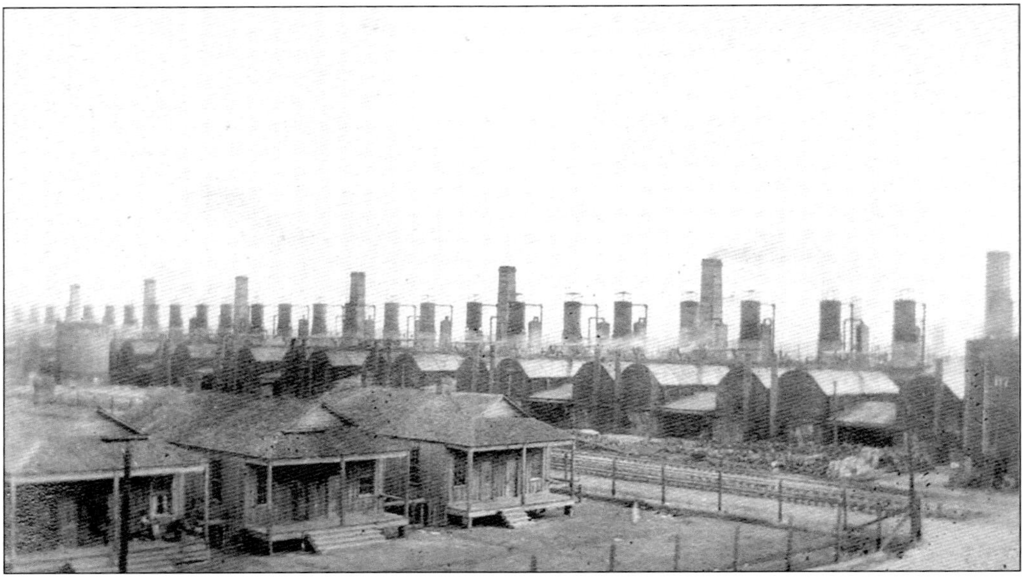

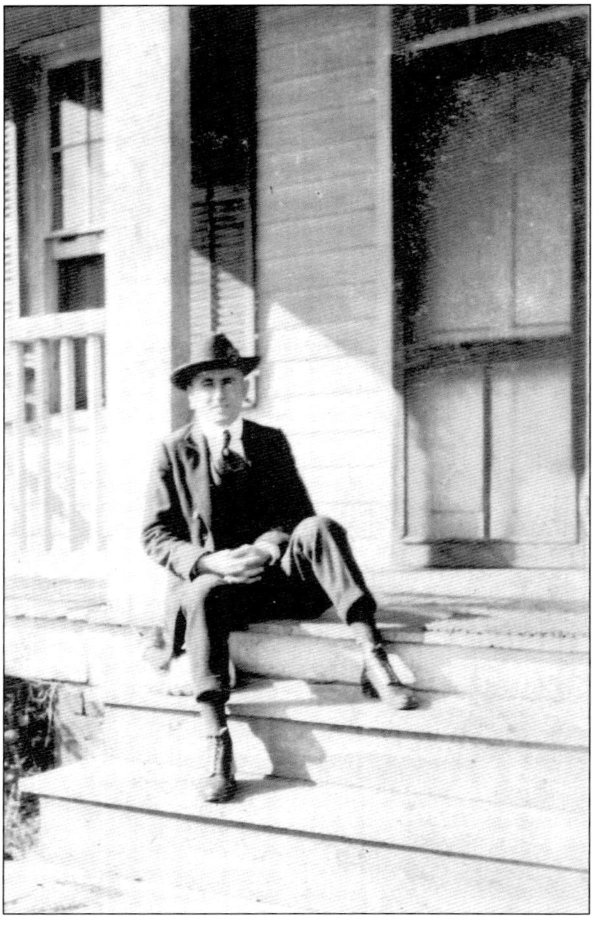

The Standard Oil Company commissioned a new refinery in Baton Rouge in 1909, after it had been rejected by the state of Texas. The huge refining complex was built on a cotton plantation to the north of downtown Baton Rouge owned by Spanish Town resident N.S. Dougherty. During the construction of the plant, the entire LSU football team was employed there as boilermakers to build up strength and stamina. (Courtesy of the Baton Rouge Room of East Baton Rouge Public Library.)

Its proximity to the refinery assured that many of Standard Oil's employees would find their home in Spanish Town. One of those was A.B. Hall, seen here on the steps of his home at 628 North Ninth Street. Hall, who started work at Standard shortly after it opened, worked for 17 years in the lighterage department as an engineer on the tug *Istrouma*. He had three sons, all of whom worked at the refinery. (Courtesy of the Foundation for Historical Louisiana.)

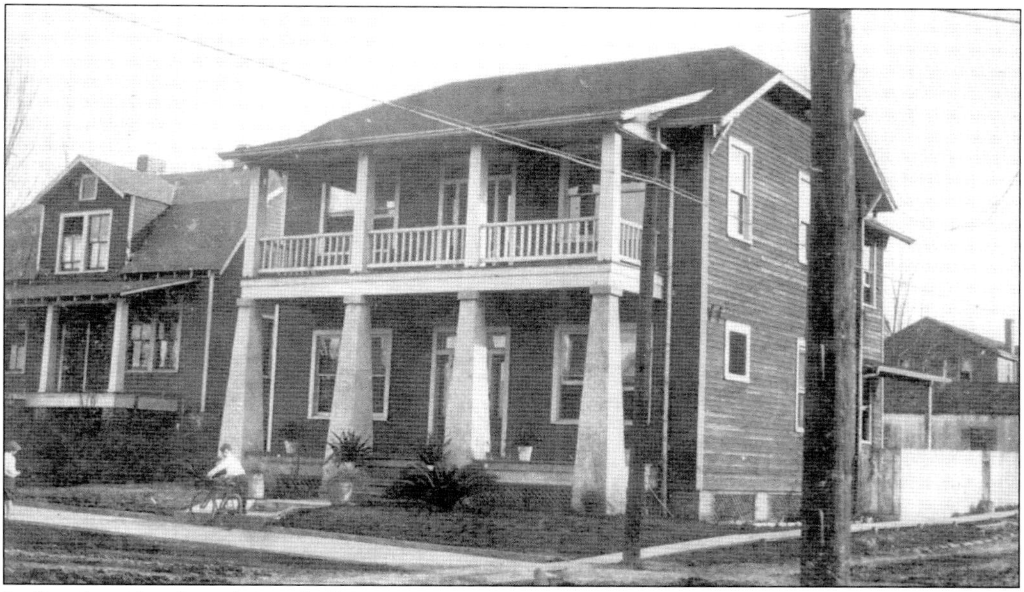

In October 1914, Joseph Mitchell Bergeron, a native of St. James Parish, moved to Baton Rouge and assumed a position as the city's building and plumbing director. He bought property at 602–604 Lakeland Drive and began construction of this house, which was completed in 1915. It is seen here in 1917. (Courtesy of Anna and Jason Hanks.)

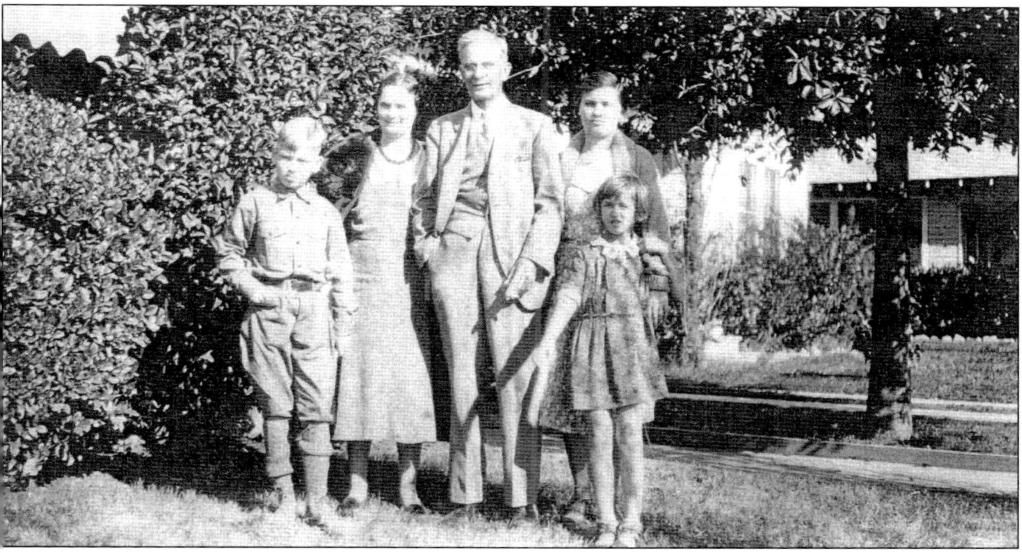

In the 1920s, the house was divided into upstairs and downstairs apartments. Bergeron's daughter Maud Florence Bergeron, third from left in this 1899 family photograph, lived in the downstairs apartment during her 41-year tenure with Iberville Parish schools. Following her retirement in 1954, she worked part time at St. Joseph Academy and moved upstairs so that her sister, Ruth Bergeron Simon, and her husband could move into the downstairs apartment. (Courtesy of Anna and Jason Hanks.)

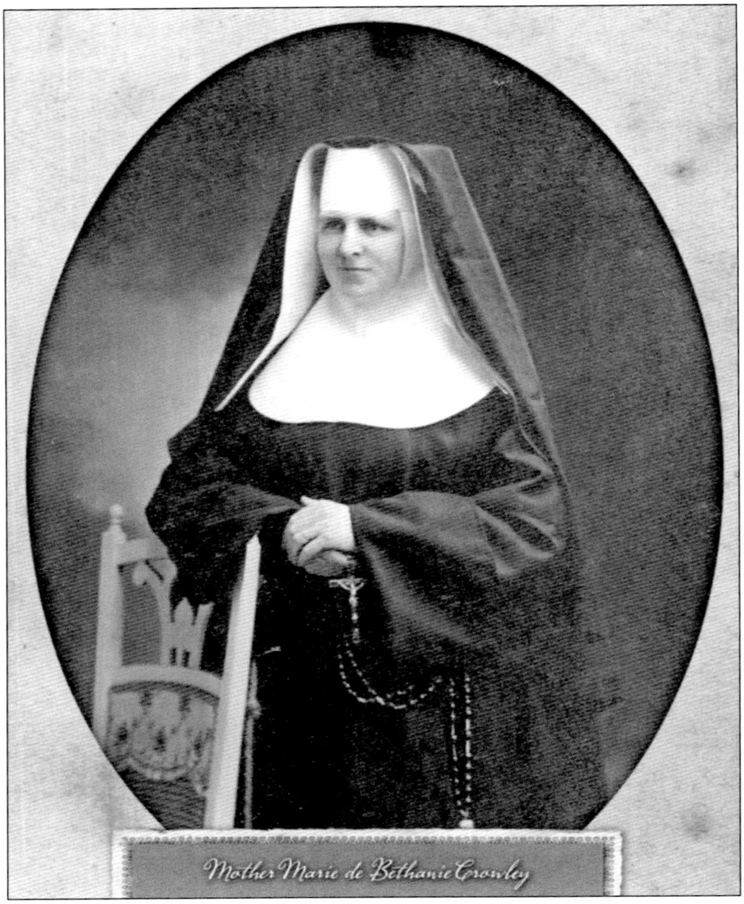

In 1911, Mother de Bethanie Crowley and five Franciscan Missionaries of Our Lady traveled to America to serve the sick and needy. Eight years after establishing a hospital in Monroe, Louisiana, Mother de Bethanie was invited to Baton Rouge by local physicians to tour the downtown area in search of a suitable location for a hospital to serve the 22,000 residents of the small river town. Mother de Bethanie insisted on a patch across University Lake from the original Louisiana State University campus. She served as administrator of the hospital until 1928. (Courtesy of the Franciscan Missionaries of Our Lady.)

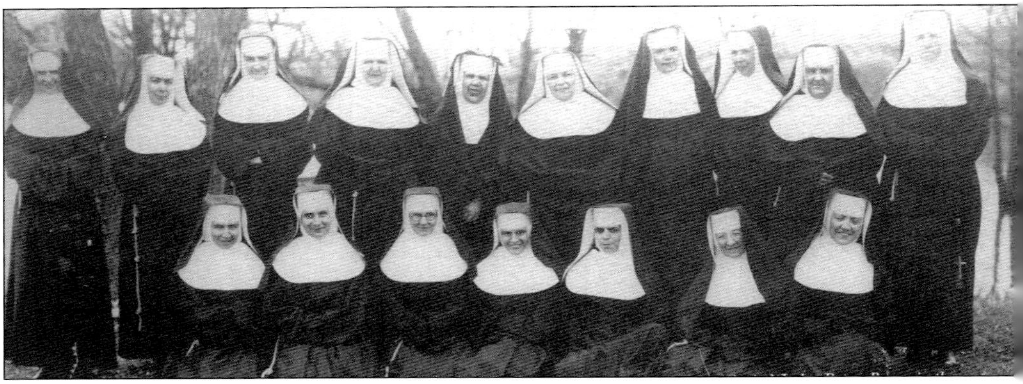

Many of the sisters who came to Louisiana in the early 1900s fell victim to the same illnesses that plagued other European immigrants. Several died of tuberculosis, and others were unable to deal with the climate and returned to Europe. As the years passed, their ranks were filled by American-born novices who carried on the work of the order. (Courtesy of the Franciscan Missionaries of Our Lady.)

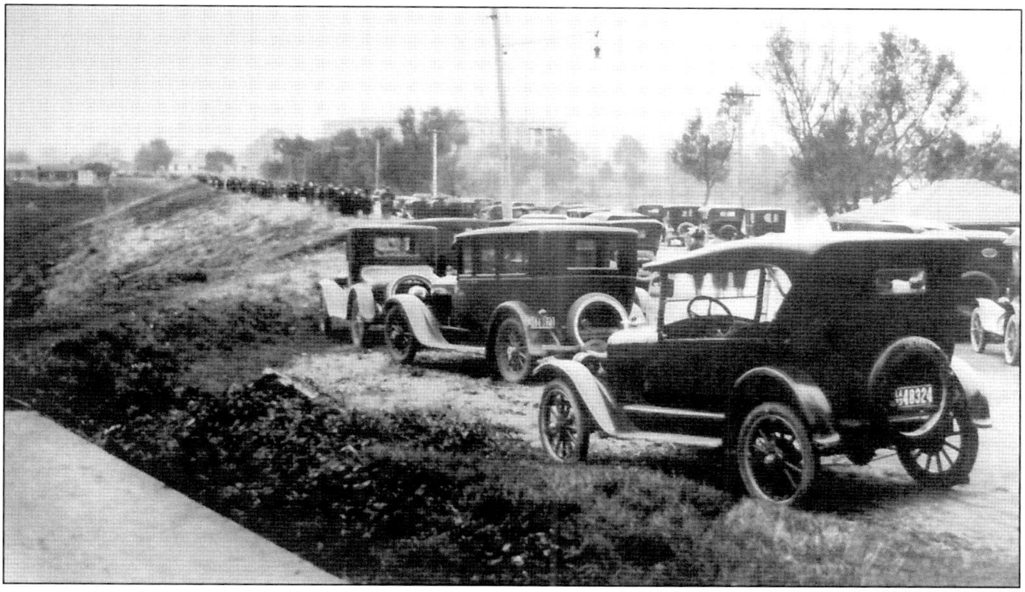

On November 4, 1923, Baton Rougeans and their cars crowded the muddy rut that would eventually become an extension of Third Street to attend the grand opening of the new Our Lady of the Lake Sanitarium. (Courtesy of the Franciscan Missionaries of Our Lady.)

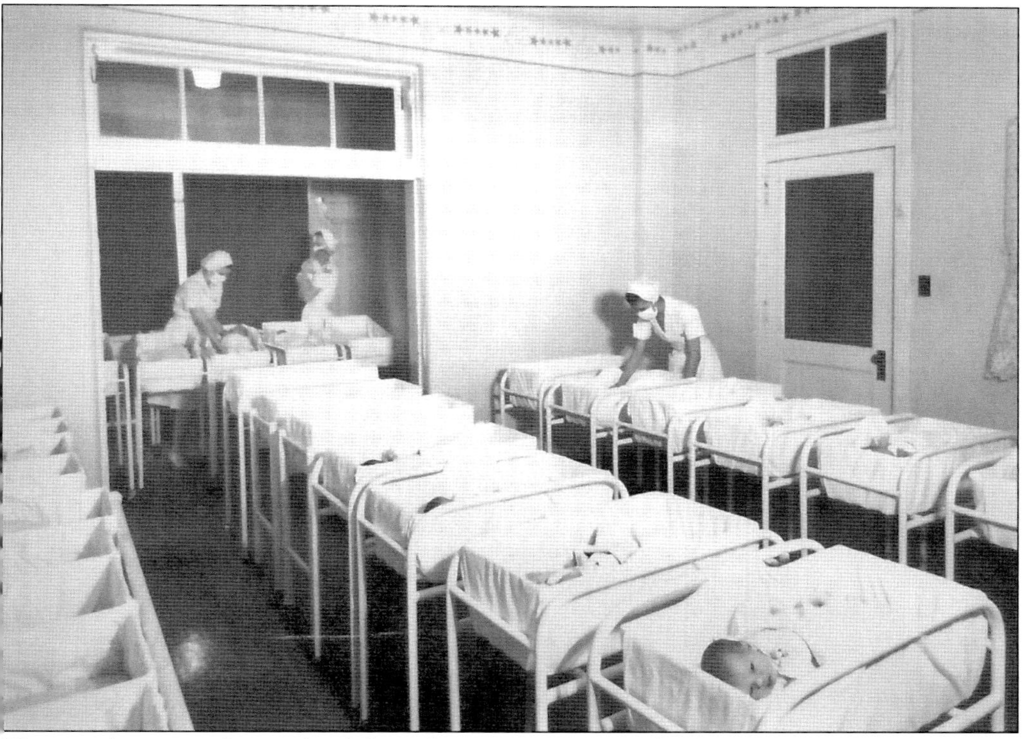

The new four-story Our Lady of the Lake Sanitarium provided hospital services that had not been available in the city, including six state-of-the-art surgery suites and a nursery for infants, pictured here. (Courtesy of the Franciscan Missionaries of Our Lady.)

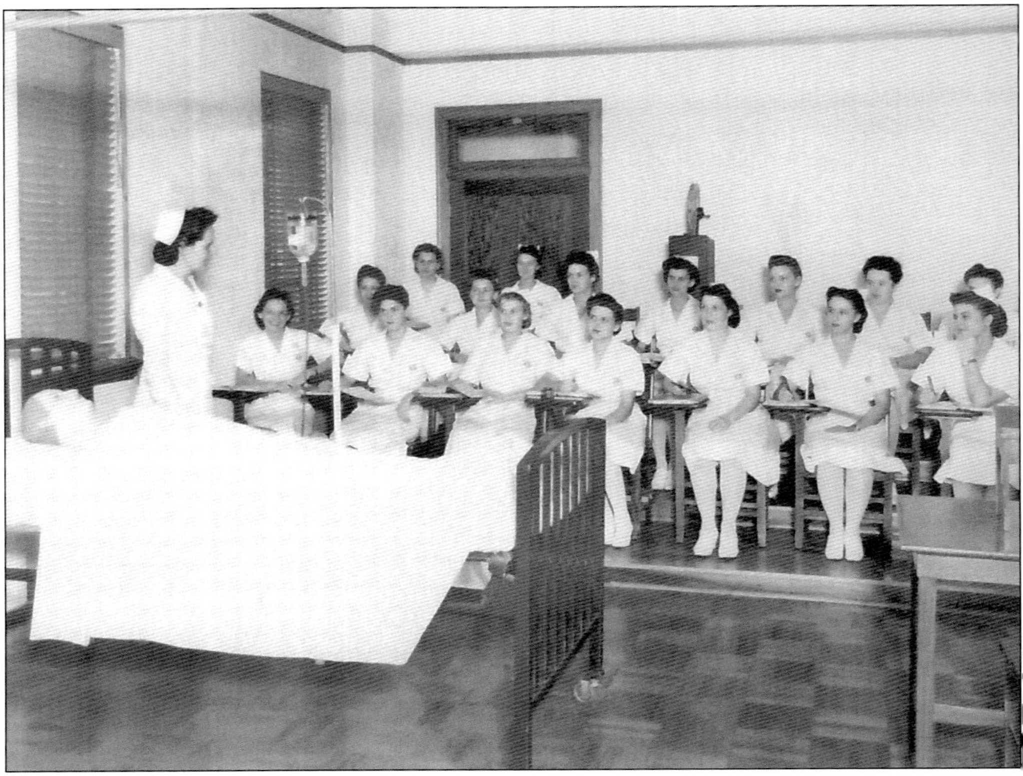

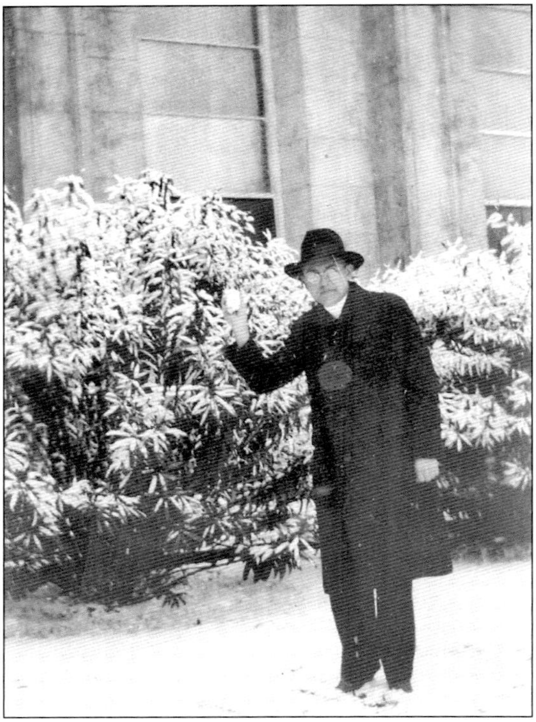

Our Lady of the Lake School of Nursing began in conjunction with the opening of the sanitarium as part of the new hospital's program of service to the community. Five students from the St. Francis Sanitarium in Monroe, Louisiana, formed part of the first class of nine students who lived, attended classes, and cared for patients in the hospital overlooking Capitol Lake. (Courtesy of the Franciscan Missionaries of Our Lady.)

In a rare 1935 snowfall, Fr. L. Abel Caillouet, a native of Thibodaux, is seen at work at Our Lady of the Lake Sanitarium. Father Abel was ordained a priest for the Archdiocese of New Orleans and later the titular bishop of Setea and auxiliary bishop of New Orleans. He served in that capacity until his retirement in 1976. (Courtesy of the Archives of the Diocese of Baton Rouge.)

Spanish Town resident Robert A. Hart was mayor of Baton Rouge between 1898 and 1902. His accomplishments included improvements to schools, roads, and other city services. At his death in 1939, he was said to be the wealthiest man in the city. (Courtesy of the Foundation for Historical Louisiana.)

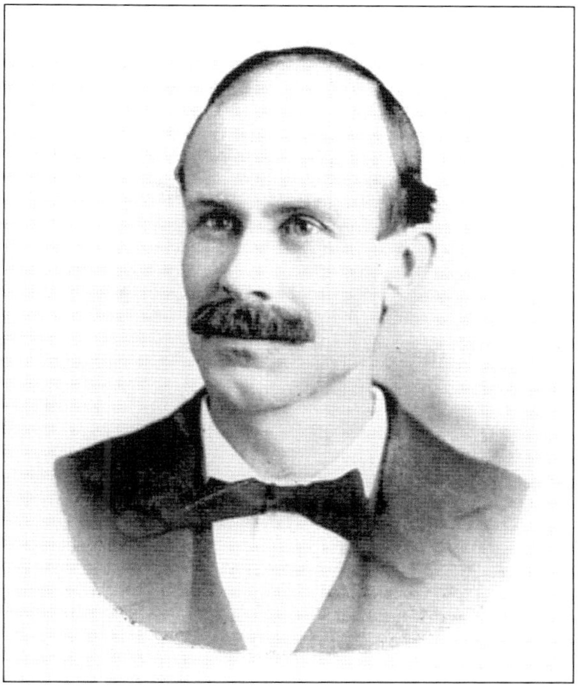

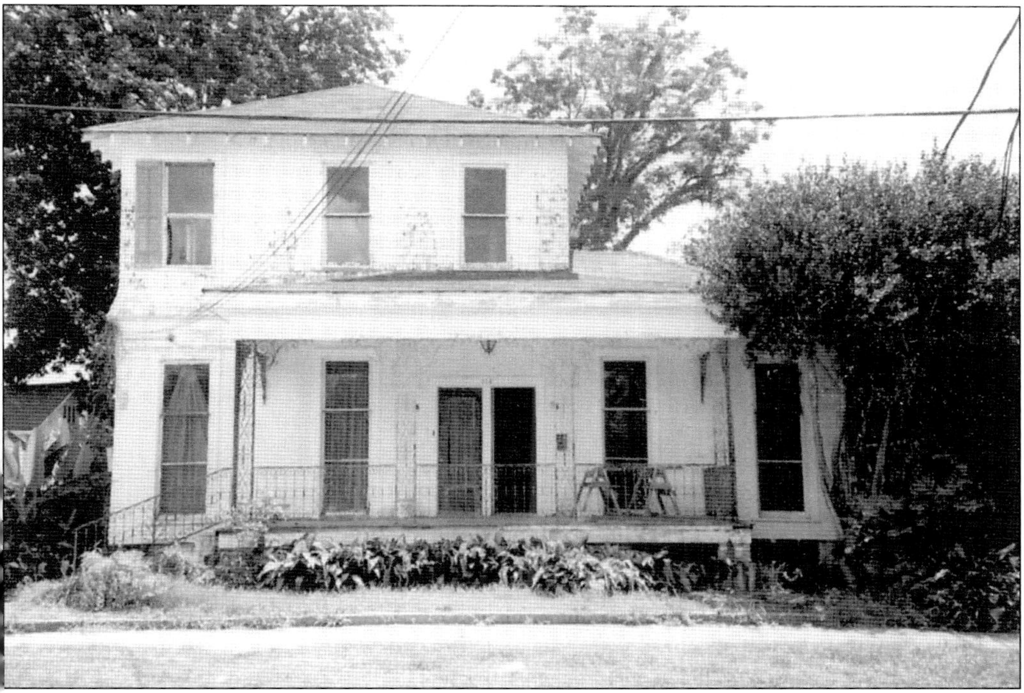

Robert A. Hart lived in this house at 732 North Fifth Street. The house was originally much more modest than it appears here in 1970. Hart sold his home in 1902 to George Arthur Evans, a St. Tammany cabinetmaker who substantially remodeled the house and added the second floor. (Courtesy of Cheryl McCormick and Derrell Cohoon.)

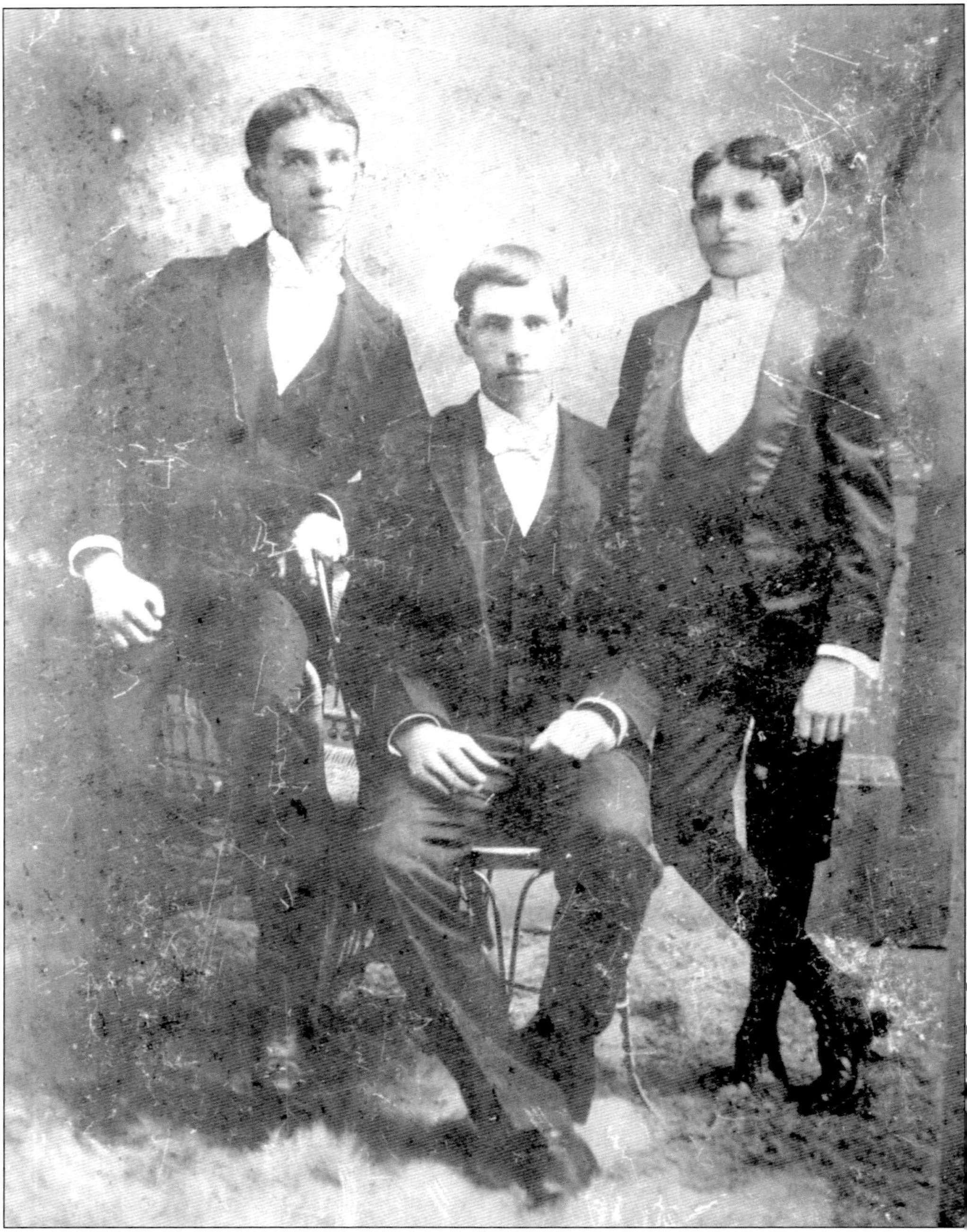

North Street between Fourth and Sixth Streets was the center of Catholic education from 1850 until the mid-20th century. Ss. Peter and Paul College, a school for boys, survived from 1850 until 1855. It reopened as St. Mary's Academy, a school for girls that closed in 1862. In 1894, St. Vincent's Academy opened on the site. The school's graduating class from that year is pictured here. (Courtesy of Catholic High School.)

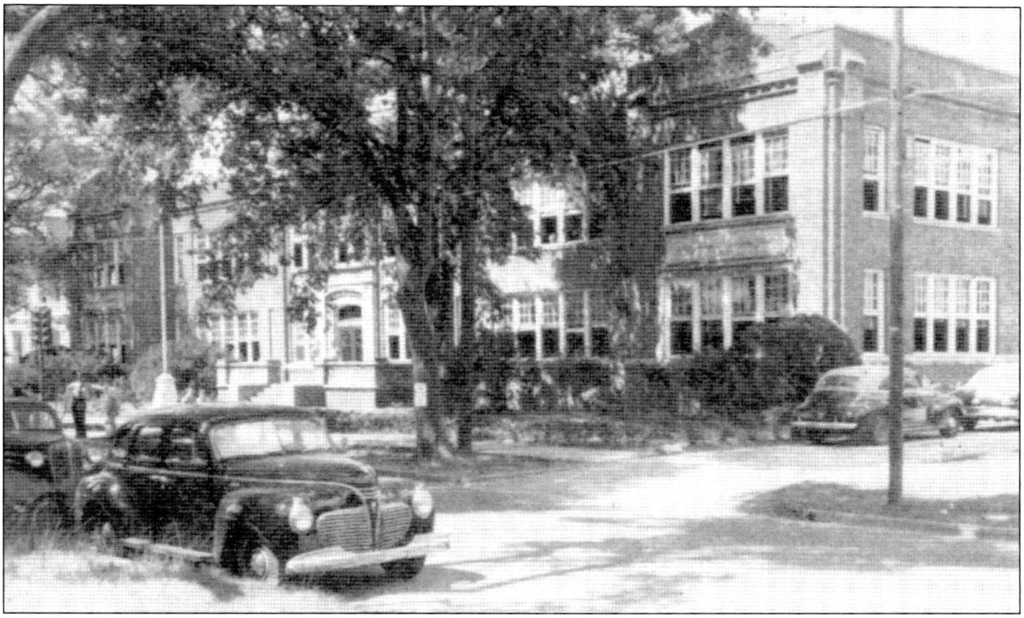

When enrollment at St. Vincent's grew to more than 300 in the mid-1920s, the Brothers of the Sacred Heart built a new $300,000 home for the school at 411 North Street. When the new school was opened in 1928, it was renamed Catholic High School. It was demolished in the 1960s to make room for a new skyscraper for the Louisiana Department of Education. (Courtesy of Catholic High School.)

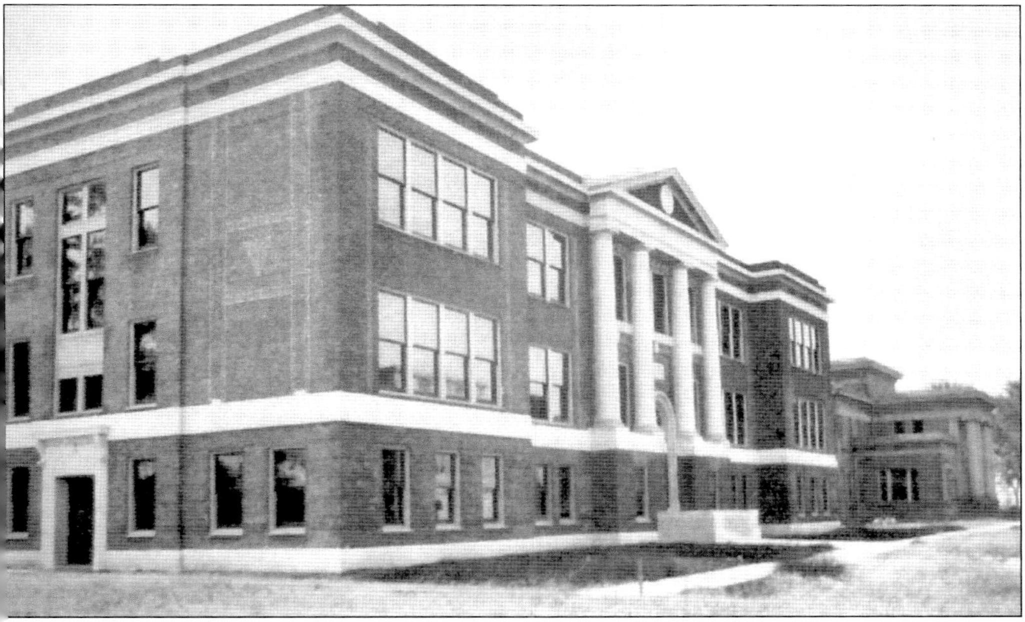

Enrollment at Catholic High School doubled to more than 600 in the 1930s. To meet the demand for additional space, the school appealed to Gov. Richard Leche to use the abandoned Peabody Hall on the old LSU campus, which had briefly housed the state archives. This photograph dates from the 1950s. (Courtesy of Catholic High School.)

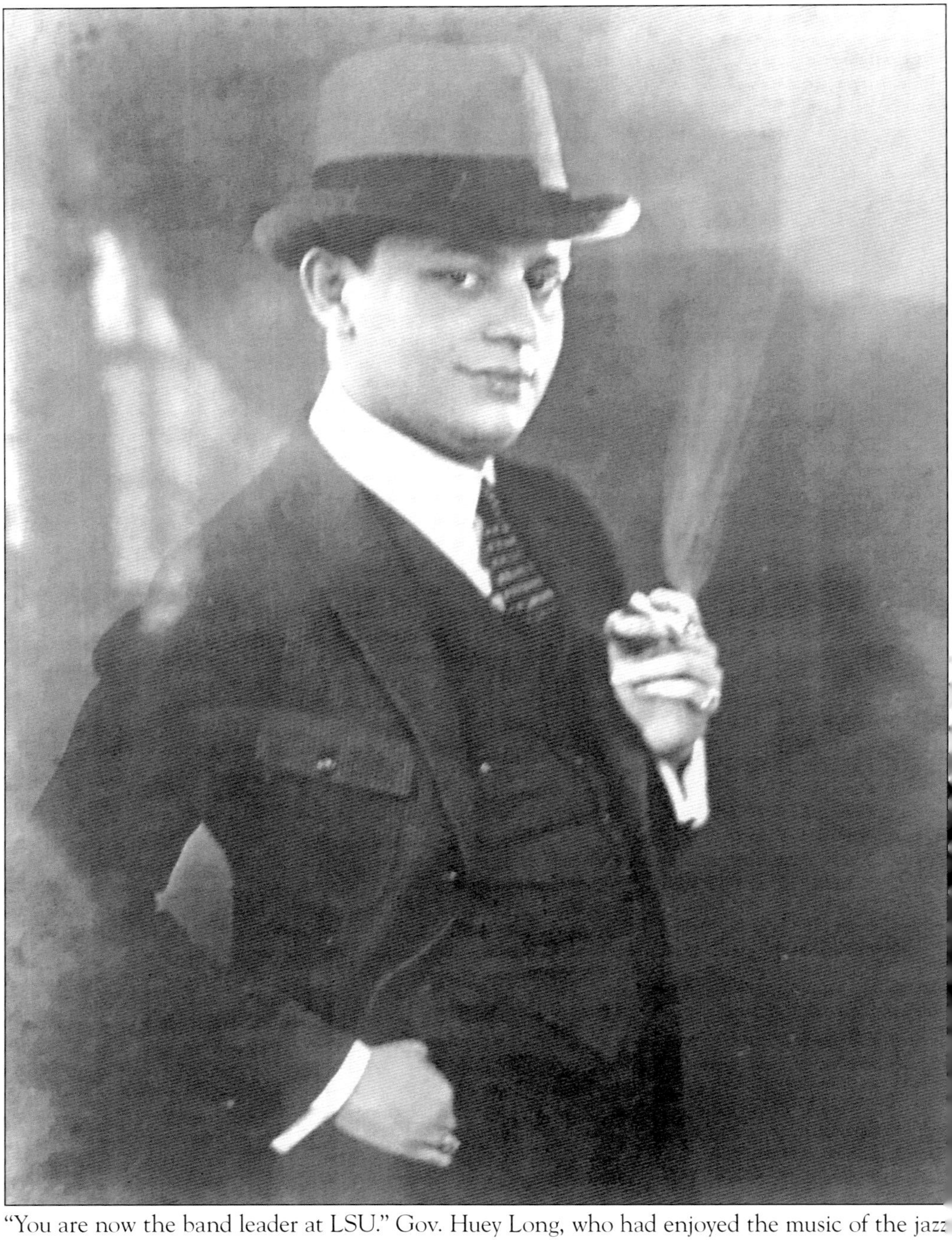

"You are now the band leader at LSU." Gov. Huey Long, who had enjoyed the music of the jazz orchestra at the Roosevelt Hotel in New Orleans in 1934, drafted Castro Carazo, the band's leader, to direct the LSU marching band. Carazo and lyricist Huey Long made one of history's more curious songwriting teams. (Courtesy of Nina Carazo Shapp.)

Carazo and Long would collaborate on a number of songs, including "Touchdown for LSU," which is still used as one of the university's fight songs. Their most successful and memorable collaboration was "Every Man a King," Long's own theme song, which the LSU band played at his funeral in 1935. (Courtesy of the Foundation for Historical Louisiana.)

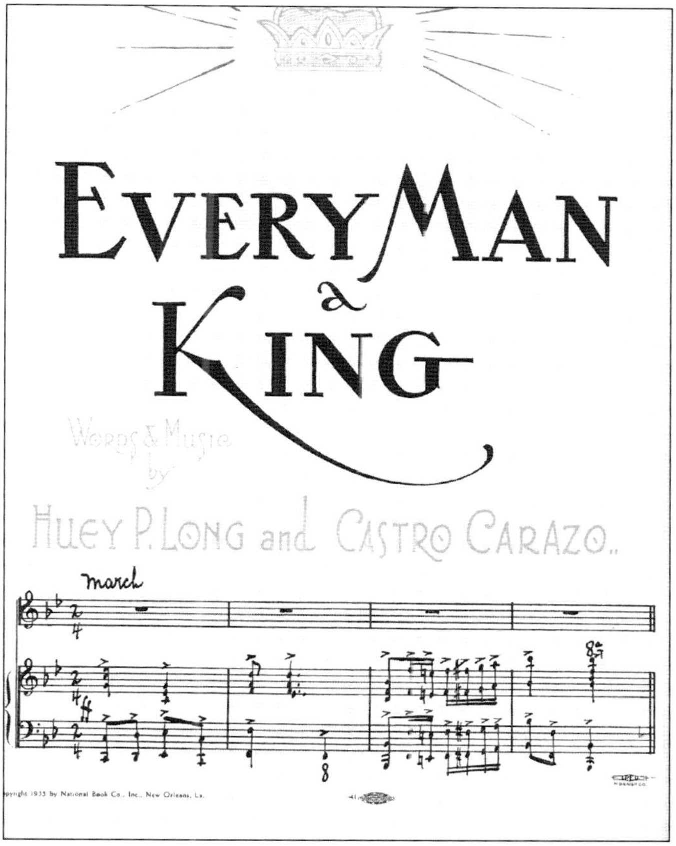

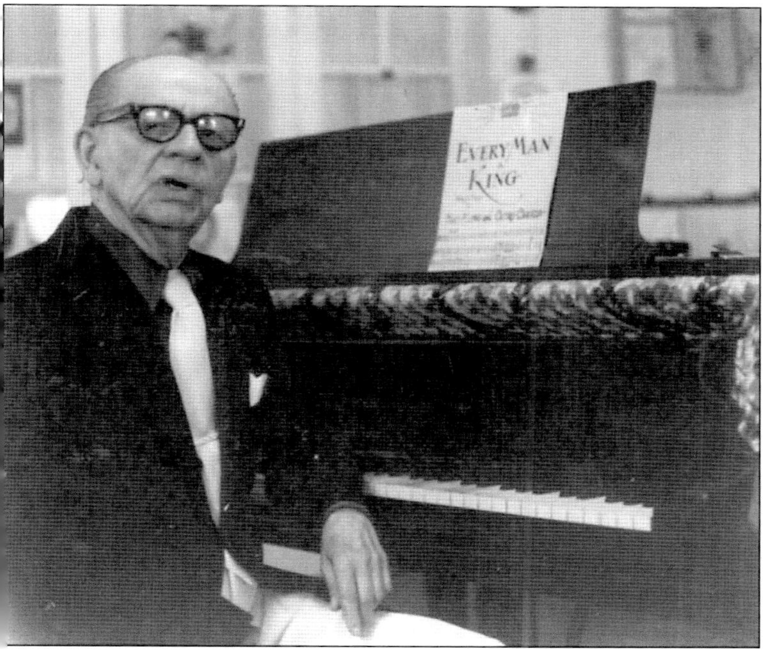

Carazo continued to direct the band until 1940. Thanks to his leadership and style, the band experienced national fame. Carazo, pictured here at age 77, lived at 660 North Eighth Street in Spanish Town. (Courtesy of the Louisiana Collection of the State Library of Louisiana.)

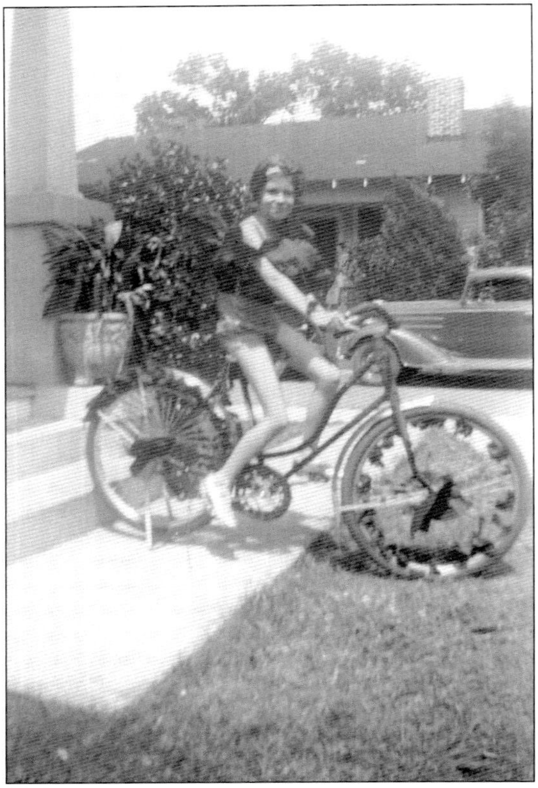

Spanish Town's Winifred Evans Byrd has spent a lifetime sharing the history of Spanish Town with neighbors and friends. During long decades when Spanish Town was a neighborhood searching for an identity, "Winnie" was a strong voice for revitalization. She is seen here in front of her home at 649 Lucilla Drive, now Lucilla Lane, in 1935. (Courtesy of Winifred Evans Byrd.)

Collett E. Woolman, a young Spanish Town resident and agent at the nearby LSU Agricultural Experimental Station in the early 1920s, nurtured an interest in agricultural aviation into a career that eventually led him to become founder and first chief executive officer of Delta Air Lines. Appropriately, his home at 830 North Sixth Street, which still stands, is an airplane bungalow. (Courtesy of Delta Air Lines.)

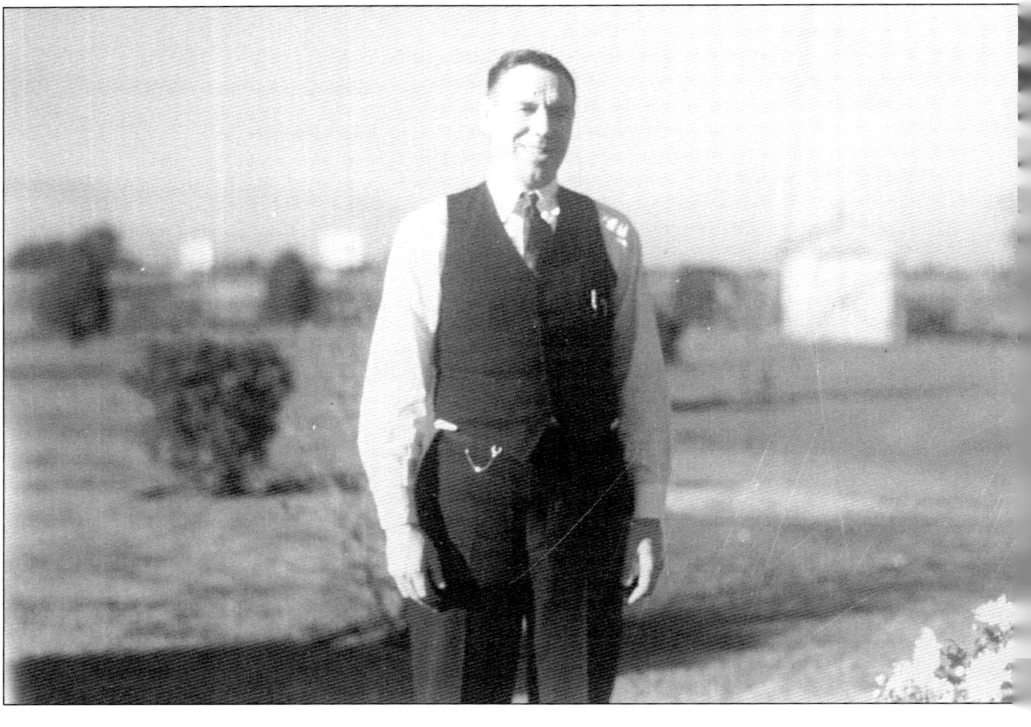

Six

The Kingfish and His Masterpiece

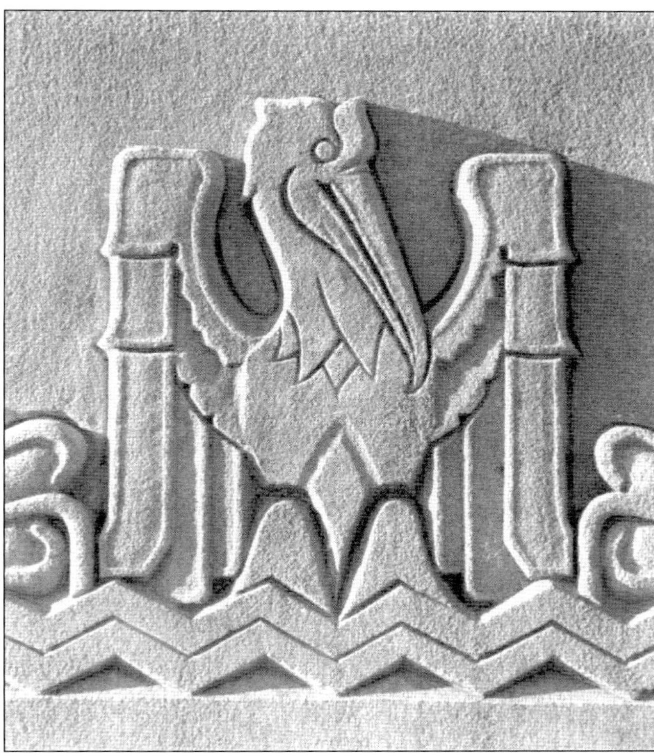

While every man might be a king in the realm of the Kingfish, only one would have the ambition and energy to build a magnificent castle, live in an apartment near its top, be murdered on its magnificent main floor, and be buried in its garden. Louisiana's State Capitol was one of the last masterpieces of Beaux Arts architecture to be built in the United States. Its walls, floors, ceilings, and gardens are adorned with works of art representing the people, flora, fauna, and history of the state. This sculpture of Louisiana's official state bird, the pelican, was carved by Ulric Ellerhusen and placed at the fifth-floor level on the north side of the building. (Courtesy of the Louisiana Collection of the State Library of Louisiana.)

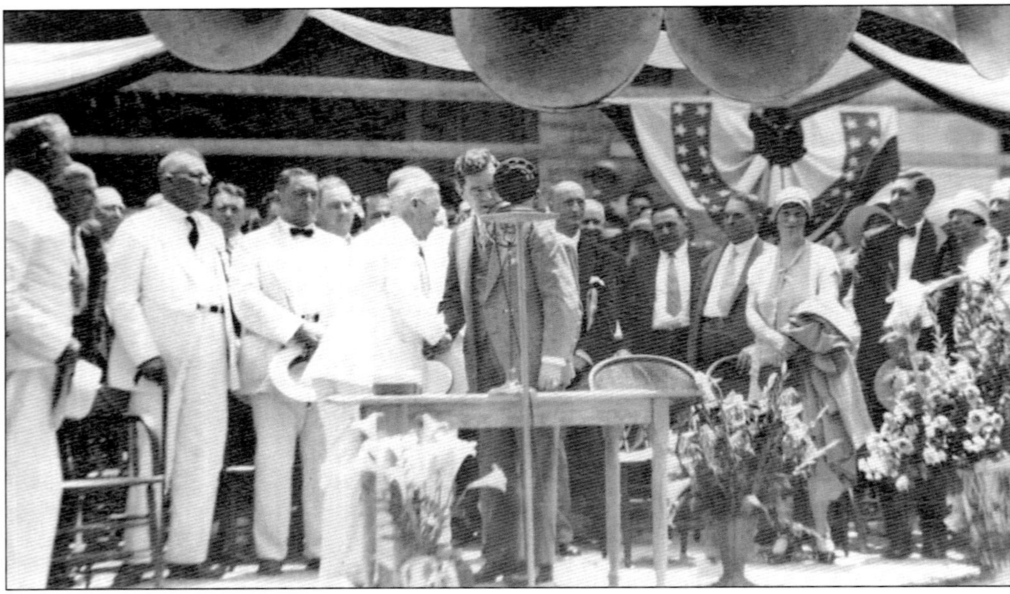

Huey Pierce Long (1893–1935) is pictured at his inauguration on May 21, 1928. Long ruled as Louisiana's governor from 1928 until his election to the US Senate in 1932. As a candidate for governor, he promised voters a new capitol that would consolidate state offices. A recalcitrant legislature fought the effort for over three years before acquiescing in 1931. (Courtesy of the Louisiana Collection of the State Library of Louisiana.)

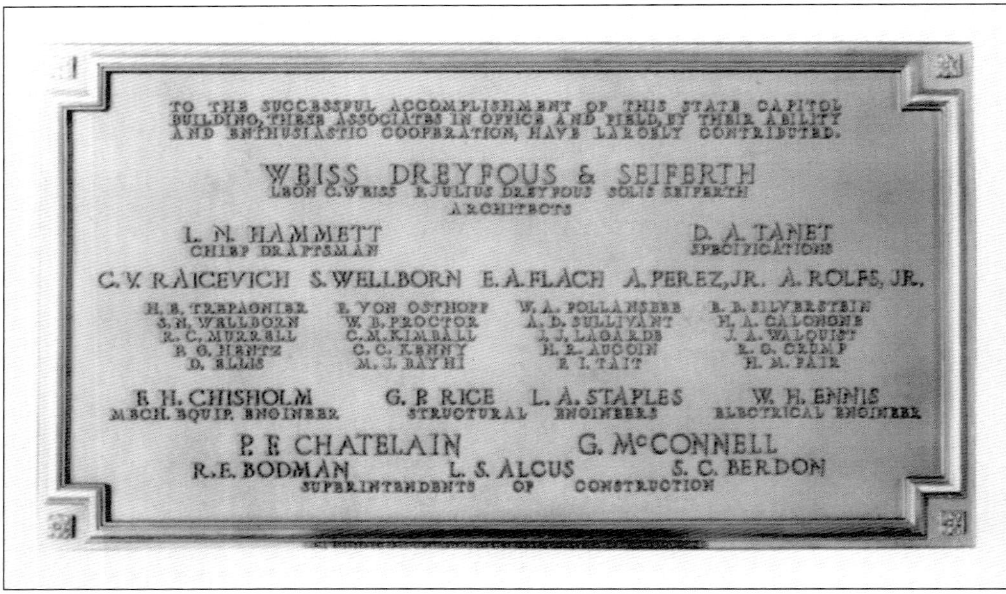

The architects of the new State Capitol were Weiss, Dreyfous, and Seiferth of New Orleans. In grand Louisiana tradition, Leon C. Weiss, the lead architect of the firm, served a prison term for fraud related to another state project. This plaque in the building's foyer lists key participants in the construction project. (Courtesy of the Louisiana Collection of the State Library of Louisiana.)

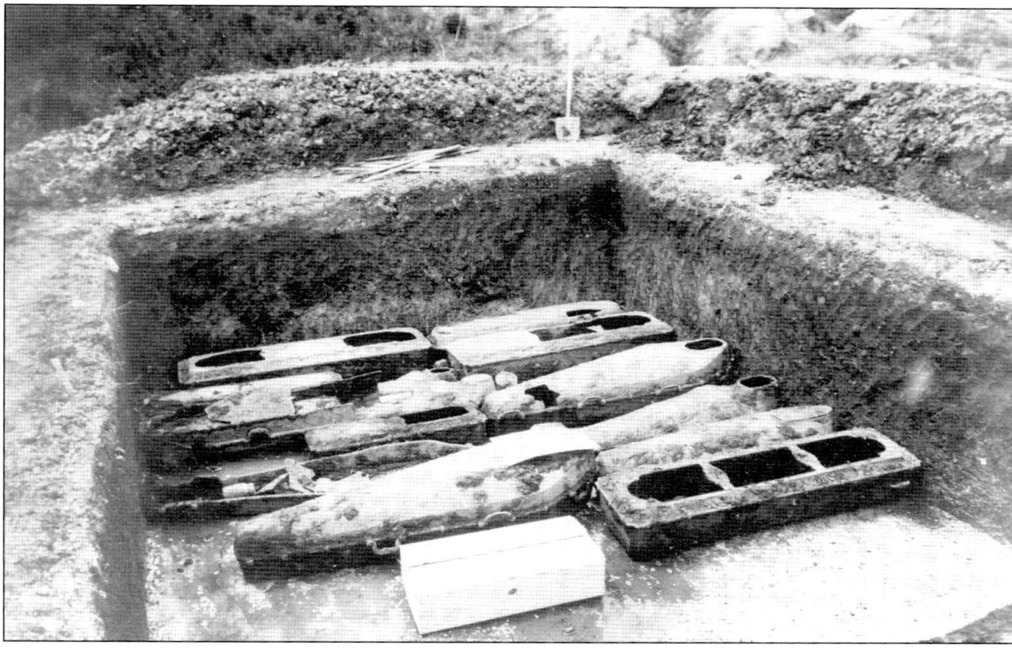

Before construction work at the capitol could begin, soil had to be moved at a site behind the Arsenal Museum. During the process, three dozen coffins containing the remains of some of the first Spanish inhabitants of Spanish Town were unearthed. The caskets were resealed and buried in an undisclosed location to protect them from vandalism. (Courtesy of the Louisiana Collection of the State Library of Louisiana.)

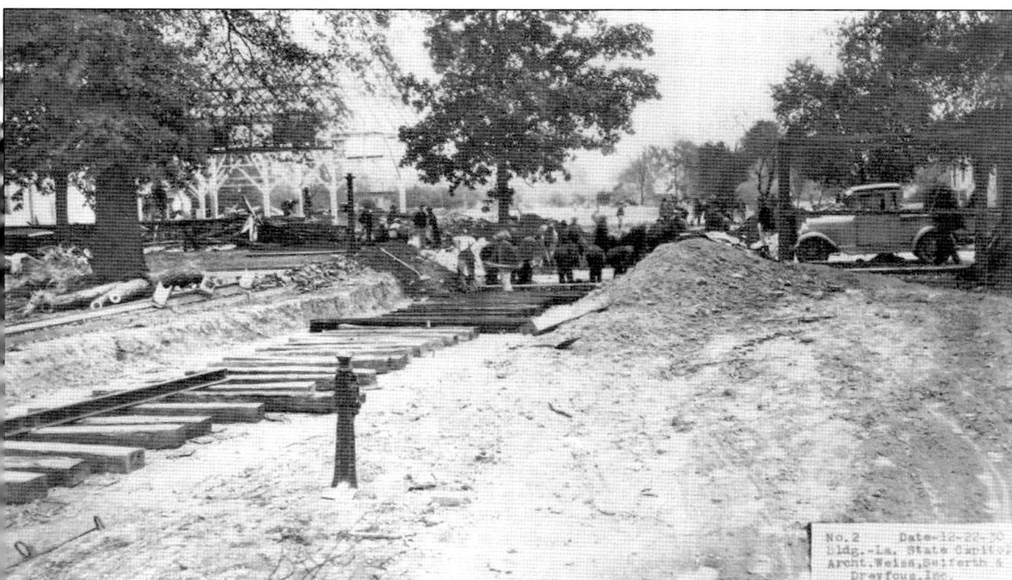

The Yazoo & Mississippi Valley Railroad built a spur that stopped at the point of construction. Approximately 2,500 carloads of materials were brought via this rail spur for use on the project, including tile, sand, gravel, limestone, cement, bricks, marble, bronze, granite, ornamental iron, and terrazzo. (Courtesy of the Louisiana Collection of the State Library of Louisiana.)

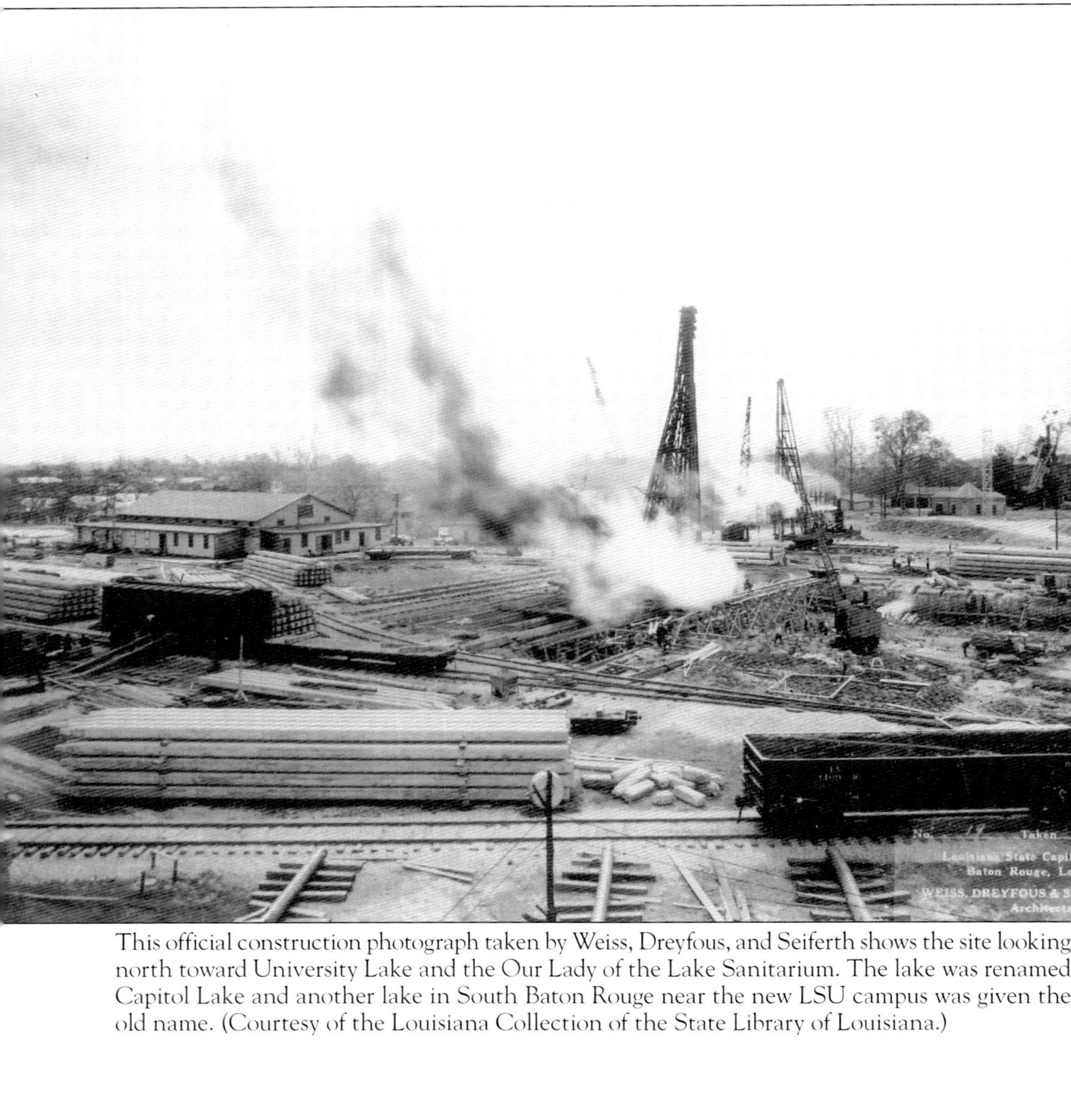

This official construction photograph taken by Weiss, Dreyfous, and Seiferth shows the site looking north toward University Lake and the Our Lady of the Lake Sanitarium. The lake was renamed Capitol Lake and another lake in South Baton Rouge near the new LSU campus was given the old name. (Courtesy of the Louisiana Collection of the State Library of Louisiana.)

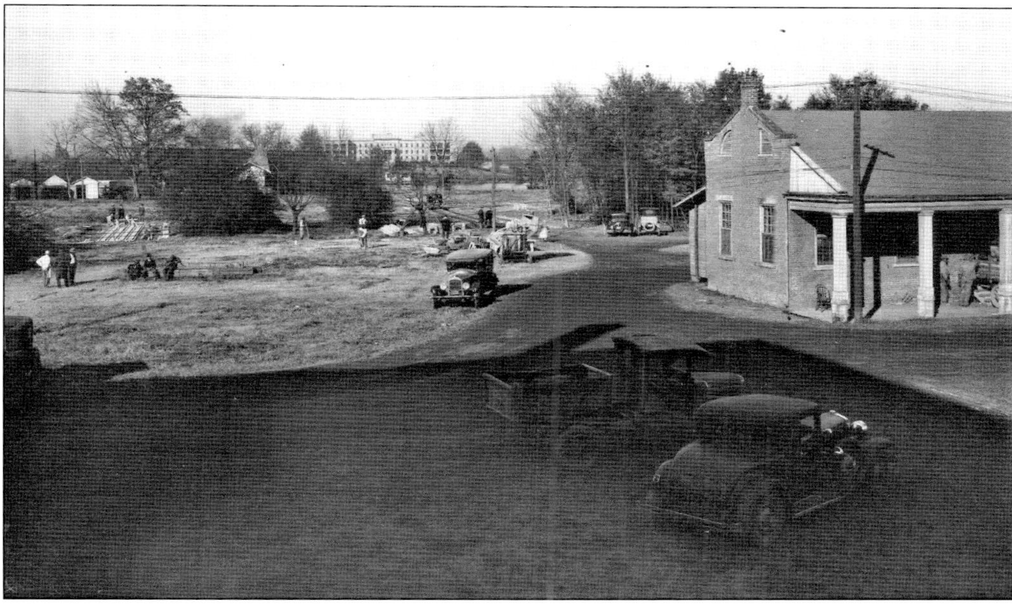

This photograph of the construction site with the Our Lady of the Lake Sanitarium in the background was taken in early 1931. Of the $5 million appropriated for the construction of the capitol, the construction contract for the building was $2,394,000. The balance of the appropriation was used for the building's distinctive Beaux Arts fixtures, bronze work, and statuary. (Courtesy of the Louisiana Collection of the State Library of Louisiana.)

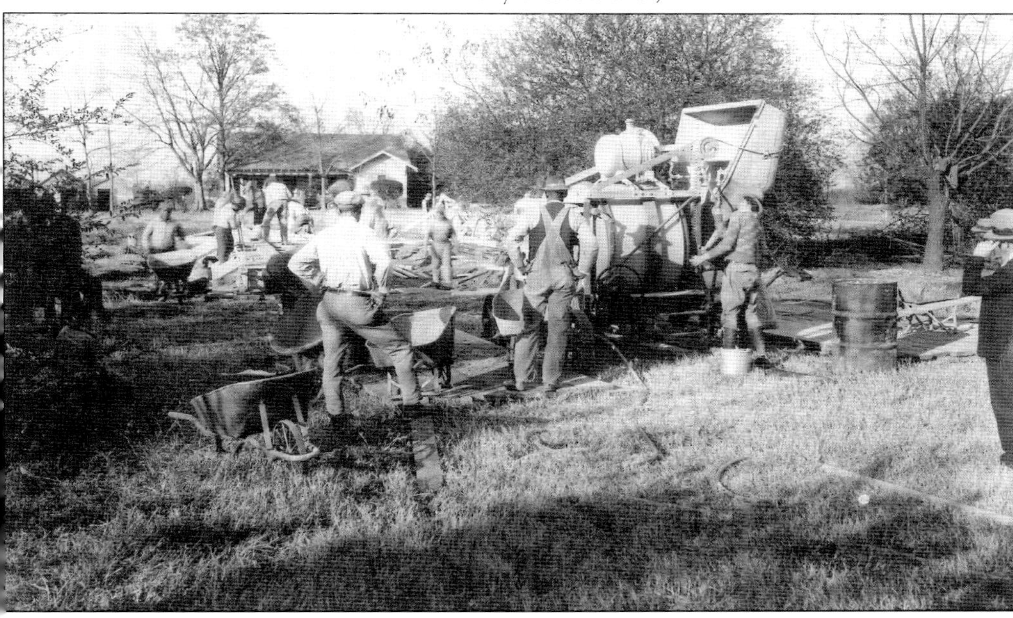

Construction was officially to begin on January 1, 1931, but ground was broken on December 15, 1930. The capitol was completed on March 1, 1932, and dedicated at the inauguration of Gov. Richard Leche on May 16, 1932. In this photograph, the first concrete for the new building is being poured in December 1930. (Courtesy of the Louisiana Collection of the State Library of Louisiana.)

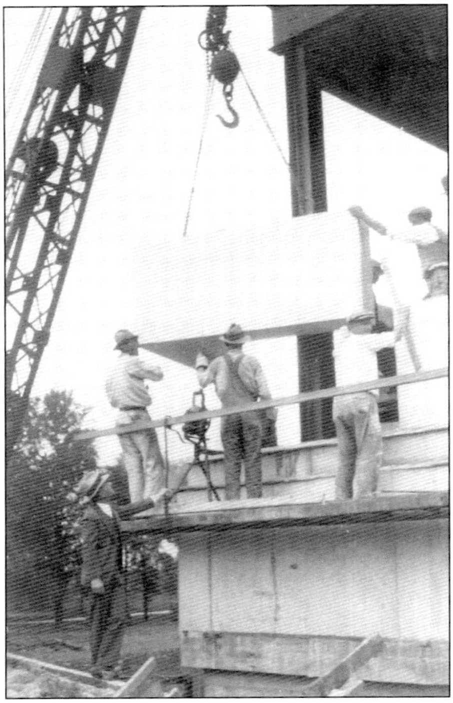

The cornerstone of the capitol was set into place on the southwest corner of the building on May 7, 1931. It contained a sealed copper box with documents related to the construction of the building, photographs of state officials, and copies of newspaper articles recounting the statewide capitol referendum in 1930. (Courtesy of the Louisiana Collection of the State Library of Louisiana.)

The cornerstone, seen here in the 1970s, is inscribed with the phrase "We Live for Those We Love," the state seal, and the dates of the Louisiana Purchase in 1803 and the setting of the cornerstone in 1931. The other side of the cornerstone is inscribed with the names of state officials and architects. (Courtesy of the Louisiana Collection of the State Library of Louisiana.)

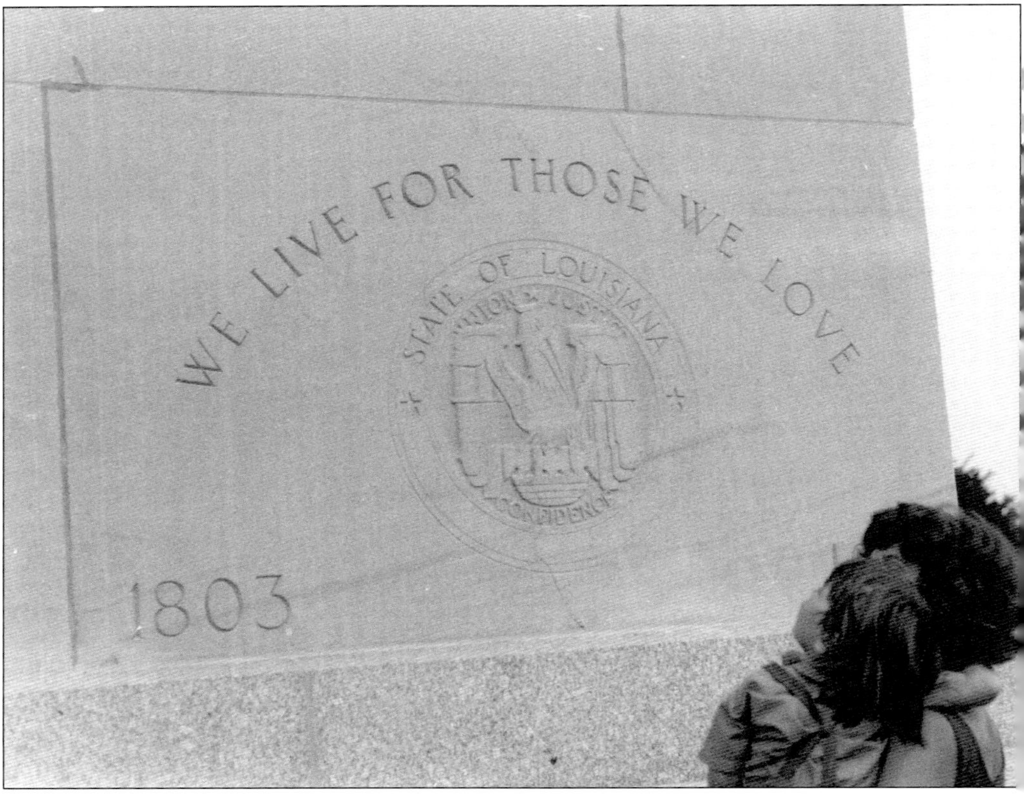

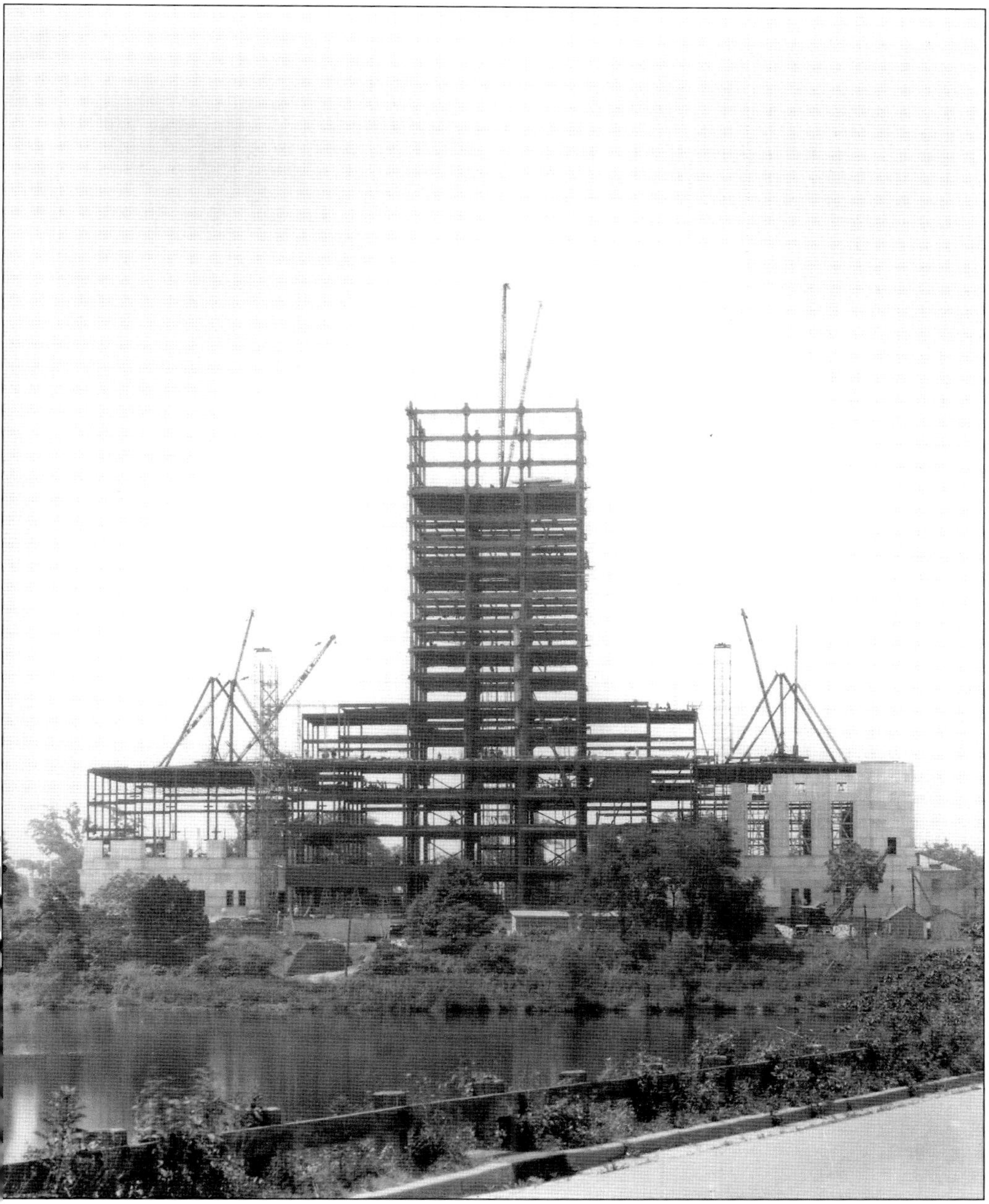

This photograph of the capitol's framework from May 1931 shows that Louisiana's capitol would become one of four skyscraper state capitols and one of only nine without a dome. At the insistence of Governor Long, the capitol would be 13 feet taller than Nebraska's skyscraper state capitol, then under construction in Lincoln. (Courtesy of the Collections of the Louisiana State Museum.)

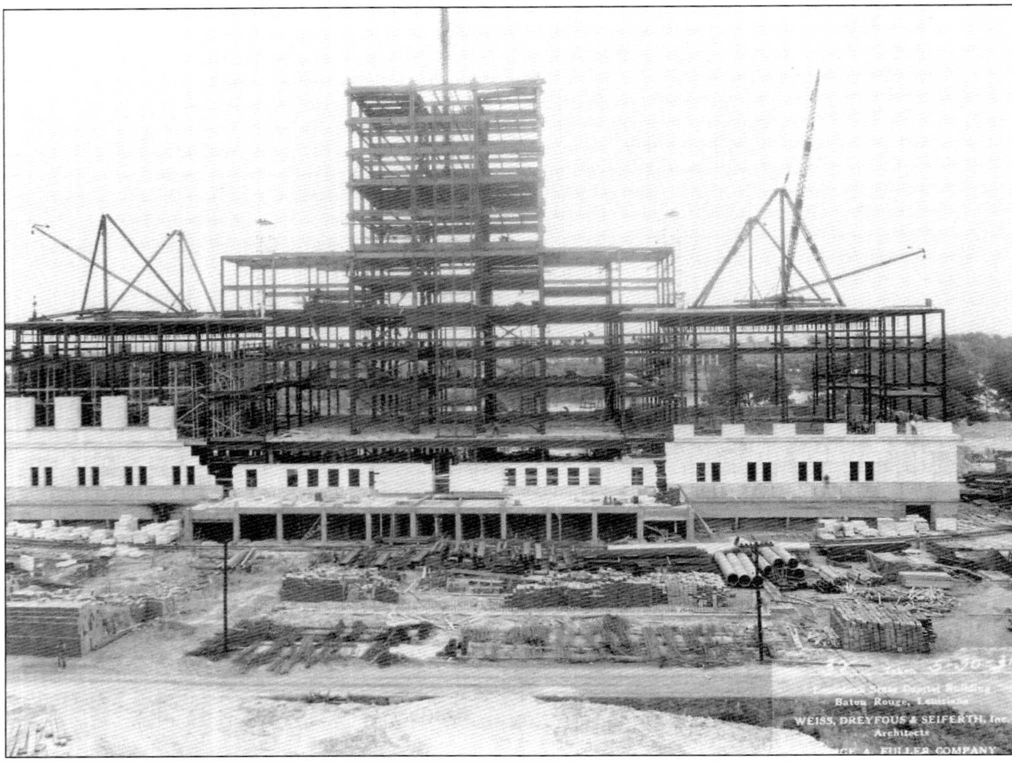

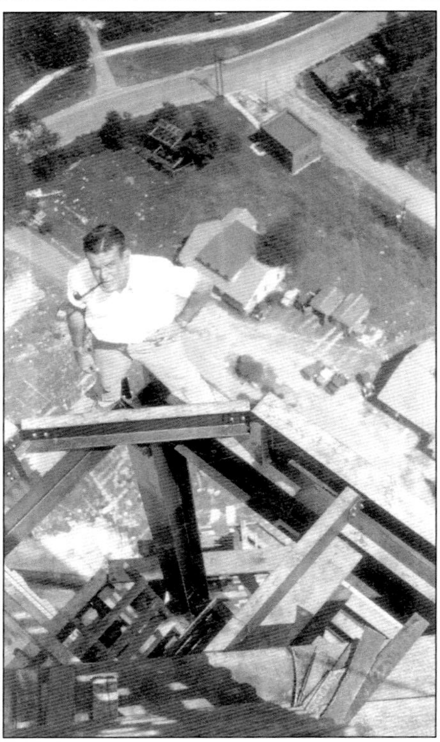

This photograph from May 1931 shows construction looking to the north. Architectural historians, including Vincent F. Kubly, who authored *The Louisiana Capitol: Its Art and Architecture*, have written that the new Louisiana State Capitol represented the end of the Beaux Arts architectural tradition in America, which sought to combine conventional elements of classicism with popular imagery of modernism. (Courtesy of the Collections of the Louisiana State Museum.)

Ralph E. Bodman, L.S. Alcus, and S.C. Burden served as the superintendents of construction for the capitol. Bodman, who opened the architectural firm of Bodman & Murrell in Baton Rouge in 1934, is seen here on the 34th floor of the capitol in mid-1931. (Courtesy of the Louisiana Collection of the State Library of Louisiana.)

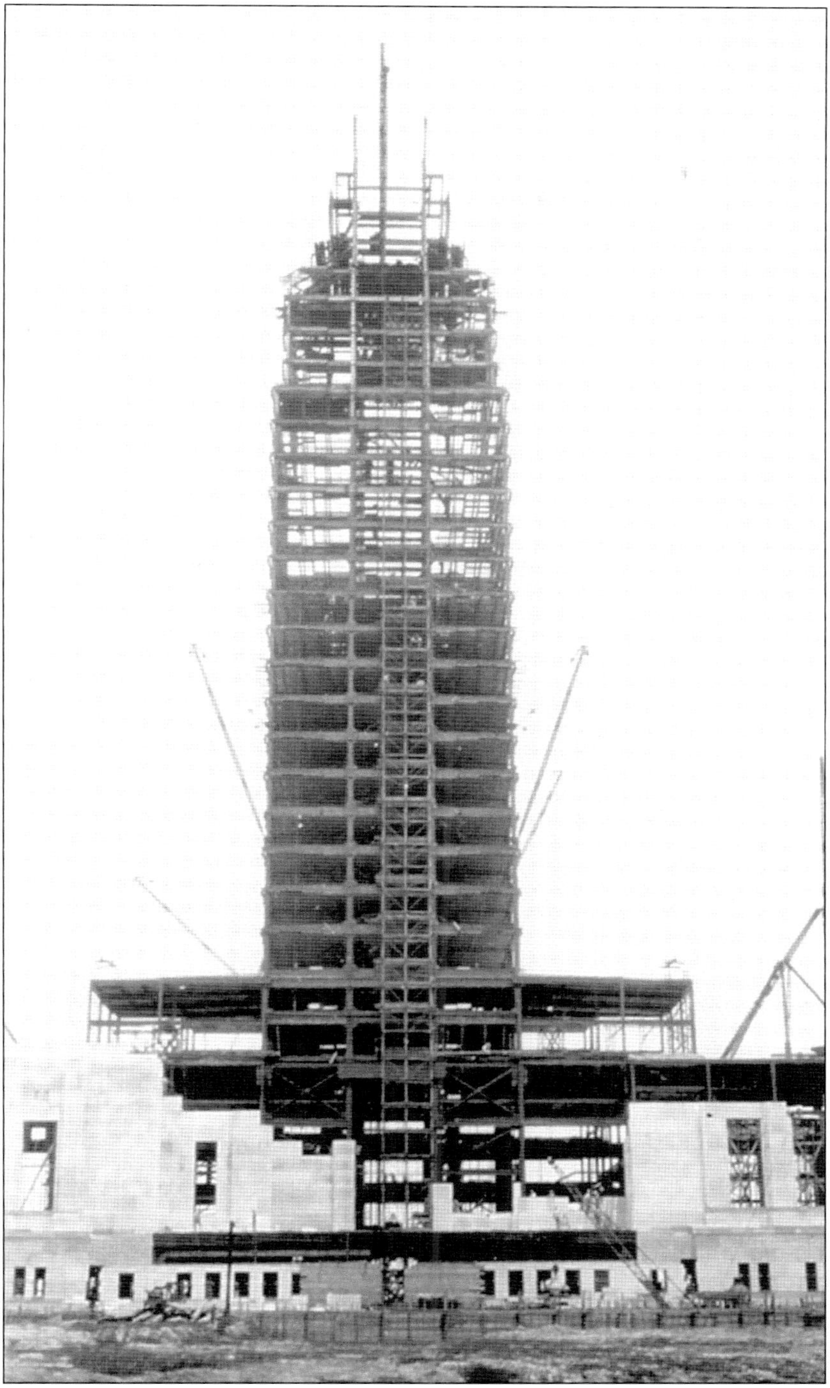

The steel framework of the tower was completed in June 1931. The tower's skeleton was designed to withstand winds of up to 110 miles per hour. At its completion, the tower contained 249,000 square feet of offices, apartments, and other amenities. (Courtesy of the Louisiana Collection of the State Library of Louisiana.)

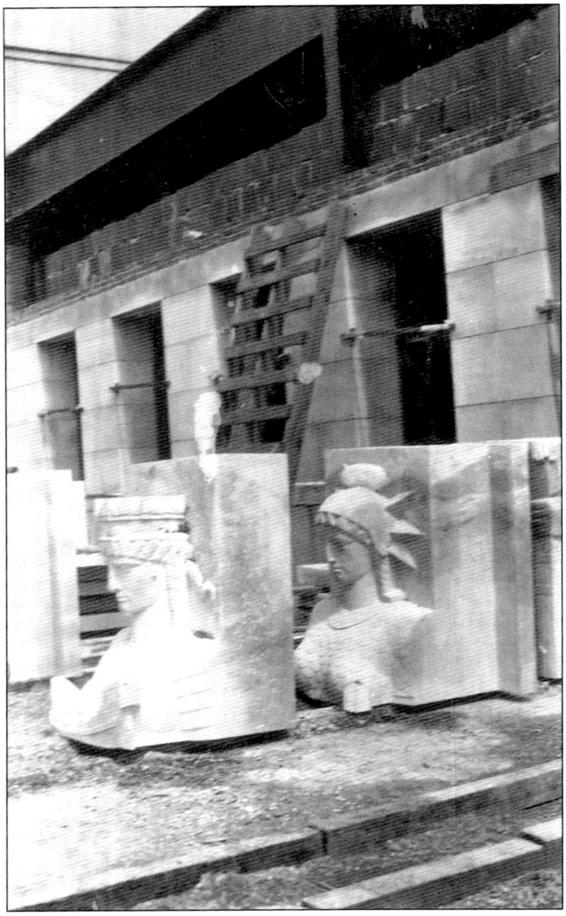

"The Dominations of Louisiana" (Indians, France, Spain, the United States, and the Confederacy) are represented in sculptures by Lee Lawrie above the capitol's main entrance. Lawrie is best known as the creator of the statue of Atlas at Rockefeller Center in New York. Spain and the United States are seen here on the sixth-floor roof awaiting placement. (Courtesy of the Louisiana Collection of the State Library of Louisiana.)

Profile plaques of 22 influential men from Louisiana history, created by New Orleans artists Angela Gregory, Albert Rieker, Juanita Gonzales, John Lachlin, and Rudolph Parducci, were placed over the large windows of the Senate and House of Representatives. Ralph E. Bodman (right), superintendent of construction, is seen here with the plaque of W.C.C. Claiborne as it awaits placement. (Courtesy of the Louisiana Collection of the State Library of Louisiana.)

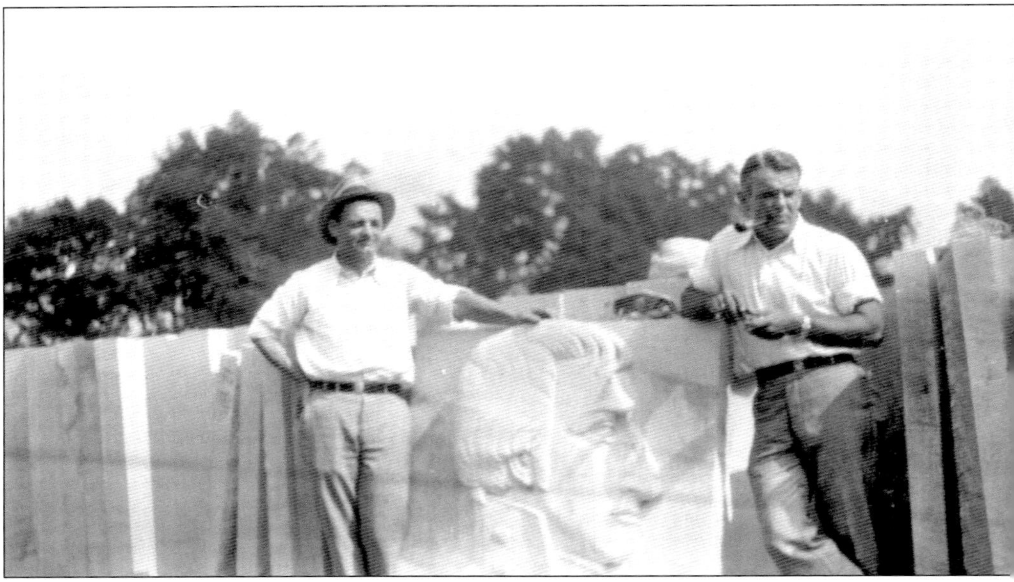

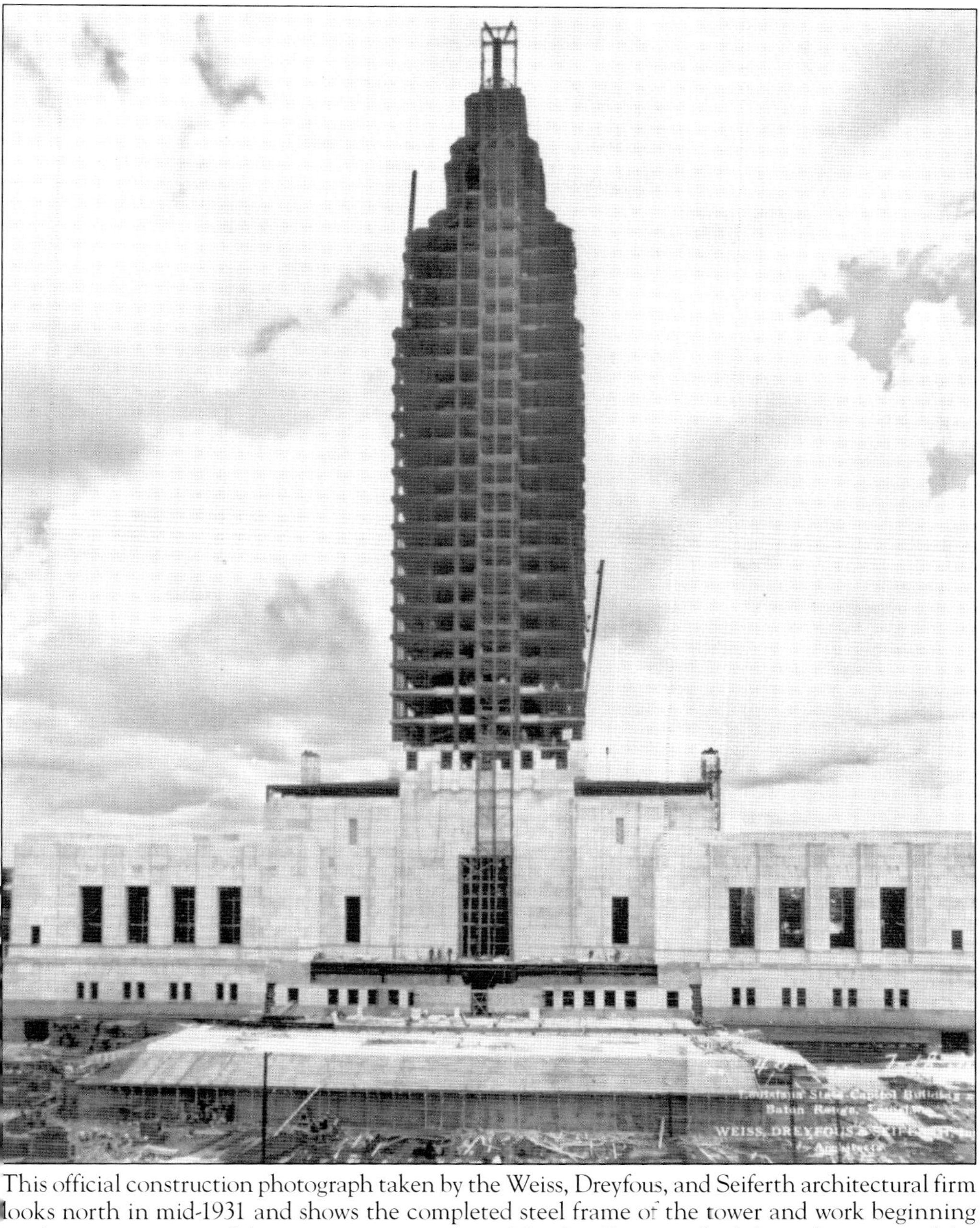

This official construction photograph taken by the Weiss, Dreyfous, and Seiferth architectural firm looks north in mid-1931 and shows the completed steel frame of the tower and work beginning on the main staircase. Minnesota granite was used for the 49 steps, which bear the names of the states of the union. (Courtesy of the Louisiana Collection of the State Library of Louisiana.)

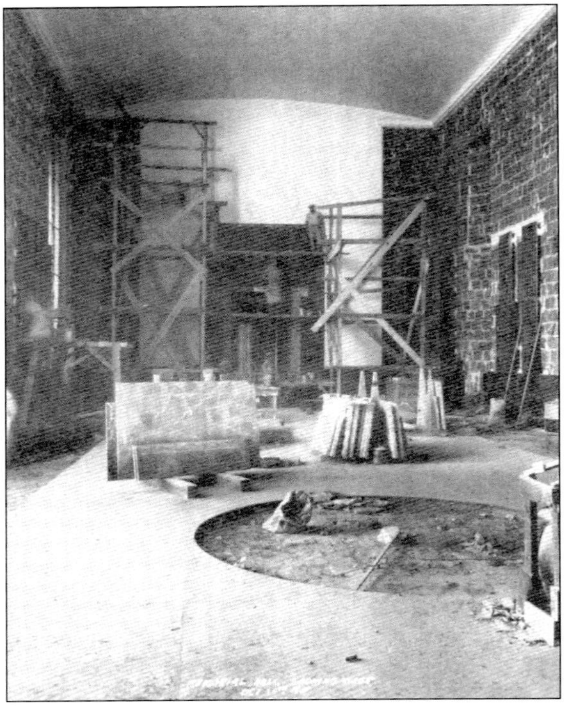

In this construction photograph of the Memorial Hall, the placement of the bronze relief map of Louisiana by architect Solis Seiferth is seen in the center of the room. Murals representing the "Abundance of the Earth" were placed over the great doors of the Senate and House of Representatives. (Courtesy of the Louisiana Collection of the State Library of Louisiana.)

This photograph from the 1950s shows the capitol's Memorial Hall, dedicated to "all of the great soldiers, statesmen, pioneers, and other benefactors, whose memory is a cherished heritage of the people of the state." The floor features two types of lava from Mount Vesuvius, and the bronze plaque on the balcony honoring Huey Long was donated by the United Confederate Veterans. (Courtesy of the Louisiana Collection of the State Library of Louisiana.)

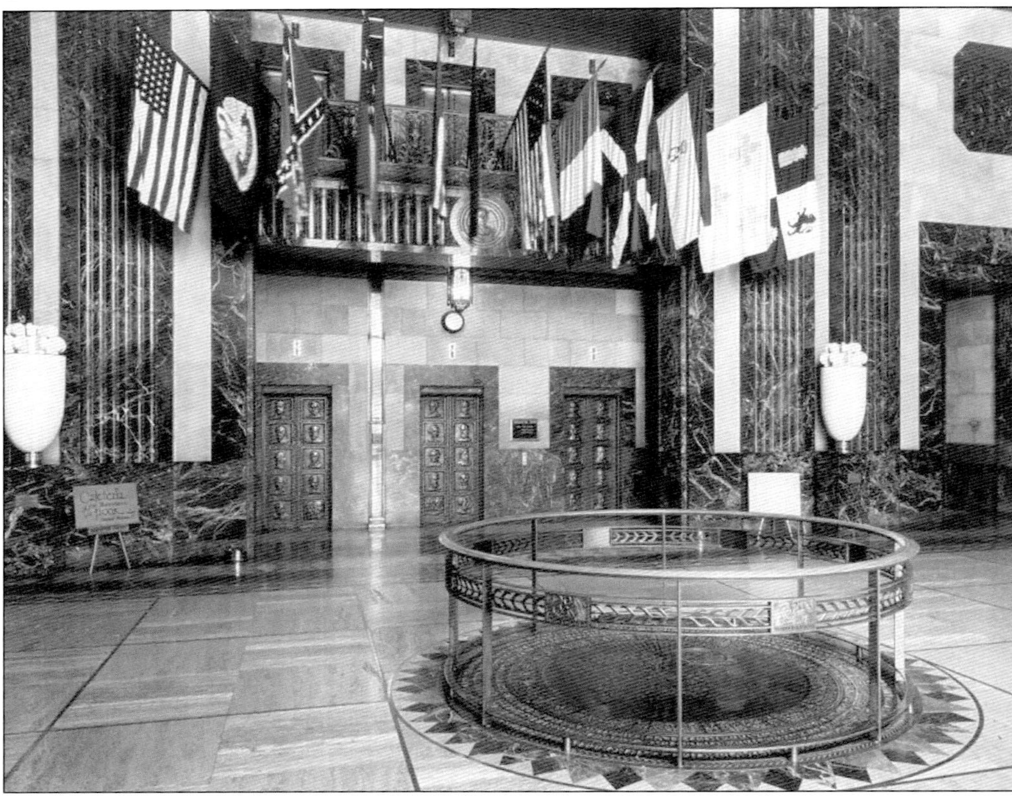

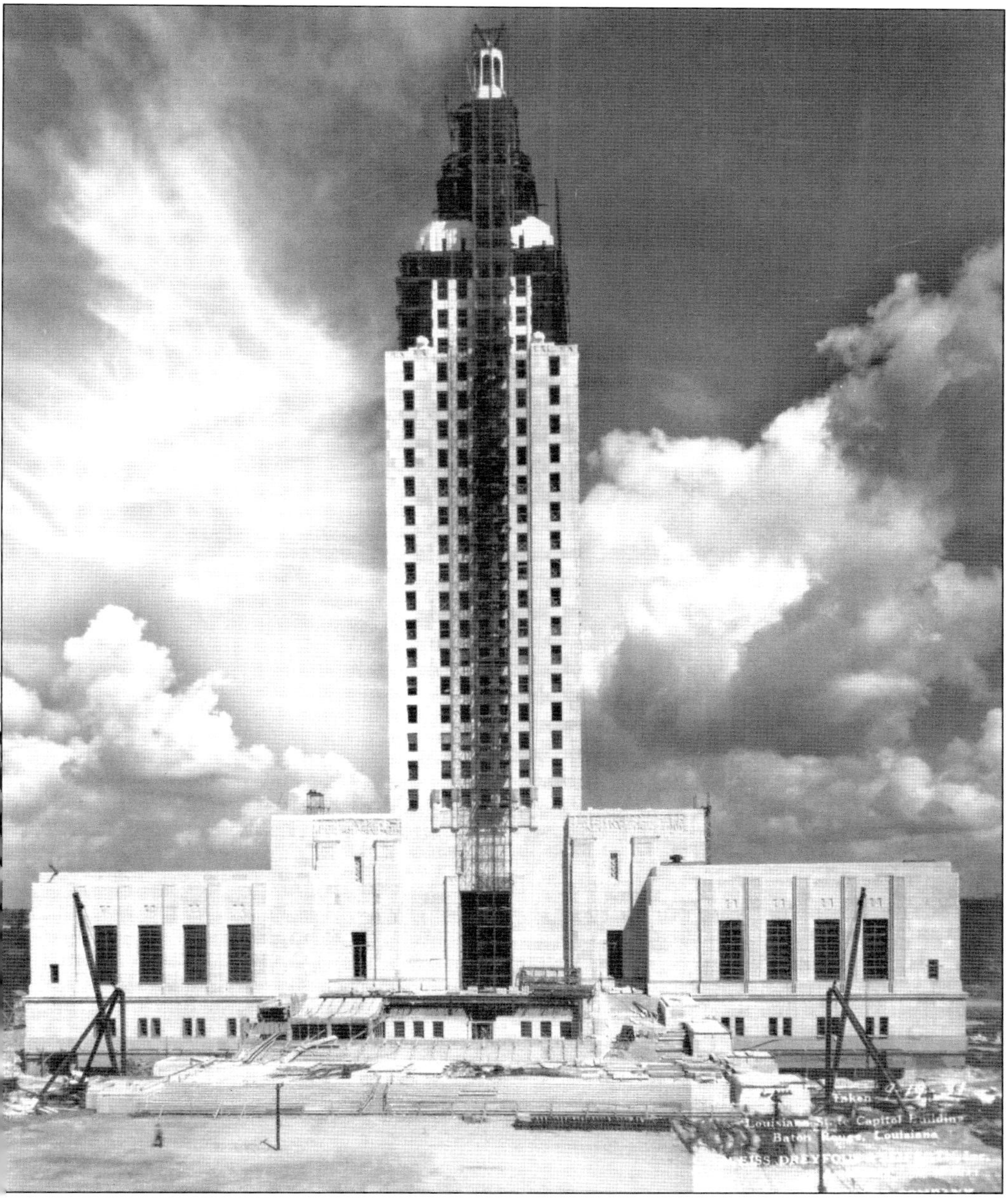

Construction of the tower nears completion in this photograph from September 19, 1931. The capitol, like the Chrysler and Empire State Buildings under construction in New York at the same time, was among the last major attempts to apply classical traditions to the skyscraper model. (Courtesy of the Louisiana Collection of the State Library of Louisiana.)

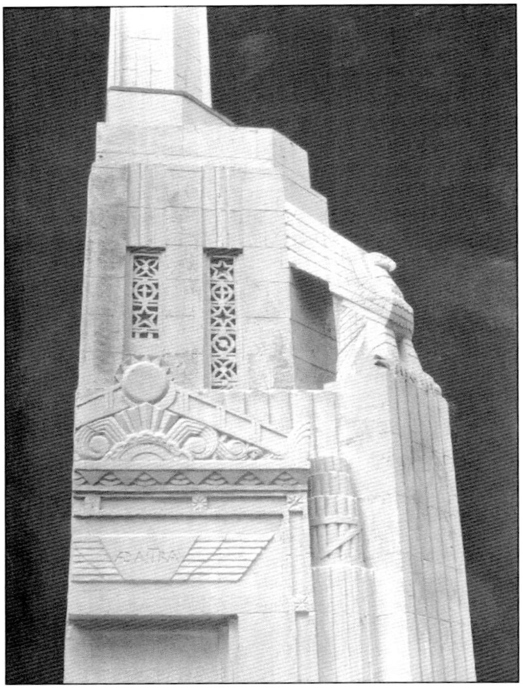

In the words of architect Seymour Weiss, the tower "rises upward and ever upward, at its topmost reaches, culminates in a spiritual 'temple' symbolizing the noblest ideals of an inspired and enlightened people." A model of the temple created by Ulric Ellerhusen is shown here. (Courtesy of the Louisiana Collection of the State Library of Louisiana.)

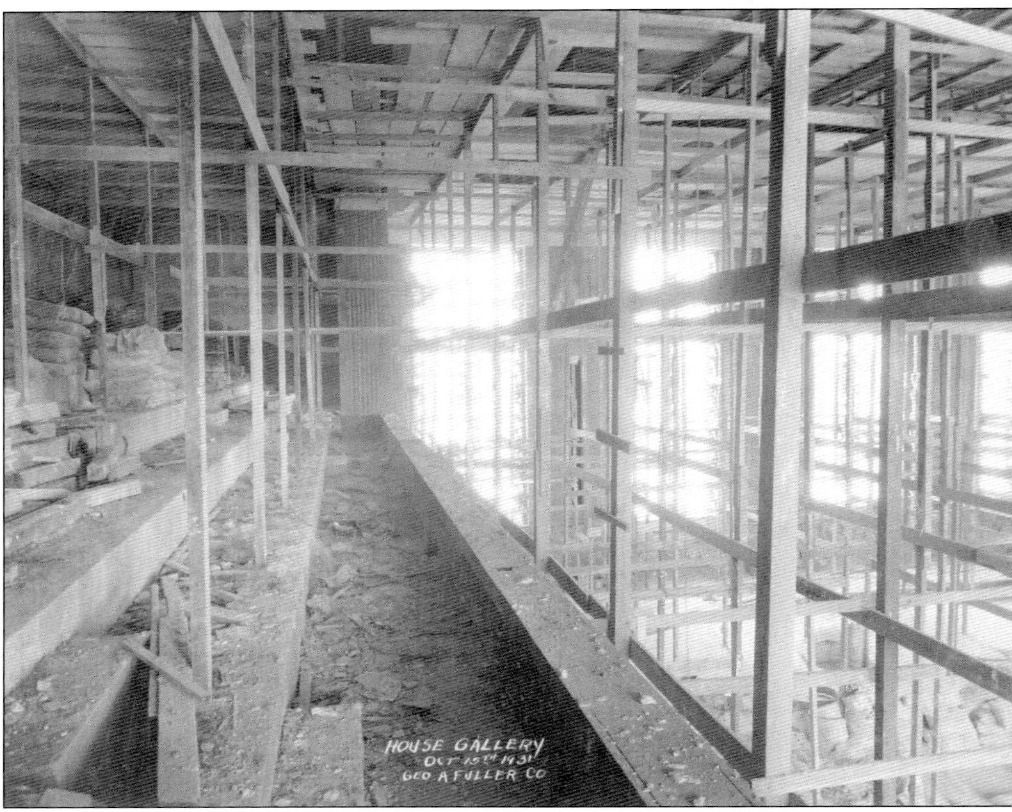

This photograph from mid-1931 shows construction of the viewers' gallery of the House of Representatives. When completed, the House chamber featured an electronic voting machine to record votes and microphones that permitted the governor to listen to the proceedings. (Courtesy of the Louisiana Collection of the State Library of Louisiana.)

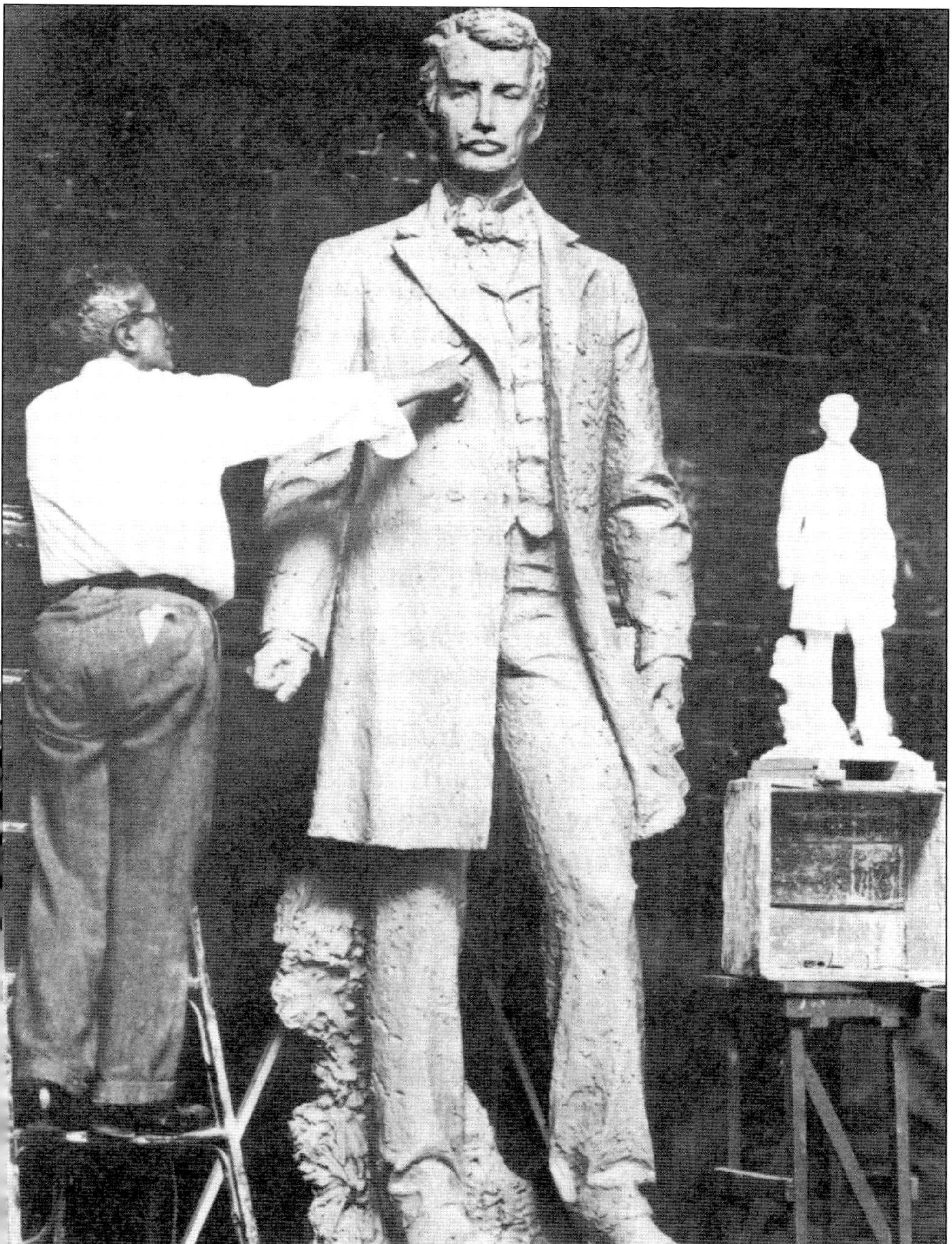

Bronze plaques featuring all of Louisiana's governors from Bienville to Huey Long are featured on elevator doors in the Memorial Hall. The plaques were modeled by Attillio Piccirilli in New York. Piccirilli (shown here) also created the statue of Gov. Henry Watkins Allen in the Memorial Hall. (Courtesy of the Louisiana Collection of the State Library of Louisiana.)

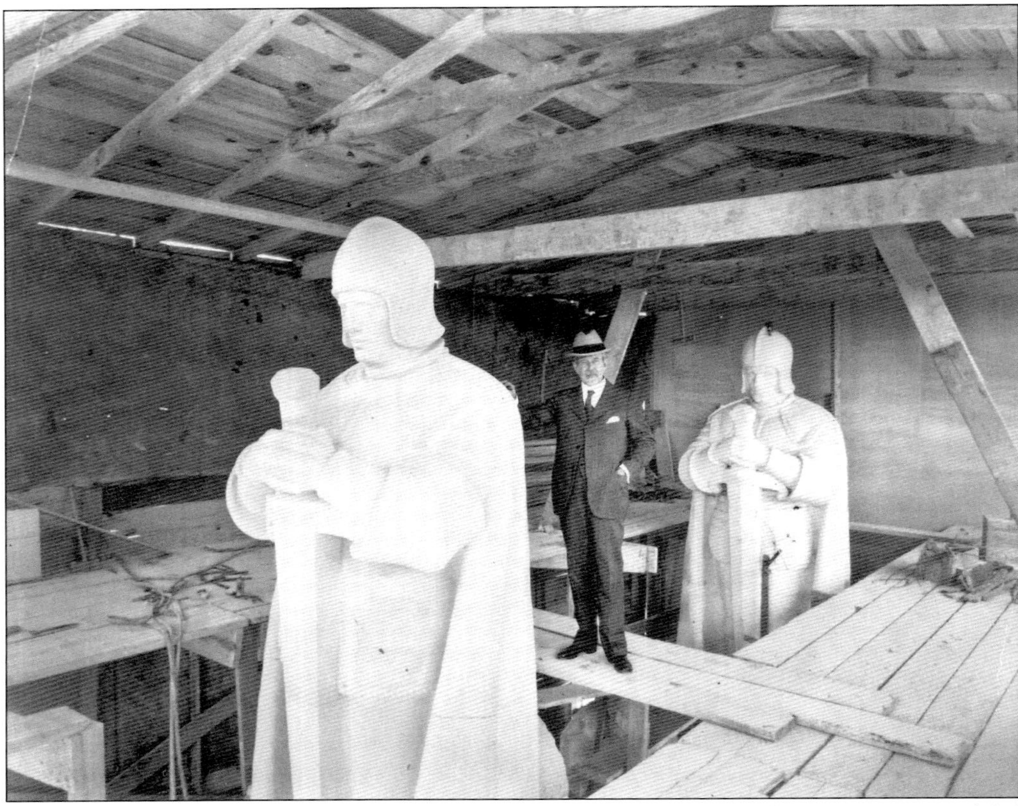

Two groups of statuary flanking the entrance to the capitol, *Patriotism* and *Pioneers*, were modeled by Lorado Taft, the "dean of American sculptors." Taft is shown in his studio with *Patriotism* and a plaster model of the statue. *Patriotism* depicts a group of mourners, including a warrior in armor, surrounding the bier of a soldier slain in battle. (Courtesy of the Louisiana Collection of the State Library of Louisiana.)

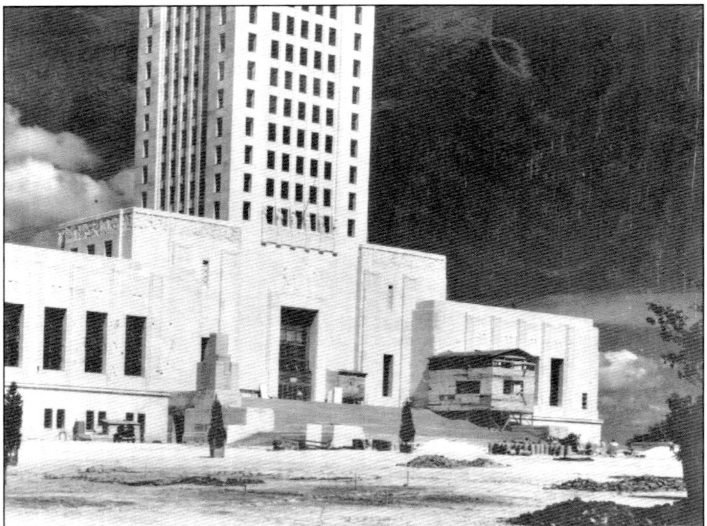

As construction of the capitol neared completion in early 1932, wooden shacks were erected on the steps to provide shelter for workers installing Taft's *Patriotism* on the east buttress. According to architect Seymour Weiss, *Patriotism* expresses "the sorrows of war, depicted in the piteous figures of the mother and father, widow and orphans of the armed defender." (Courtesy of the Louisiana Collection of the State Library of Louisiana.)

In this photograph from the 1970s of *Pioneers* on the west buttress of the capitol, a woman depicting the Spirit of Adventure stands atop a pair of iron-bound treasure chests surrounded by LaSalle, DeSoto, the priests who followed in the wake of the Spanish and French explorers, a frontiersman in buckskins, a Spanish conquistador, French settlers, and Indians. (Courtesy of the Louisiana Collection of the State Library of Louisiana.)

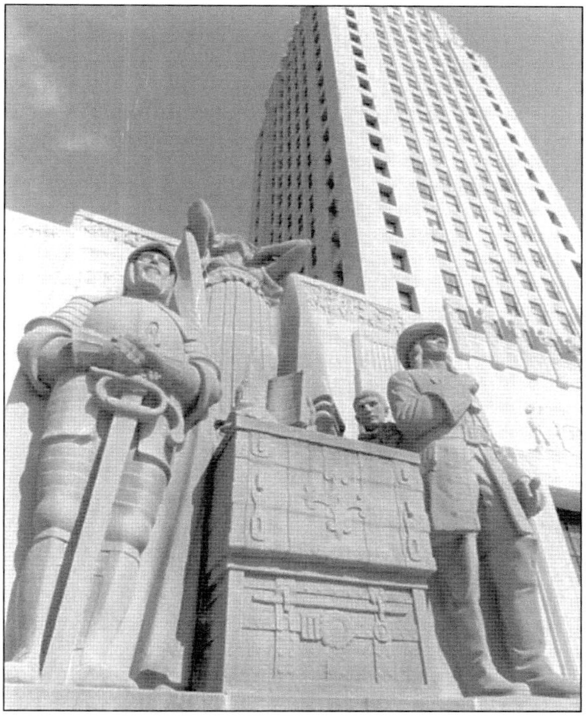

The Italian marbles (violet brocatelle, fomosa violet, and travertine) used in the Senate chamber are among the 26 marbles from Belgium, France, Germany, Italy, Spain, and the United States used in the building. The ceilings of the legislative chambers were made of celotex, a fiber extracted from bagasse, or sugarcane waste. (Courtesy of the Louisiana Collection of the State Library of Louisiana.)

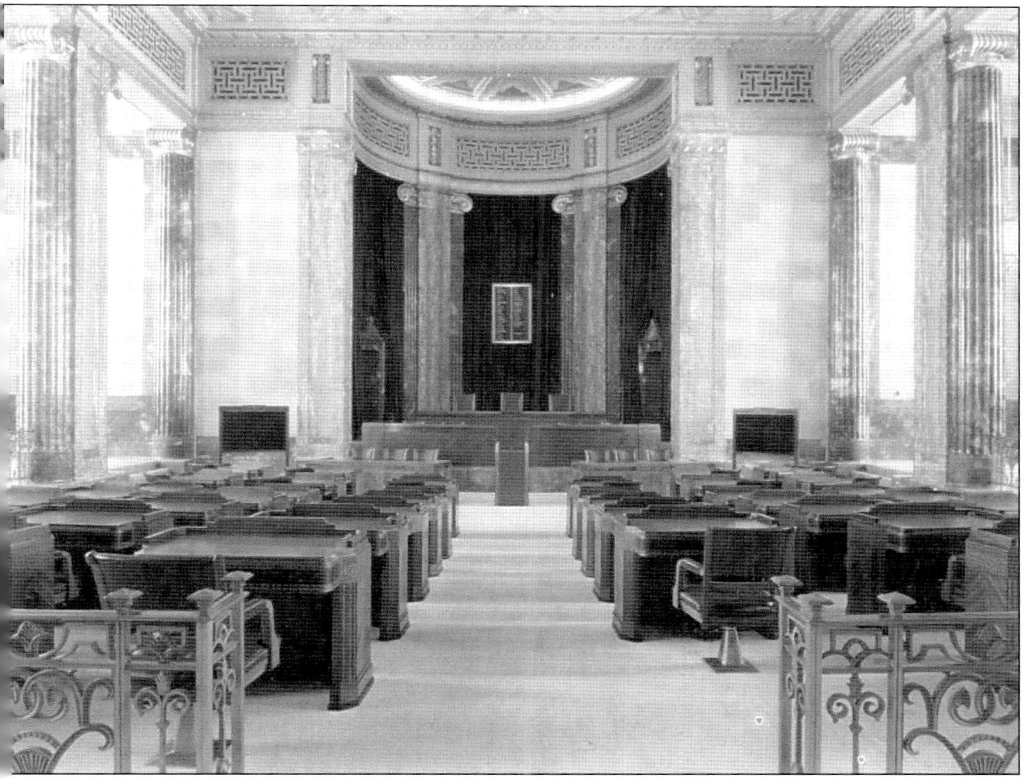

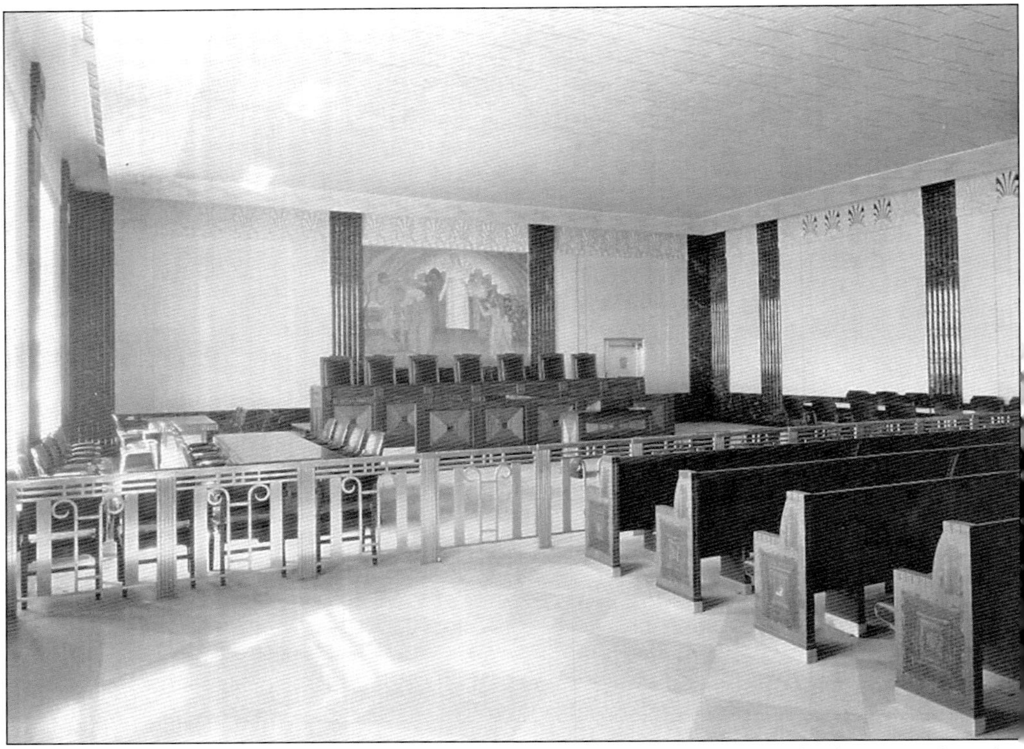

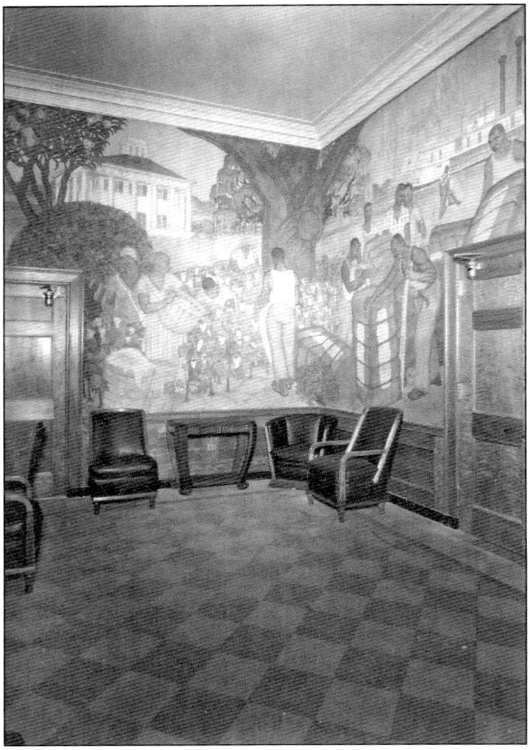

When the capitol was built, it was thought that the state supreme court would forsake its home in New Orleans to move to the capitol's fourth floor. When that did not happen, the fourth floor became the governor's office. This photograph shows the original courtroom featuring a Conrad Albrizio mural representing Psalm 94:15. (Courtesy of the Louisiana Collection of the State Library of Louisiana.)

New York–born artist Conrad Albrizio created six murals for the State Capitol, of which only one survives. This mural depicting Louisiana plantation life originally decorated the waiting room of the governor's office on the first floor. Albrizio taught art at LSU from 1935 until his retirement in 1954. (Courtesy of the Louisiana Collection of the State Library of Louisiana.)

A hallmark of the Beaux Arts style was incorporating images from the history of Louisiana into every facet of the construction of the building from the outer limestone sheath to the interior adornments. This sculpture of a Native American is on the north side of the building. (Courtesy of the Louisiana Collection of the State Library of Louisiana.)

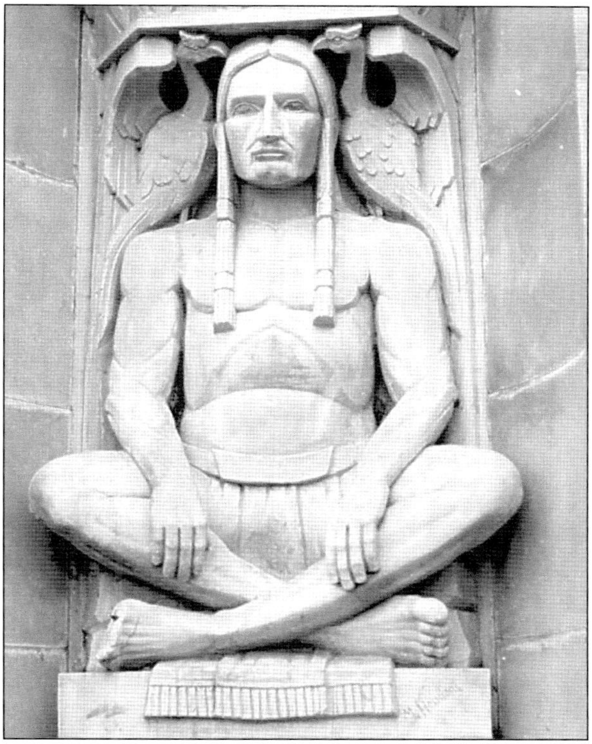

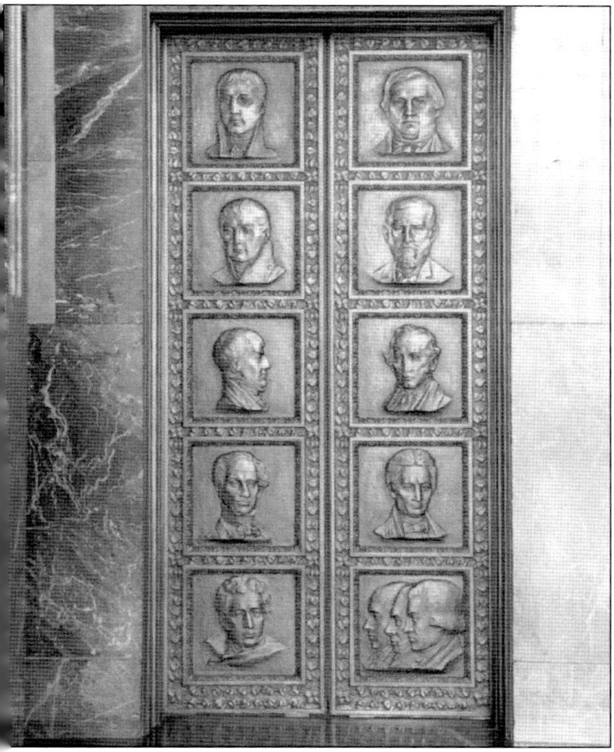

In addition to several of the statues at the capitol, the Piccirilli studio in New York also created most of the elaborate bronze work that adorns the public spaces of the building. Elevator doors in the Memorial Hall feature relief portraits of Louisiana's governors from Bienville to Huey P. Long. (Courtesy of the Louisiana Collection of the State Library of Louisiana.)

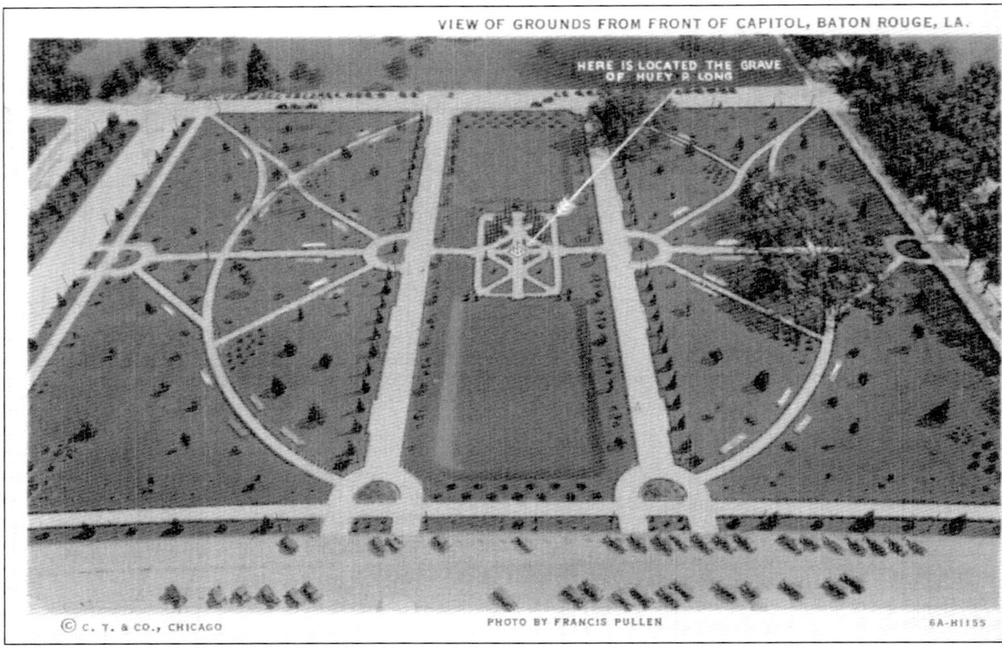

Landscaping for the capitol's 27 acres of grounds was executed by Jungle Gardens of Avery Island, Louisiana, and included over 10 miles of walks and drives. Plantings include azaleas, camellias, and magnolias, the state flower. Live oaks were transplanted to complement the existing oaks, several of which were more than 200 years old. (Courtesy of the Baton Rouge Room Collection of East Baton Rouge Public Library.)

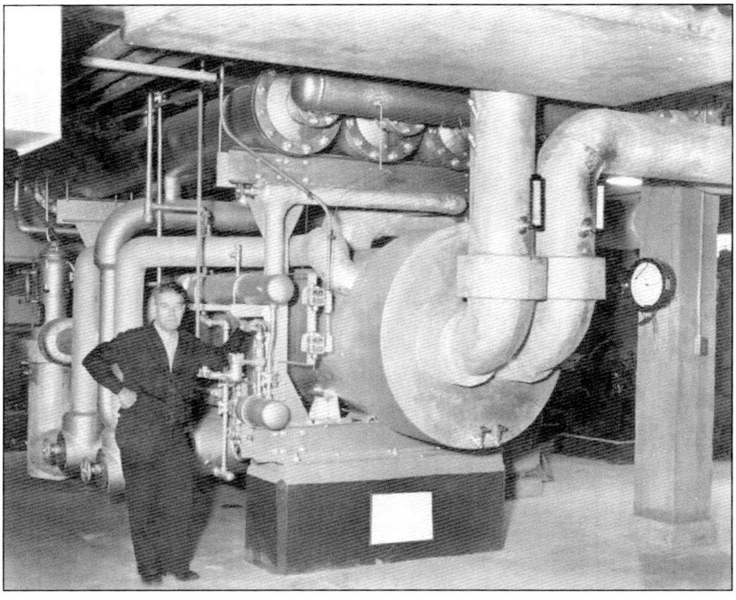

When it was completed in 1932, the State Capitol was the tallest building in the South and featured many modern novelties of the age, such as air-conditioning. Massive chillers for air-conditioning equipment for the capitol are seen in this photograph from the 1940s. The engineer is Joseph Hemsteader of New Orleans. (Courtesy of the Louisiana Collection of the State Library of Louisiana.)

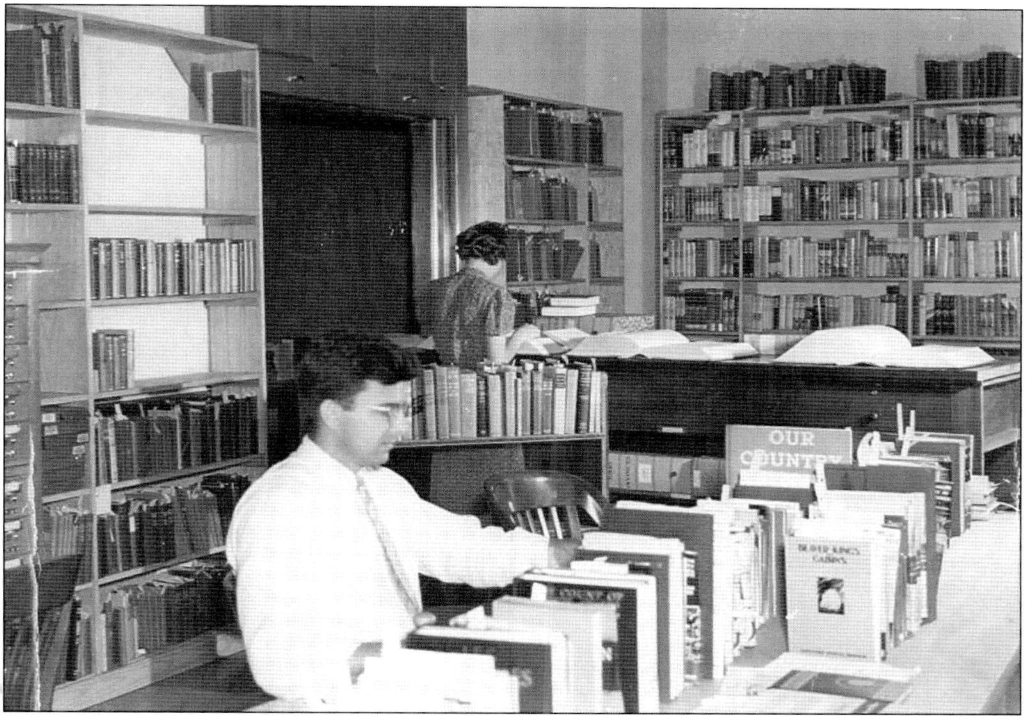

The State Library of Louisiana, which had opened at the Old State Capitol in 1925, moved to offices on the 18th floor of the new capitol in 1932. The library remained at the capitol until 1940, when it moved to the old LSU Hill Memorial Library building on Third Street. (Courtesy of the Louisiana Collection of the State Library of Louisiana.)

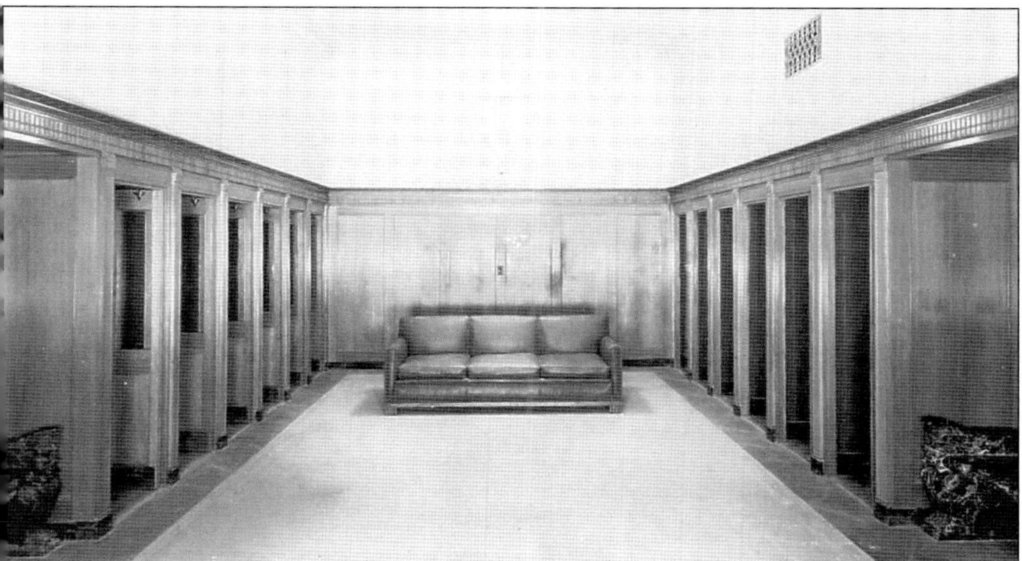

Cellular technology was still 50 years in the future when the State Capitol opened in 1932. To provide telephone service to legislators and others, this telephone office was located in the basement of the building. (Courtesy of the Louisiana Collection of the State Library of Louisiana.)

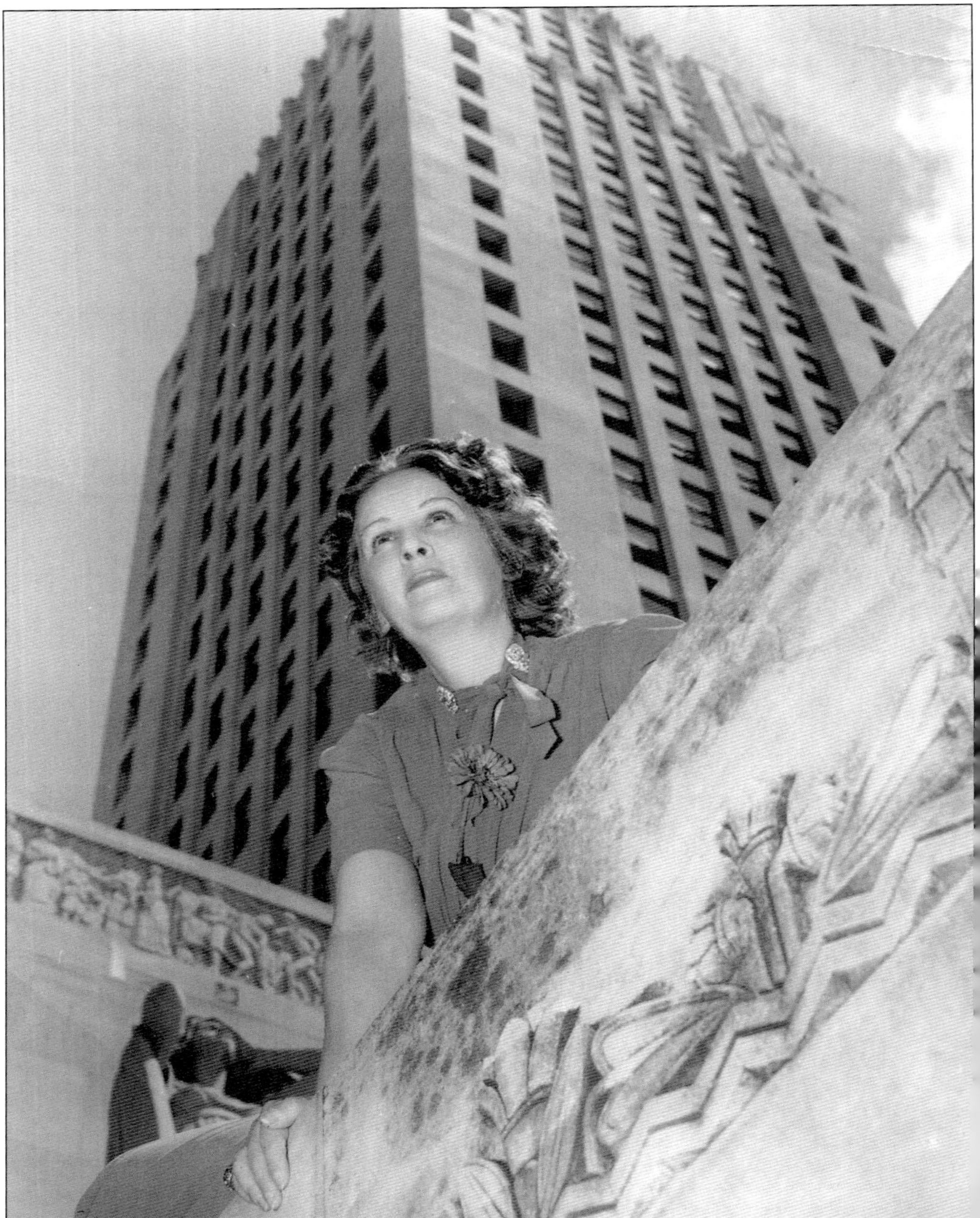

One of the most gracious features of the new State Capitol was its official hostess, Helen Wurzlow Wurzlow served as tour guide and also wrote a handbook for visitors titled *Louisiana Its Capitol* She was born in Houma and lived for a time in a boardinghouse in Spanish Town. In later years she wrote for newspapers in New Orleans and Houma. (Author photograph.)

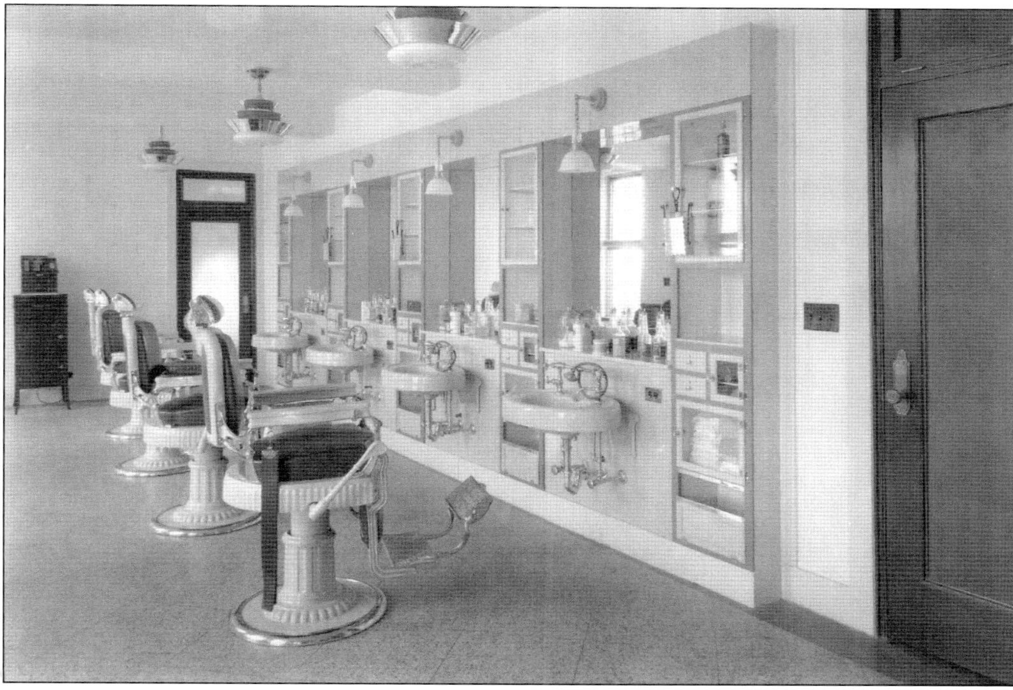

In addition to the state library and other government offices, the capitol's amenities in 1932 included a post office, dining room, and barbershop. This photograph of the barbershop on the building's seventh floor was taken shortly after the building's completion. (Courtesy of the Louisiana Collection of the State Library of Louisiana.)

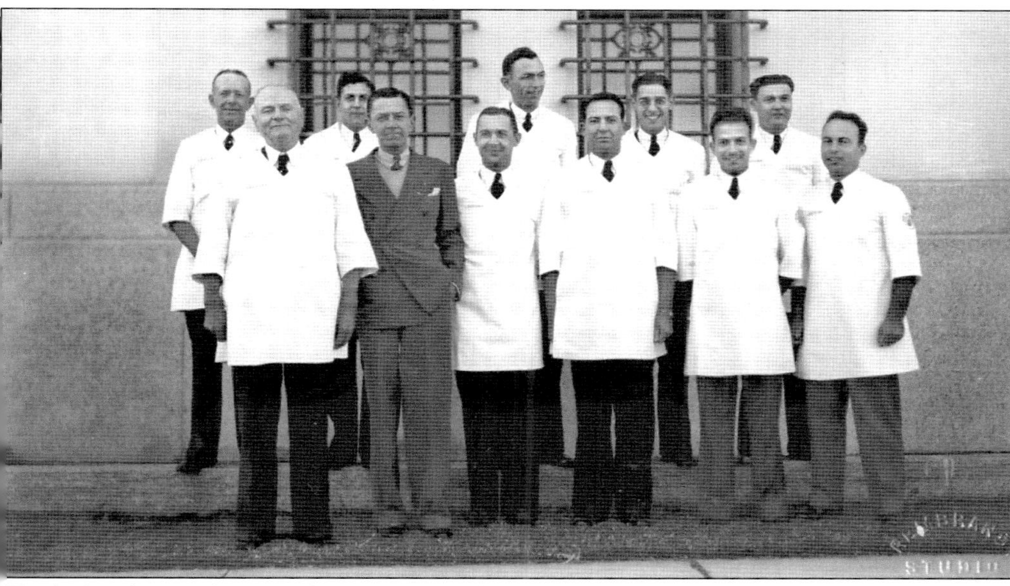

The barbershop at the capitol was a center of social activity where visitors could glean the news and rumors of the day as they waited for a trim. As indicated in this photograph from the 1940s, the shop was a substantial enterprise, employing no fewer than 11 people at one time. (Courtesy of the Baton Rouge Room Collection of East Baton Rouge Public Library.)

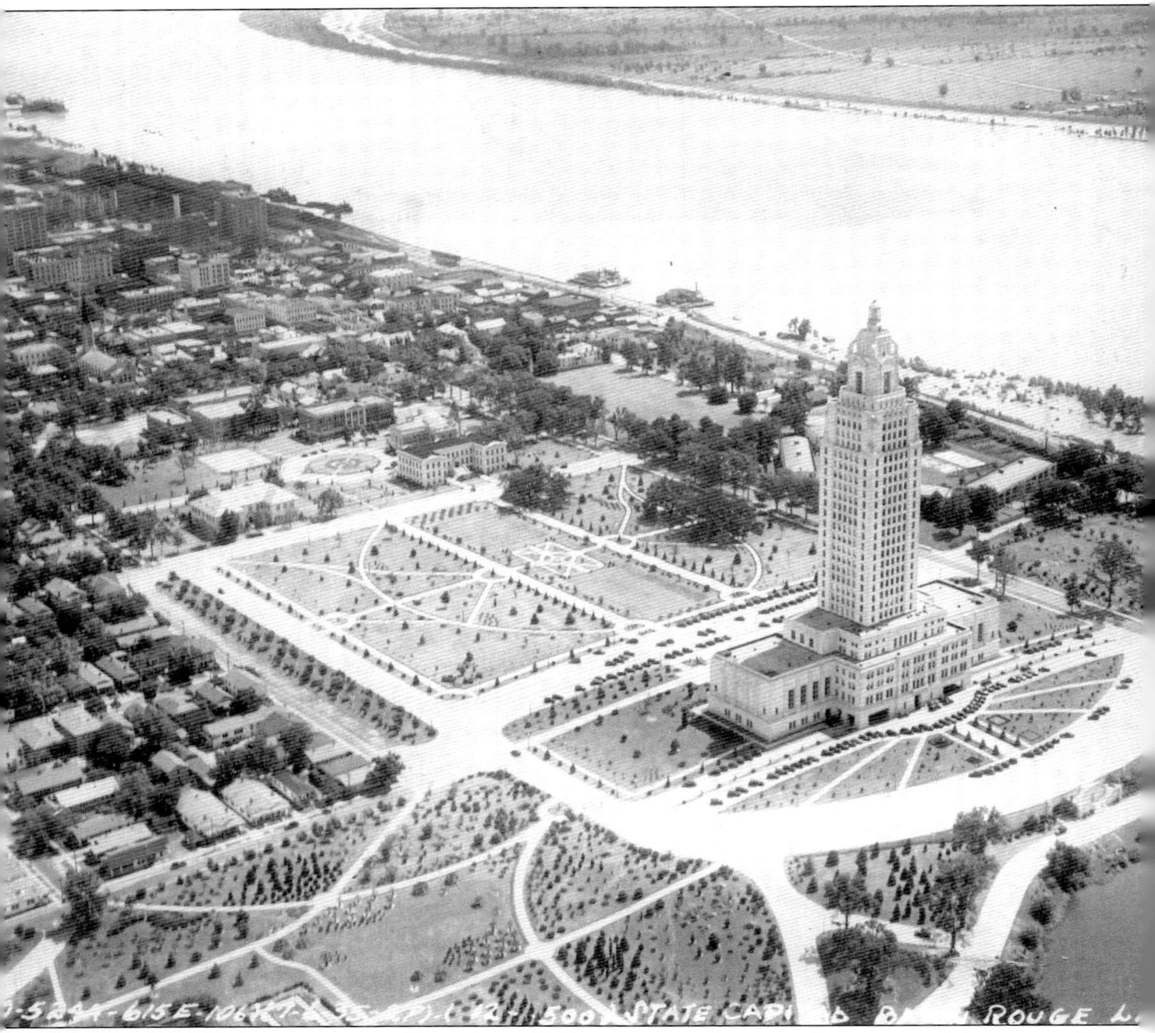

Completion of the State Capitol in 1932 began a gradual transformation of downtown Baton Rouge. Older buildings of the LSU campus, still seen in this aerial photograph taken shortly after completion, would gradually be replaced over the next 30 years. By the 1960s, the only buildings remaining from campus days were the Arsenal Museum and the Pentagon Barracks. (Courtesy of the Collections of the Louisiana State Museum.)

The short life and violent death of Dr. Carl Austin Weiss, alleged assassin of Sen. Huey P. Long, unfolded in what is now Capitol Park and Spanish Town. After graduation from St. Vincent's Academy and LSU, he attended medical school at Tulane and completed post-graduate work in New York and Vienna before returning to Baton Rouge in 1932. (Courtesy of the Foundation for Historical Louisiana.)

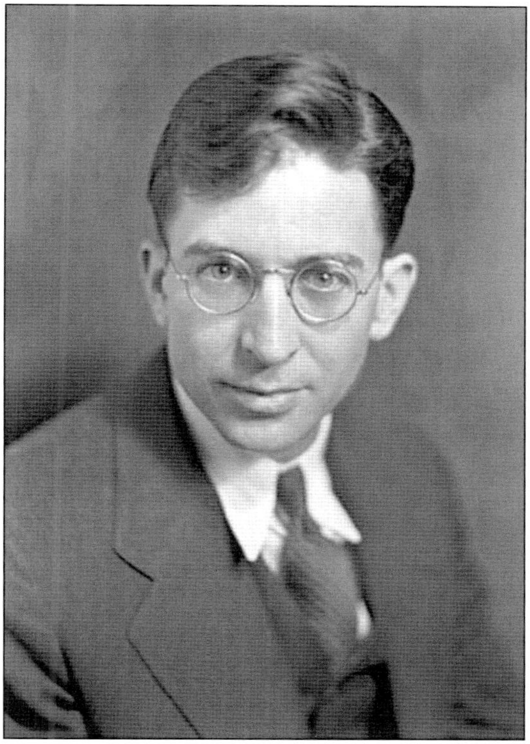

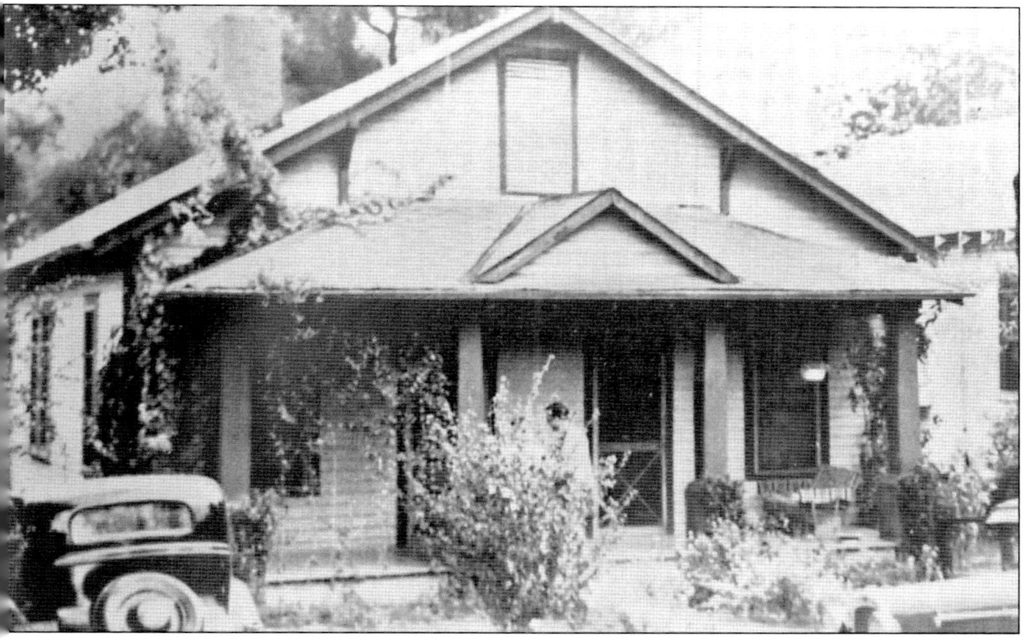

Weiss lived at this modest house on Lakeland Drive in Spanish Town, two blocks from the capitol. On September 8, 1935, he ambushed Long in the first-floor hallway of the capitol, outside the doors to what was then the governor's office. After firing one shot, Weiss was mowed down by 62 bullets fired by the senator's bodyguards. (Courtesy of the Foundation for Historical Louisiana.)

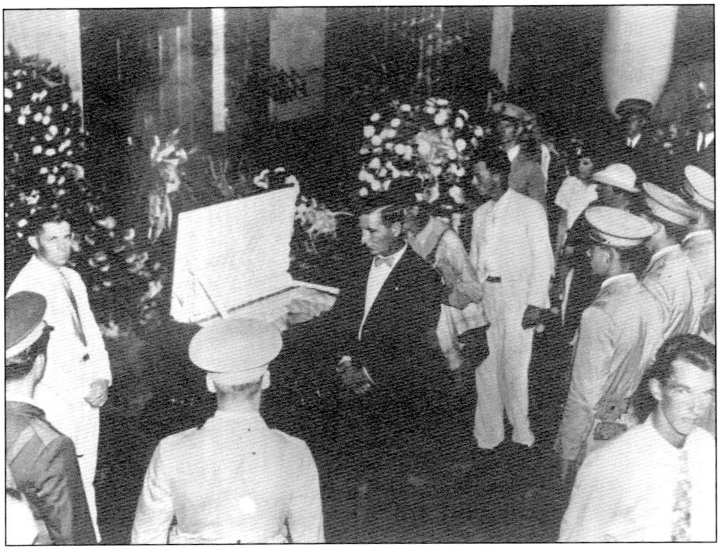

After he was shot, Long was carried into the governor's office and later to the nearby Our Lady of the Lake Sanitarium, where he died the following day. His body was dressed in a tuxedo, and his open double casket was placed in the State Capitol Memorial Hall. State police and LSU football players stood guard as 10,000 mourners filed past the casket. (Courtesy of the Collections of the Louisiana State Museum.)

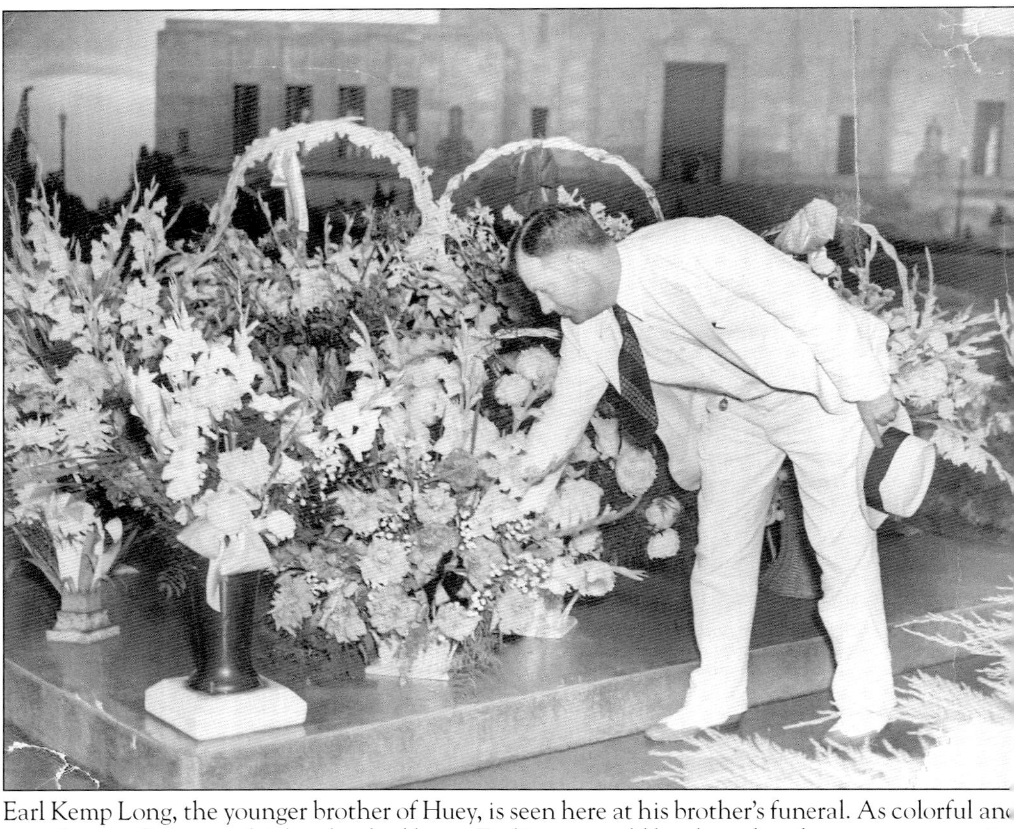

Earl Kemp Long, the younger brother of Huey, is seen here at his brother's funeral. As colorful and complex a politician as his brother had been, Earl Long would be elected to three nonconsecutive gubernatorial terms in 1939, 1948, and 1956. (Courtesy of the Louisiana Collection of the State Library of Louisiana.)

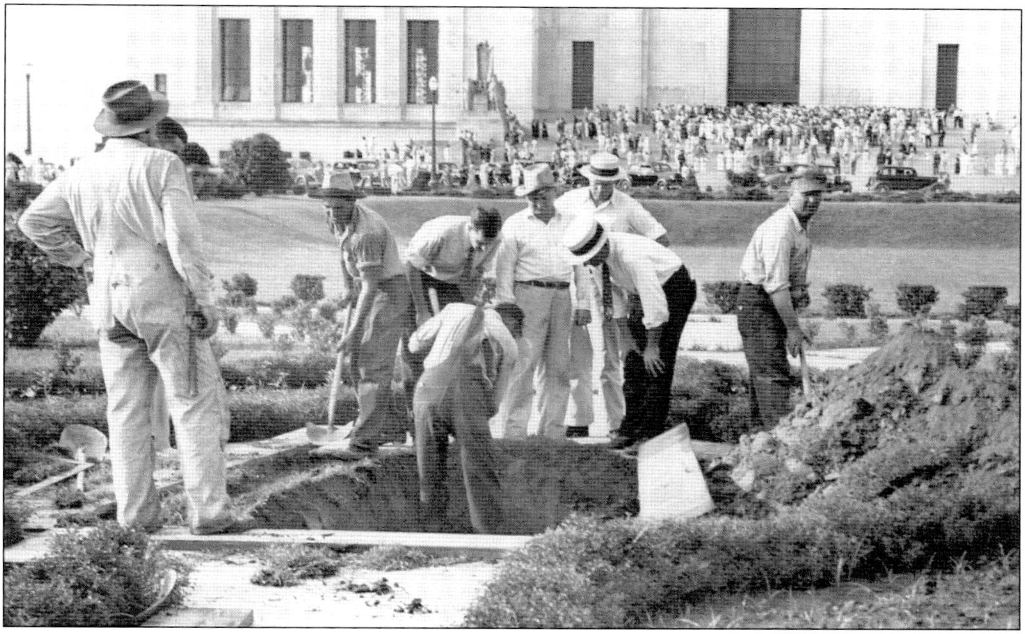

As part of the crowd of mourners gathers on the steps of the capitol to view Long's body on September 11, 1935, workers from Rabenhorst Funeral Home in Baton Rouge dig the grave where he would be buried the following day. (Courtesy of the Collections of the Louisiana State Museum.)

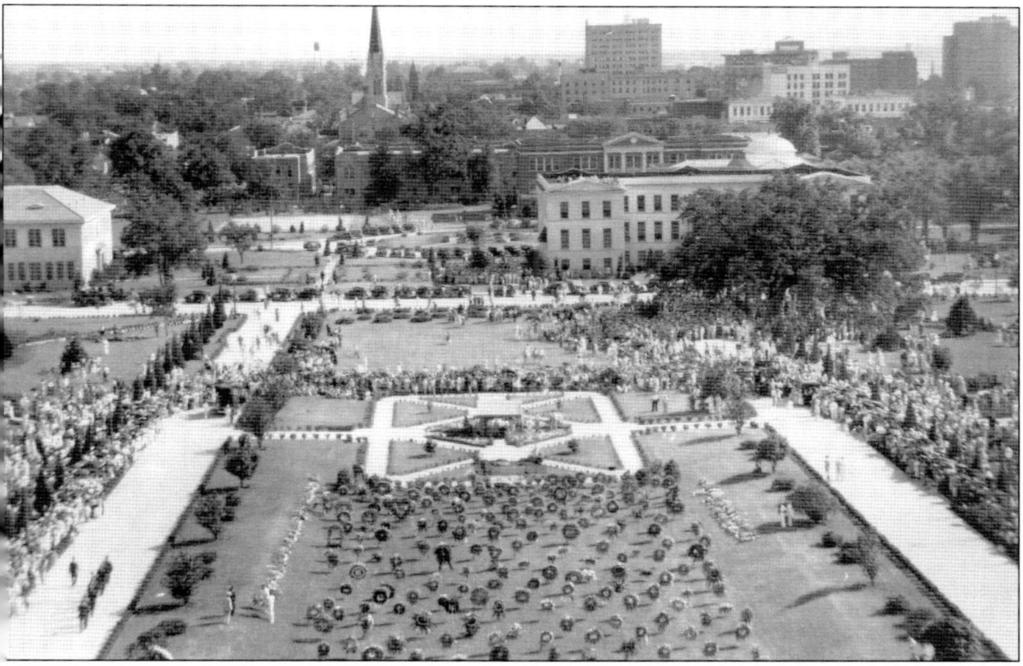

In this photograph, taken from an upper floor of the capitol, Long was buried in a ceremony attended by thousands. Editor and author Hodding Carter, no admirer of Long, wrote, "Close beside the bier crowded the thieves and sycophants of the inner circle. Beyond wept the poor." (Courtesy of the Louisiana Collection of the State Library of Louisiana.)

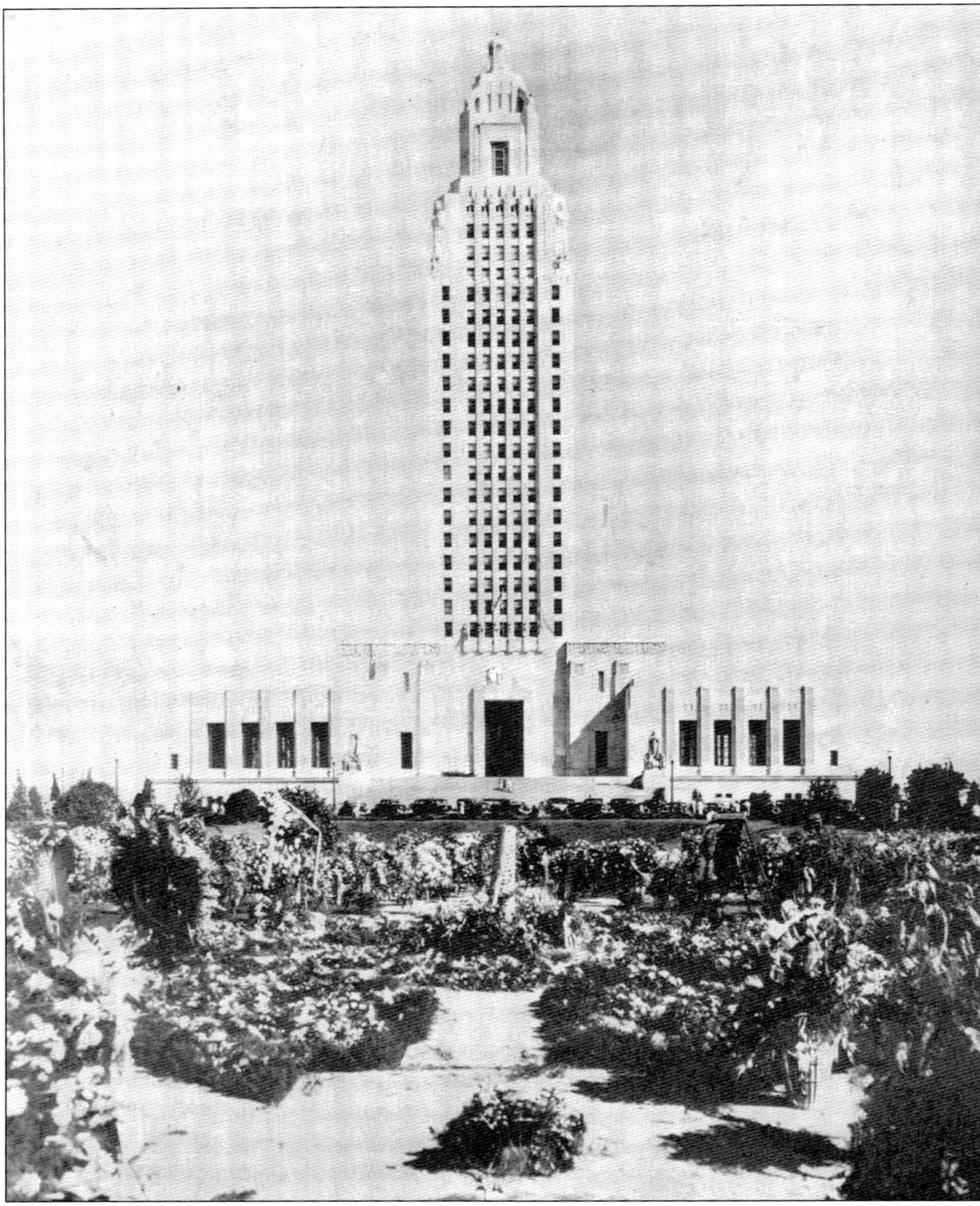

Flowers for Long's funeral were sent from all over the world and trucked into Baton Rouge from throughout Louisiana to carpet the capitol's garden at Long's funeral on September 12, 1935. (Courtesy of the Collections of the Louisiana State Museum.)

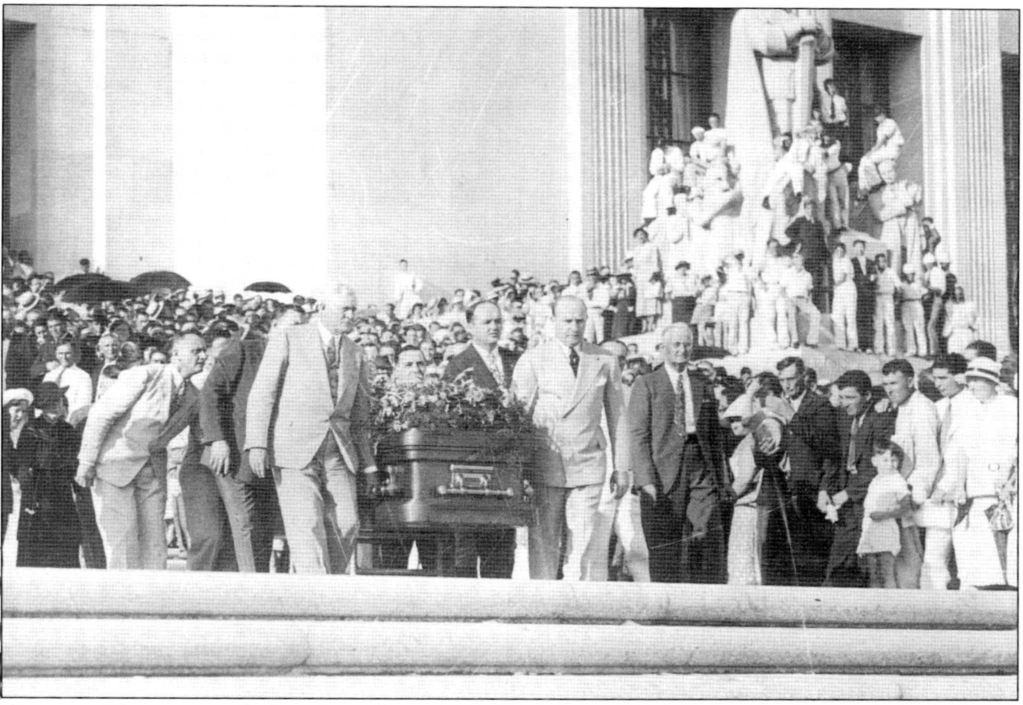

Eleven pallbearers, including Gov. Oscar K. Allen, carried the massive lead-lined coffin of Sen. Huey P. Long down the broad steps of the capitol. Schools and businesses were closed for the funeral, and additional trains were scheduled to bring mourners to Baton Rouge from every corner of the state. (Courtesy of the Collections of the Louisiana State Museum.)

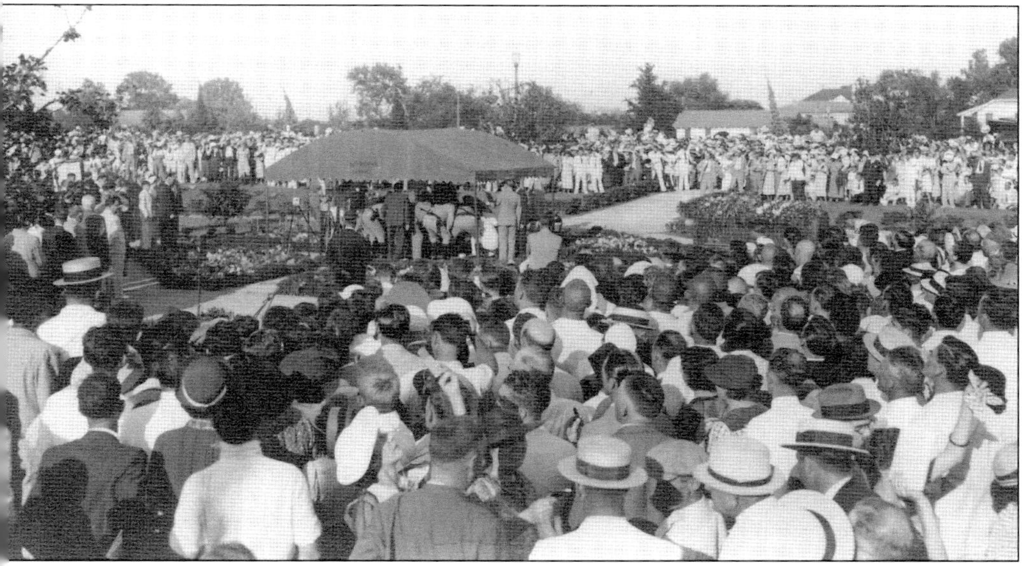

The funeral service was led by Gerald L.K. Smith, cofounder of the Share Our Wealth program. He said, "This place marks not the final resting place of Huey. . . . His spirit shall never rest as long as hungry bodies cry for food, as long as human frames stand naked, as long as homeless wretches haunt this land of plenty." (Courtesy of the Collections of the Louisiana State Museum.)

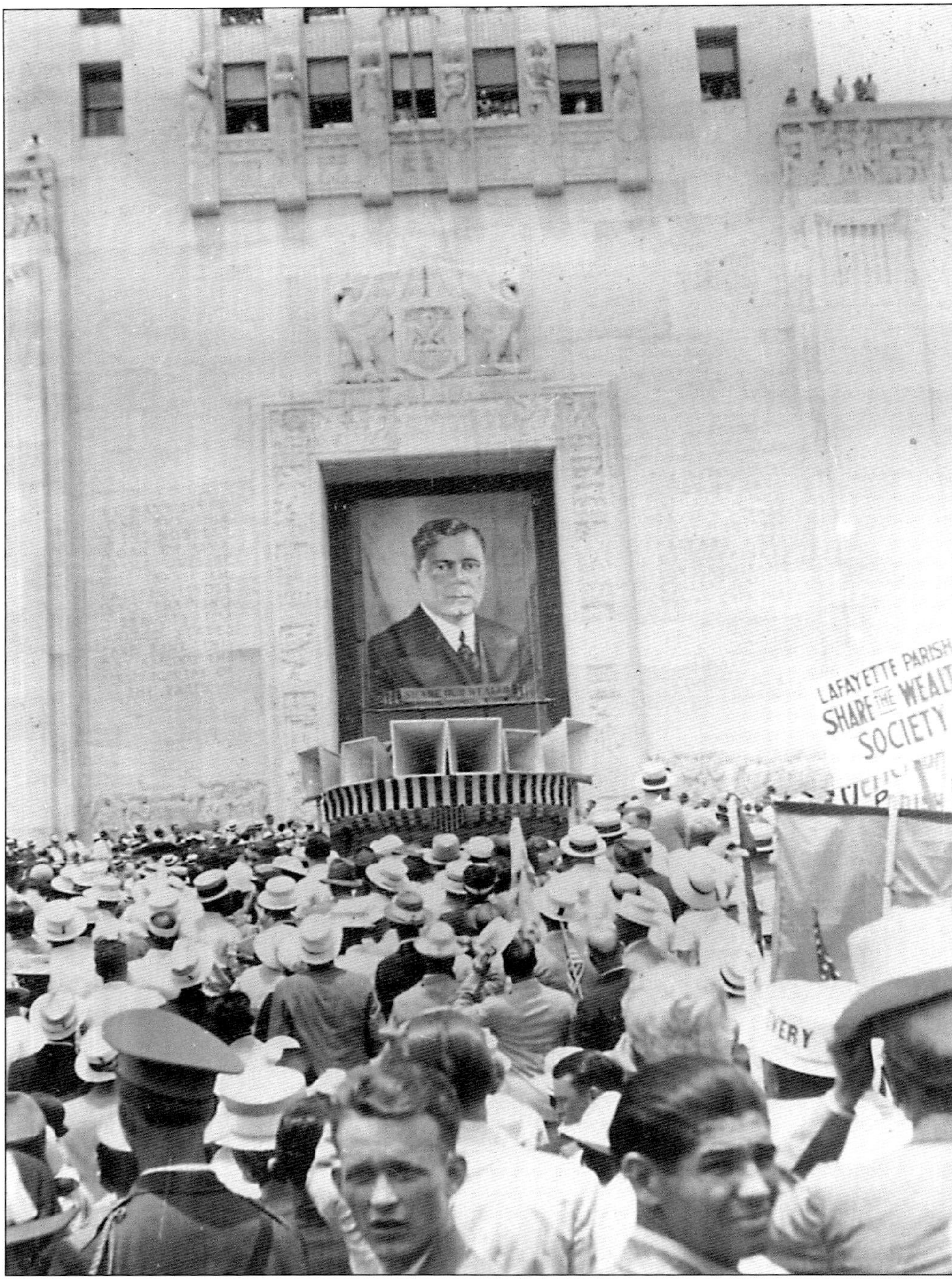

Anticipating a run at the presidency, Long had set up Share Our Wealth clubs around the country By mid-1935, more than 27,000 clubs with 7.5 million members had been formed. The club would not long survive their founder, but this photograph shows a Share Our Wealth banner a the inauguration of Long crony Richard Leche as governor in 1936. (Courtesy of the Louisian Collection of the State Library of Louisiana.)

Five years after the assassination of Sen. Huey P. Long in 1935, the legislature agreed that a fitting memorial to the slain senator would be a bronze statue at his grave site on the capitol grounds. Sculptor Charles E. Keck was given the commission, and the finished statue was lifted into place in March 1940. (Courtesy of the Louisiana Collection of the State Library of Louisiana.)

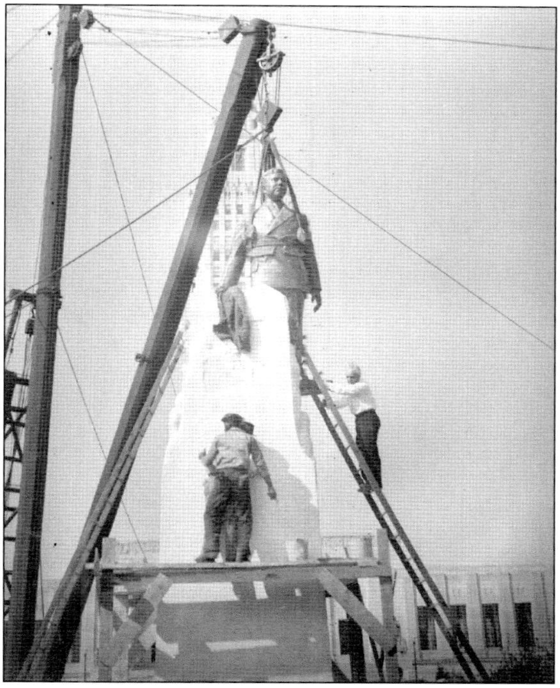

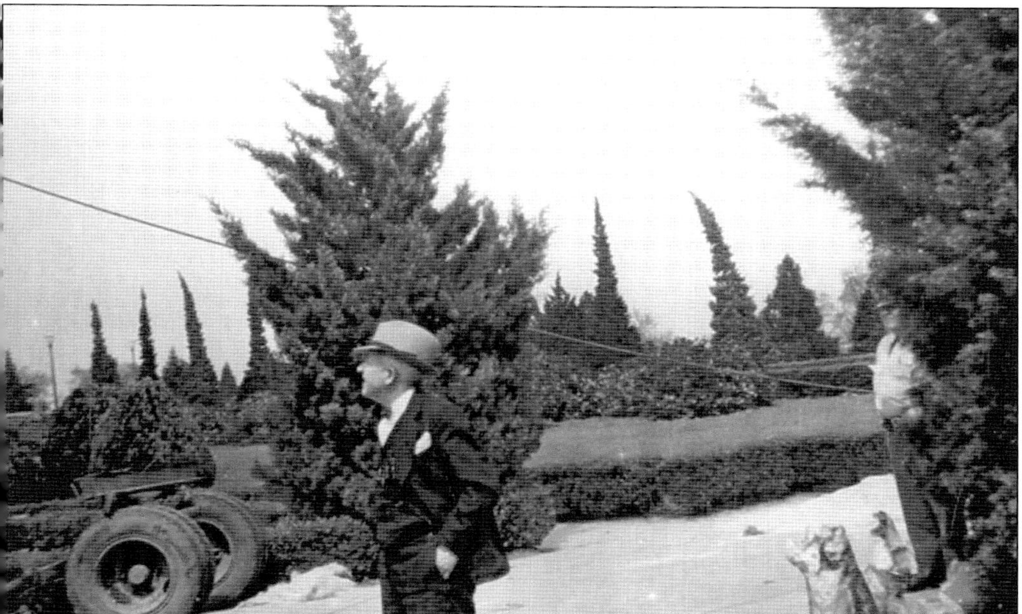

The statue at Long's grave was one of the last commissions of New York sculptor Charles E. Keck, who had once worked as an assistant to Augustus Saint-Gaudens. Previous commissions included the Waldorf-Astoria Hotel and the George Rogers Clark Memorial in Ohio. Here, Keck is overseeing the placement of the statue in April 1940. (Courtesy of the Louisiana Collection of the State Library of Louisiana.)

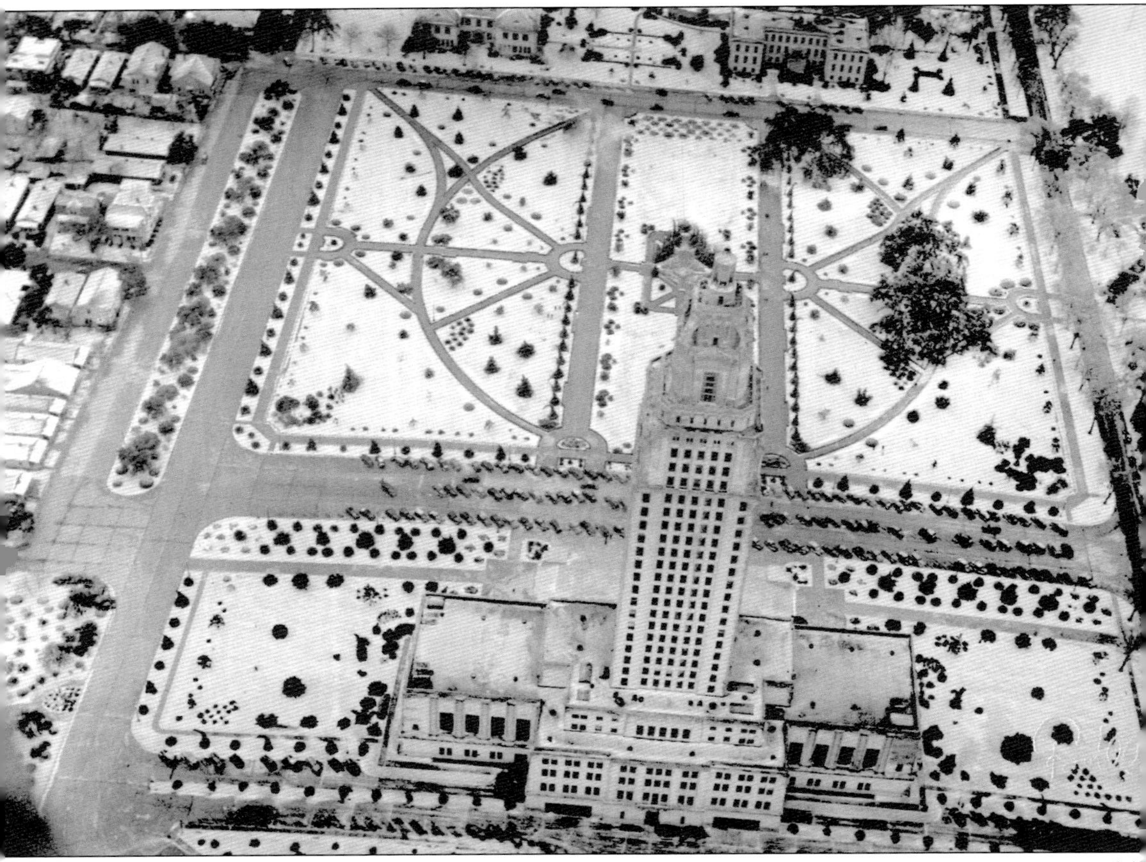

By the time this aerial photograph of the capitol was taken during a rare Baton Rouge snowfall in 1935, the Capitol Annex had been built. While not visible in the picture, its sidewalk can be seen at far right. (Courtesy of the Foundation for Historical Louisiana.)

Seven

After World War II

In the years after the Second World War, Louisiana state government exploded in size, and new buildings to house its offices were built, torn down, and rebuilt in the area that had once been the US Army garrison and the campus of Louisiana State University. It was not until the late 1990s that the area would be named Capitol Park during the administration of Gov. Mike Foster. This aerial photograph from the 1970s shows the old powder magazines, which were renovated in the 1960s, as well as the new Governor's Mansion and Department of Transportation and Development Building. Meanwhile, new construction in the Spanish Town neighborhood languished as young people with families opted to forego being close to their state government or refinery jobs for the perception of a better life in the suburbs. Their decisions were made much easier by the construction of Interstate Highway 110, which cut off Spanish Town and the capitol area from the rest of the city. (Courtesy of the Louisiana Collection of the State Library of Louisiana.)

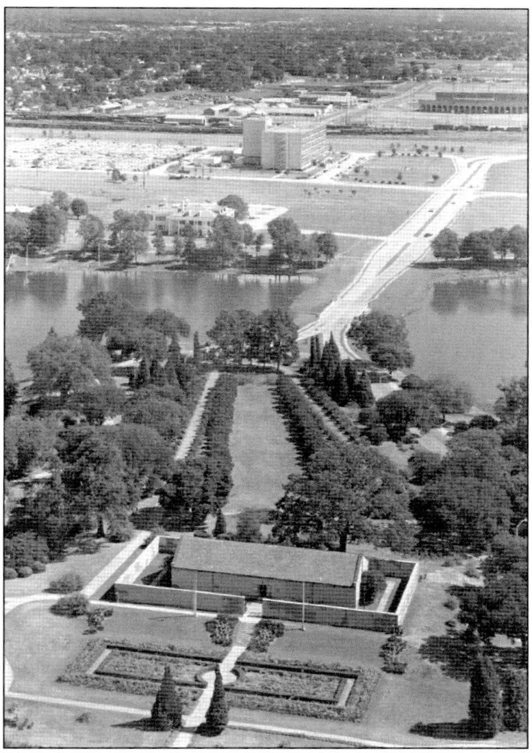

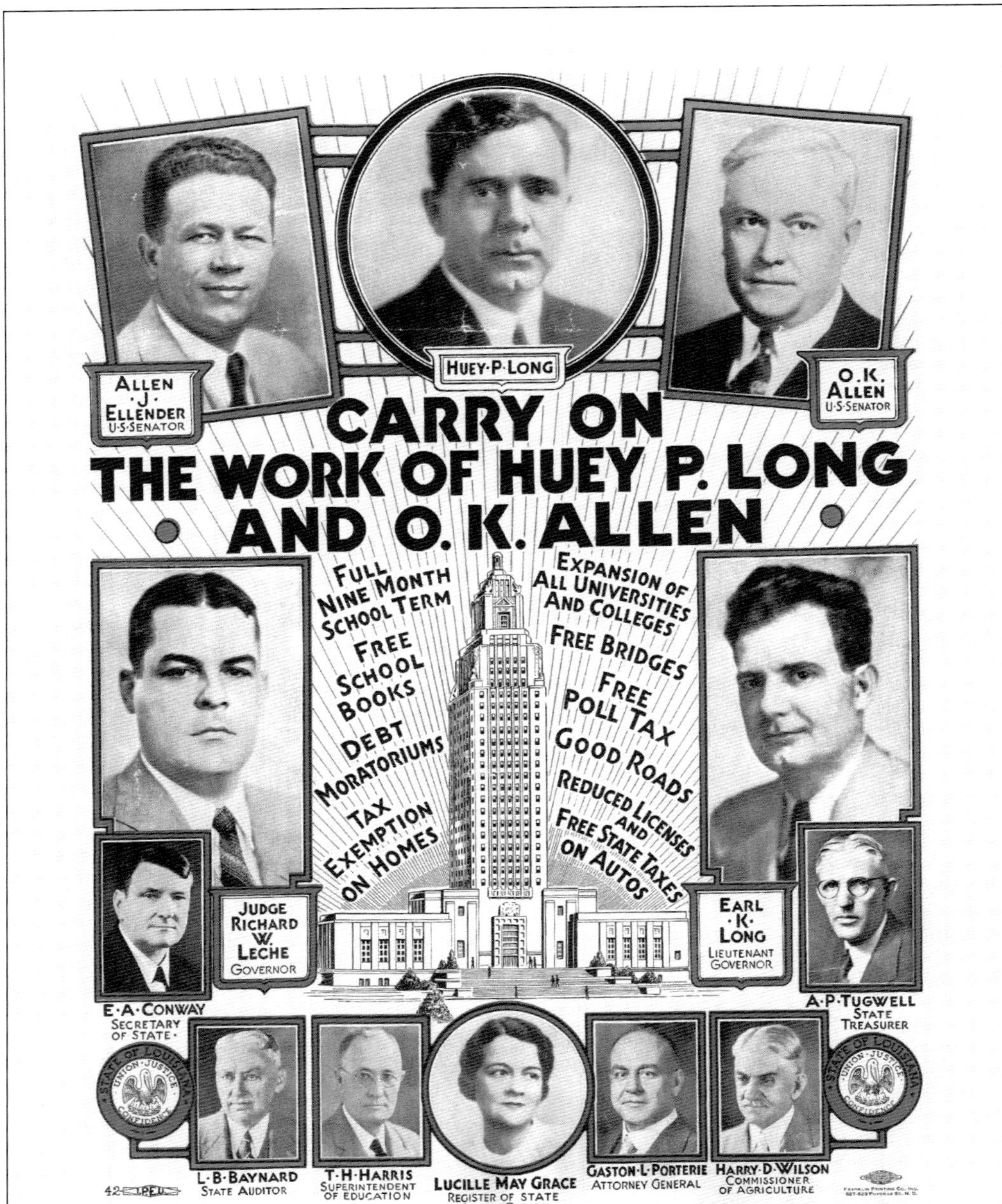

Within five months of Long's death, Gov. O.K. Allen was dead after suffering a brain hemorrhage in January 1936. To continue Long's work, his machine selected Richard W. Leche to run for governor. This campaign poster from the election features the candidates running on the "Long Ticket," including Spanish Town resident Lucille May Grace, Louisiana's first female statewide elected official as register of the state land office. (Courtesy of the Foundation for Historical Louisiana.)

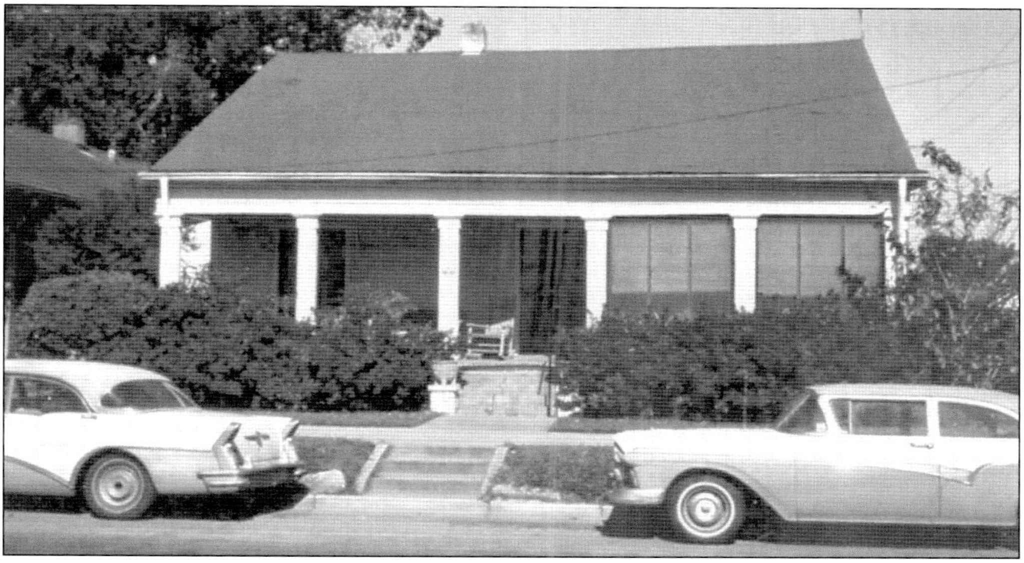

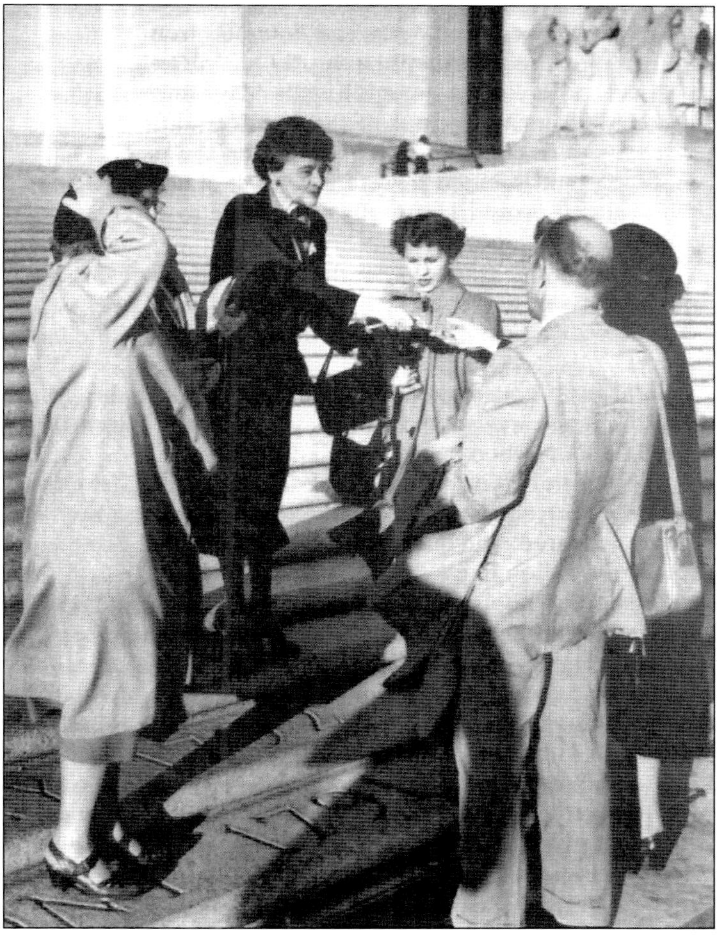

Grace was the daughter of Spanish Town resident Fred Grace, Louisiana's state land registrar, who died in office in 1931. The Graces lived at this house at 781 North Street built in 1857 for Don Manuel Moreno. (Courtesy of the Baton Rouge Room of East Baton Rouge Public Library.)

Grace ran for governor in 1952 and accused one of her rivals, US representative Hale Boggs, of Communist sympathies during his student days at Tulane University. These, she claimed, forbade him from holding office under the state's constitution. Her complaint was heard at the capitol. Here, "Miss Grace" is seen with supporters on the capitol steps after the hearings. (Courtesy of the Foundation for Historical Louisiana.)

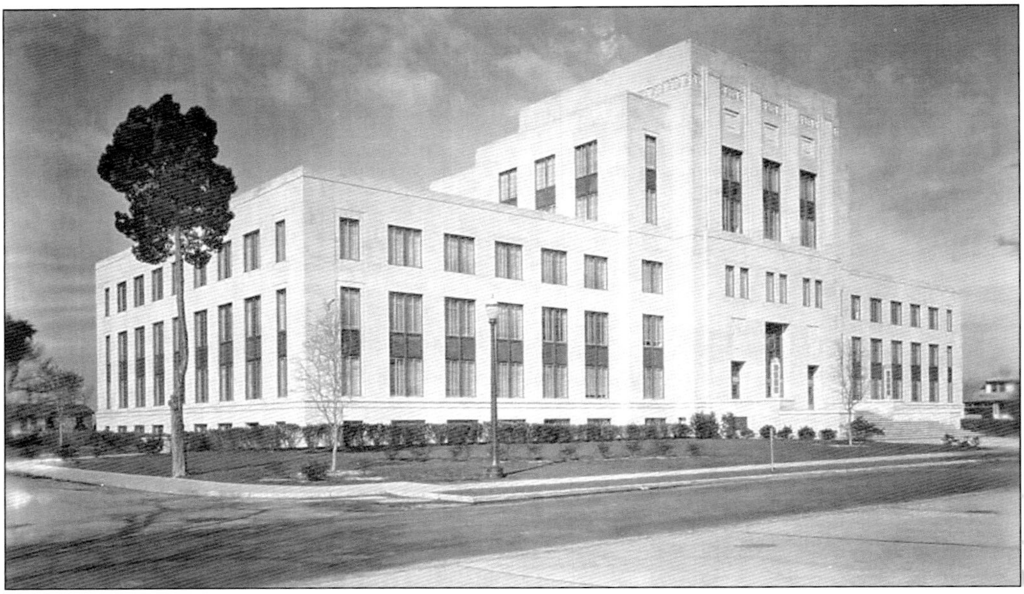

At the time the new capitol was constructed, it was considered large enough to house virtually all of the administrative offices and departments of state government. This assumption proved to be incorrect, and the State Office Building, often referred to as the Capitol Annex, was erected across the street. (Courtesy of the Louisiana Collection of the State Library of Louisiana.)

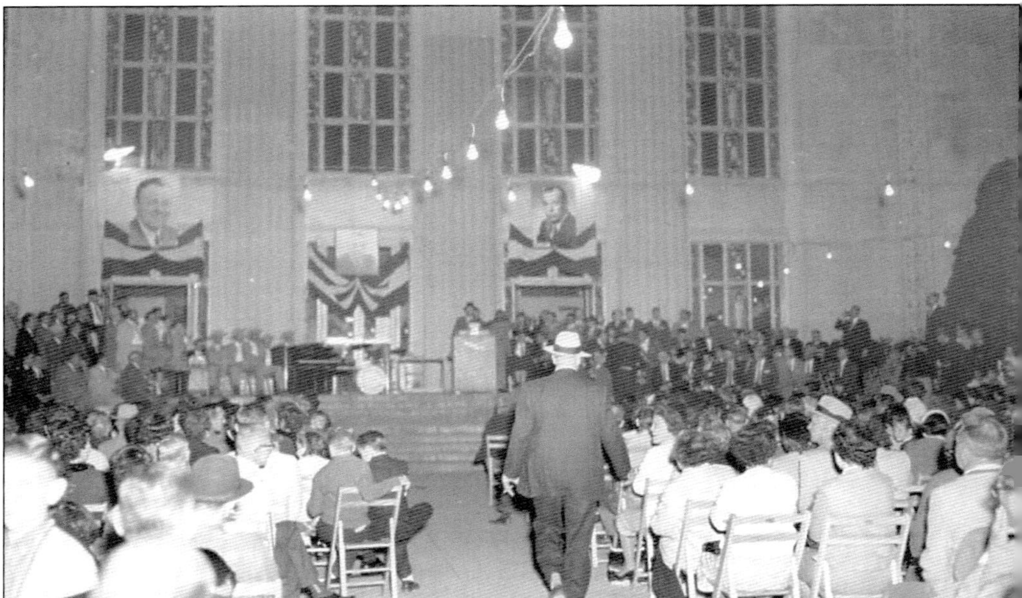

The Capitol Annex served as the backdrop for the inauguration of Gov. Jimmie Davis in 1944. The annex was completed in August 1938 at a construction cost of $1,104,395 and a project cost of $1,190,525. It featured a reinforced concrete frame and exterior masonry walls faced with limestone that matches as closely as possible the limestone used on the capitol building. (Courtesy of the Louisiana Collection of the State Library of Louisiana.)

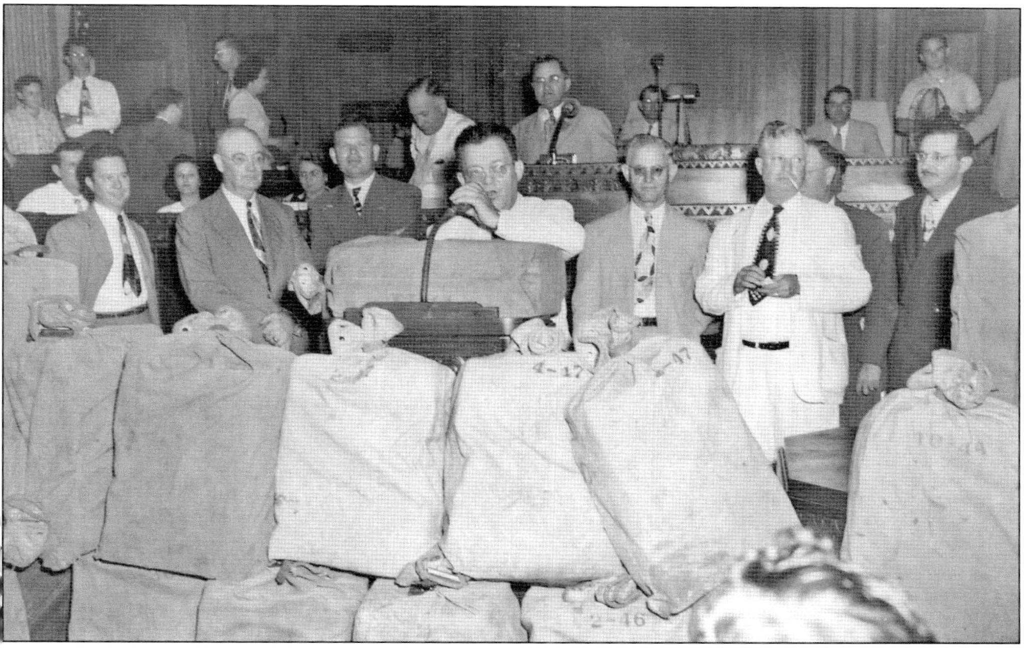

One of Louisiana's most colorful figures was Dudley J. "Couzan Dud" LeBlanc of LeBlanc, Louisiana. In addition to inventing a patent medicine named Hadacol because he "had to call it something," he served four terms in the Senate. In the Senate chamber in 1949, he stands over the first bags of pension checks soon to be mailed to senior citizens. (Courtesy of the Louisiana Collection of the State Library of Louisiana.)

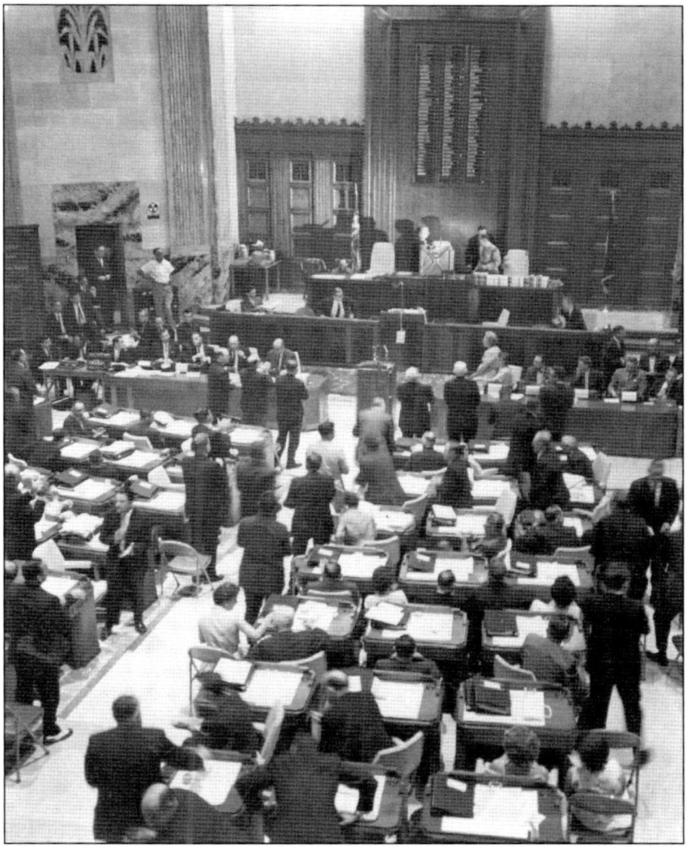

By the time this photograph of the Louisiana House of Representatives was taken in the 1960s, the legislature was on the cusp of major reform. Powerful political machines from the Long era were beginning to crumble, and voters were clamoring for a more open legislative process. (Courtesy of the Louisiana Collection of the State Library of Louisiana.)

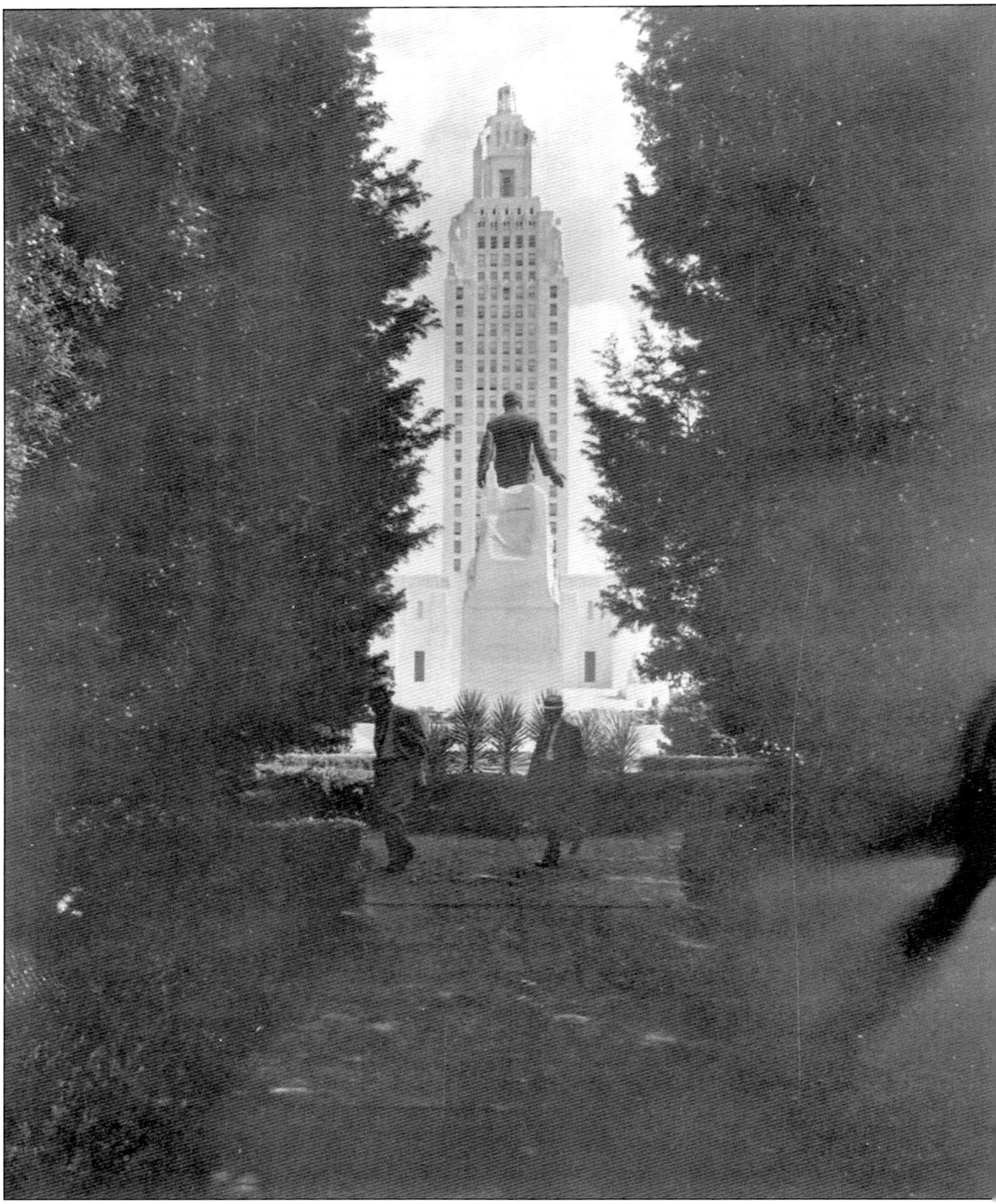

By the 1950s, the capitol's lush landscaping from the 1930s was starting to look overgrown. Several of the cypresses that lined the center sidewalks of the gardens seen here were removed in a landscaping project in the 1980s. (Courtesy of the Louisiana Collection of the State Library of Louisiana.)

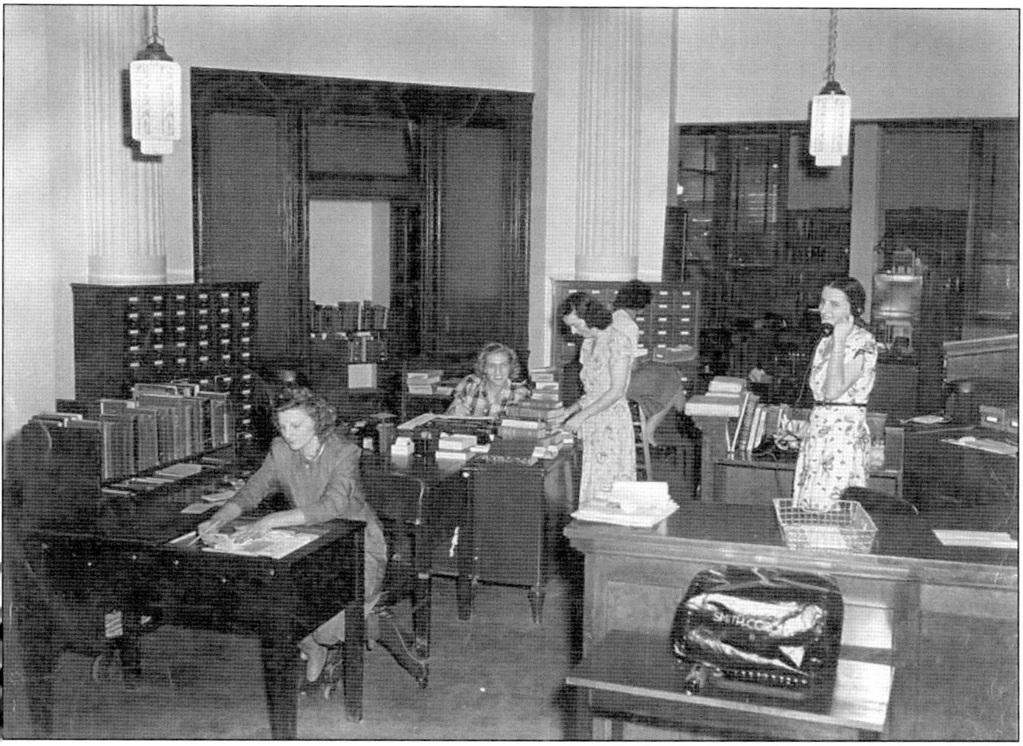

Since moving from the capitol to the Hill Memorial Library in 1940, the State Library of Louisiana has remained a fixture in Capitol Park. This 1947 photograph shows the library's reference desk. (Courtesy of the Louisiana Collection of the State Library of Louisiana.)

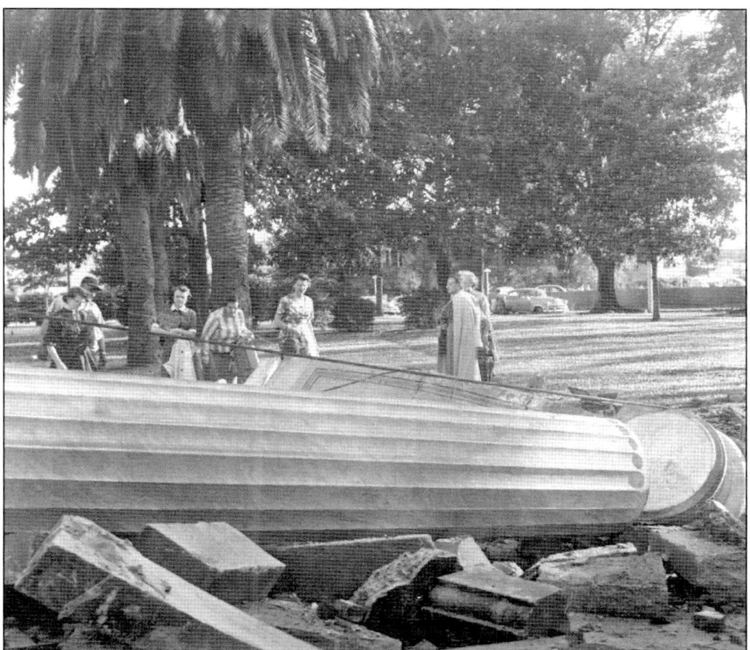

This photograph from 1957 shows the demolition of Hill Memorial Library. The state library moved from the old building to a modern building on the current site. Since 1925, only four people have held the position of state librarian: Essae Martha Culver (1925–1968), Sallie Farrell (1968–1981), Thomas Jaques (1981–2005), and Rebecca Hamilton (2005–present). (Courtesy of the Louisiana Collection of the State Library of Louisiana.)

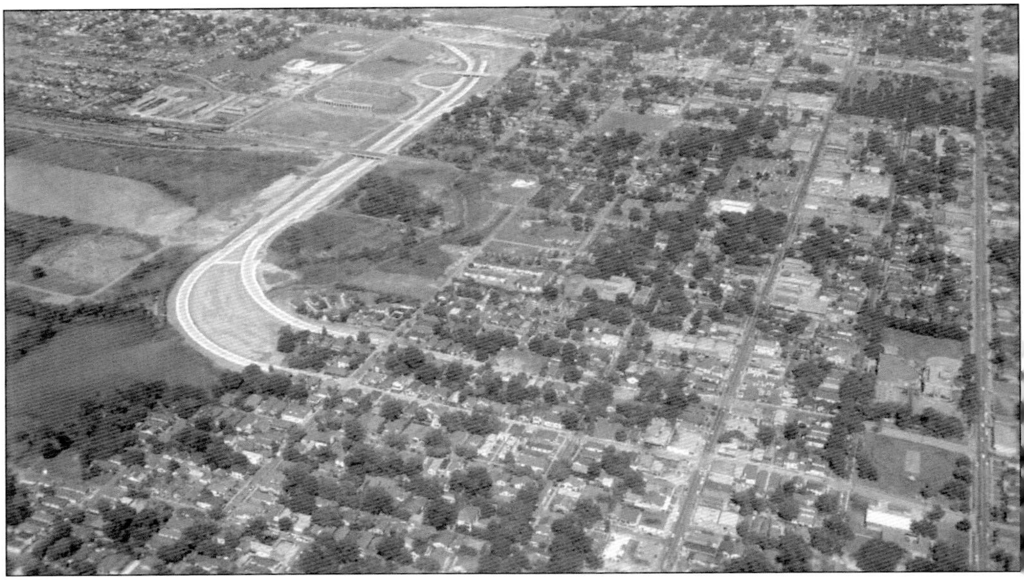

The creation of the Interstate Highway System in the 1950s was a mixed blessing for downtown Baton Rouge and the Spanish Town neighborhood. While new highways like the Baton Rouge Expressway (later I-110), seen here, brought workers from outside the city center to work, they also took them away at the end of the workday. (Courtesy of the Louisiana Collection of the State Library of Louisiana.)

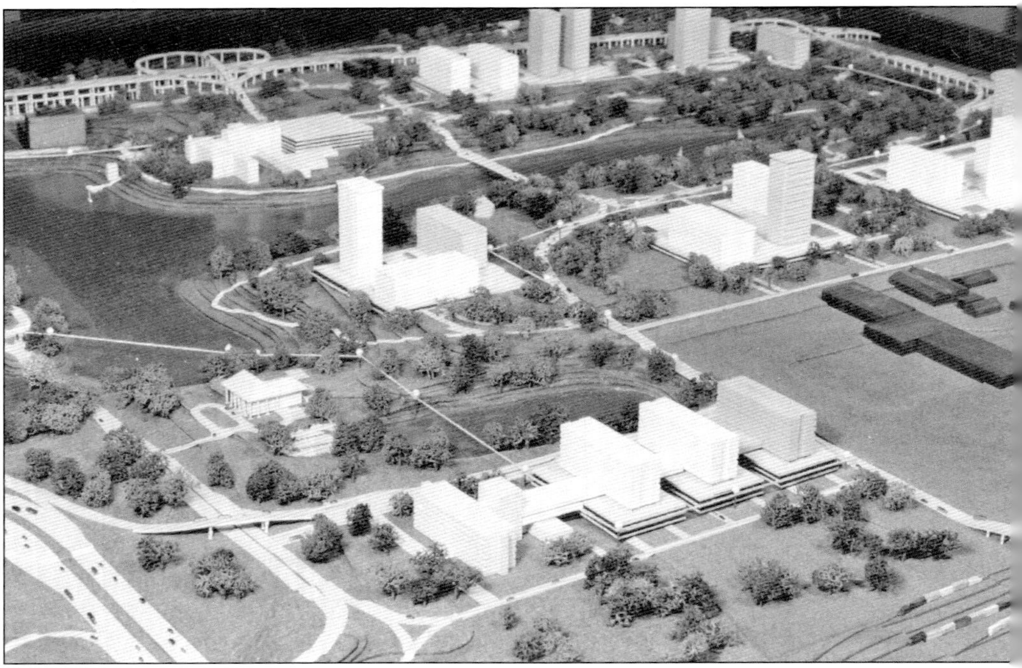

In the 1960s, a comprehensive plan for a new complex of state office buildings to be constructed to the north and east of Capitol Lake was created. This model from the period looks from east to west. The current Department of Transportation and Development Building and Governor's Mansion are in the foreground. (Courtesy of the Louisiana Collection of the State Library of Louisiana.)

In the second half of the 20th century, suitable hotel accommodations for visitors to the State Capitol and downtown Baton Rouge were scarce. Groundbreaking was held in February 1962 for the new Lakeshore Motor Hotel near the capitol on Third Street. This photograph was taken during construction prior to the opening in early 1964. (Courtesy of the Louisiana Collection of the State Library of Louisiana.)

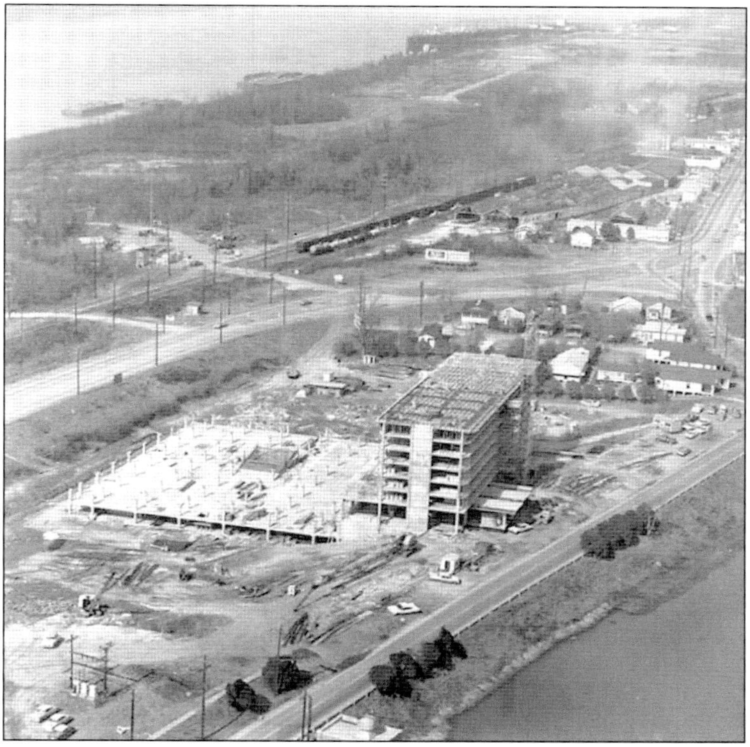

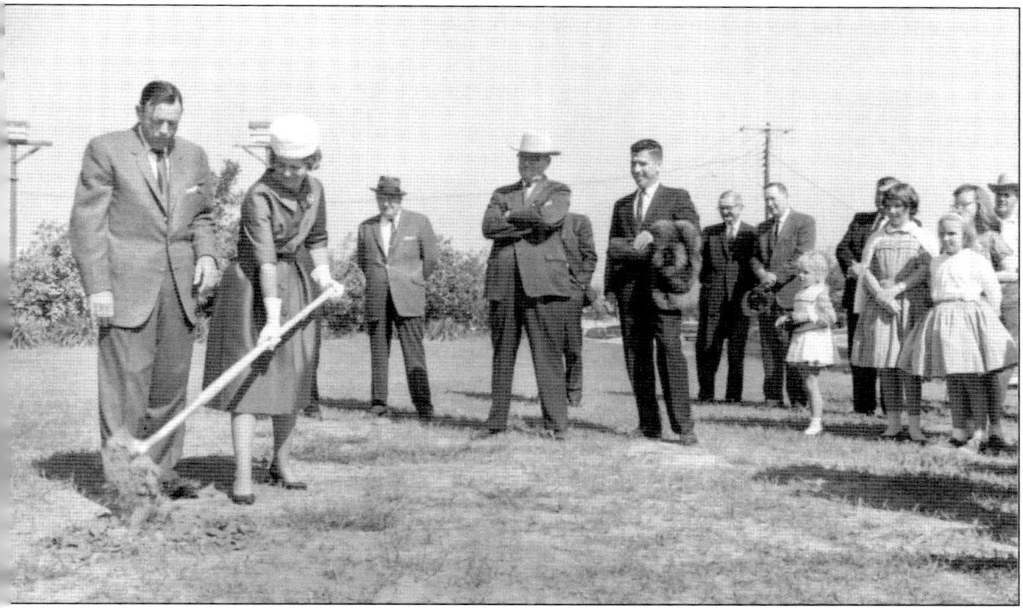

n the 1960s, Louisiana's governors were still living in a house that had been built on North 3oulevard in the 1930s. The old house was considered too small to meet the requirements of a overnor's home, so a new site was chosen east of the capitol. In this photograph from early 1963, 3ov. Jimmie and Alvern Davis attend the ground breaking of the new mansion. (Courtesy of the ouisiana Collection of the State Library of Louisiana.)

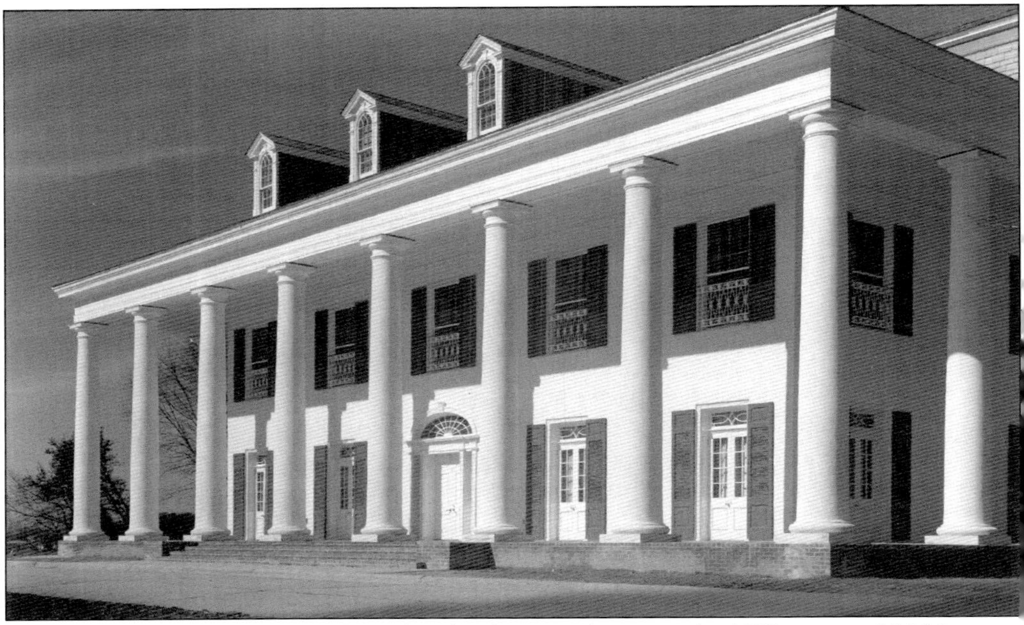

The Governor's Mansion, seen here shortly after completion in the 1970s, covers 25,000 square feet and was built at a cost of $893,000. The floor plan includes 12 bedrooms, 18 baths, two kitchens and one kitchenette, two dining rooms, a receiving room for state affairs and another for routine business, a living room, a sitting room, and other amenities. (Courtesy of the Louisiana Collection of the State Library of Louisiana.)

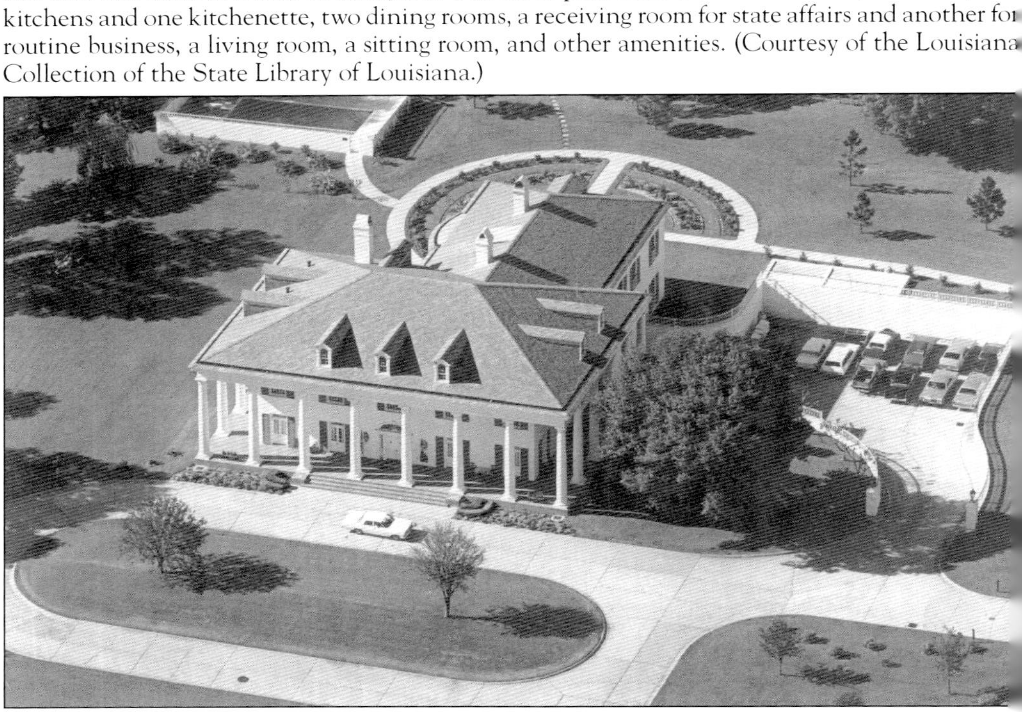

The expansive grounds of the new Governor's Mansion afforded an opportunity for Louisiana governors to entertain on a lavish level. During the 1980s and 1990s, parties at the mansion frequently featured enormous outdoor stages, seated dinners for hundreds in elaborate tents, and hot air balloons. (Courtesy of the Louisiana Collection of the State Library of Louisiana.)

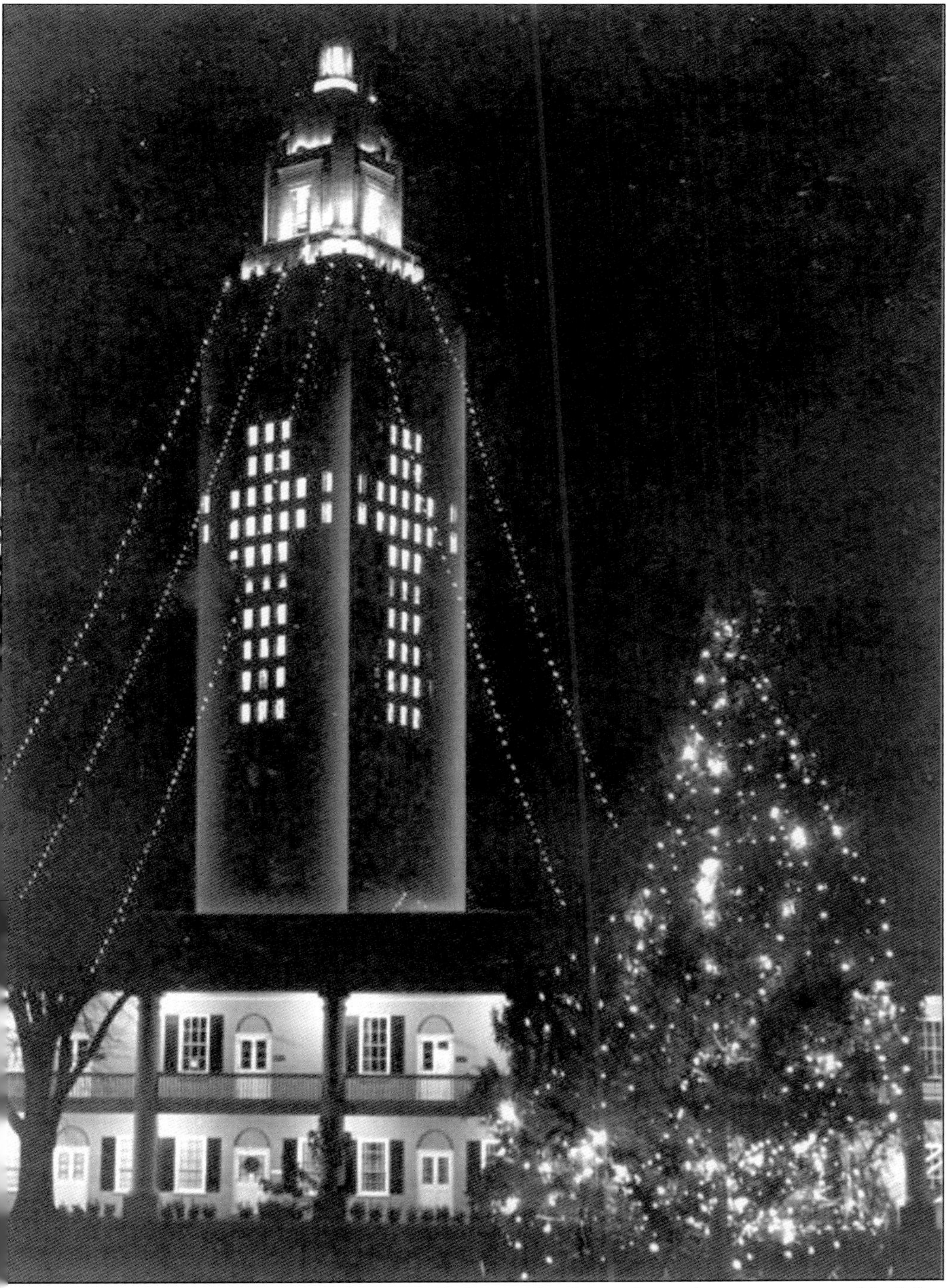

n the years after World War II, Christmas lights at the State Capitol were an annual holiday eature in Baton Rouge. This 1970 photograph shows the Christmas tree in the courtyard of the 'entagon Barracks with the capitol in the background. (Courtesy of the Louisiana Collection of he State Library of Louisiana.)

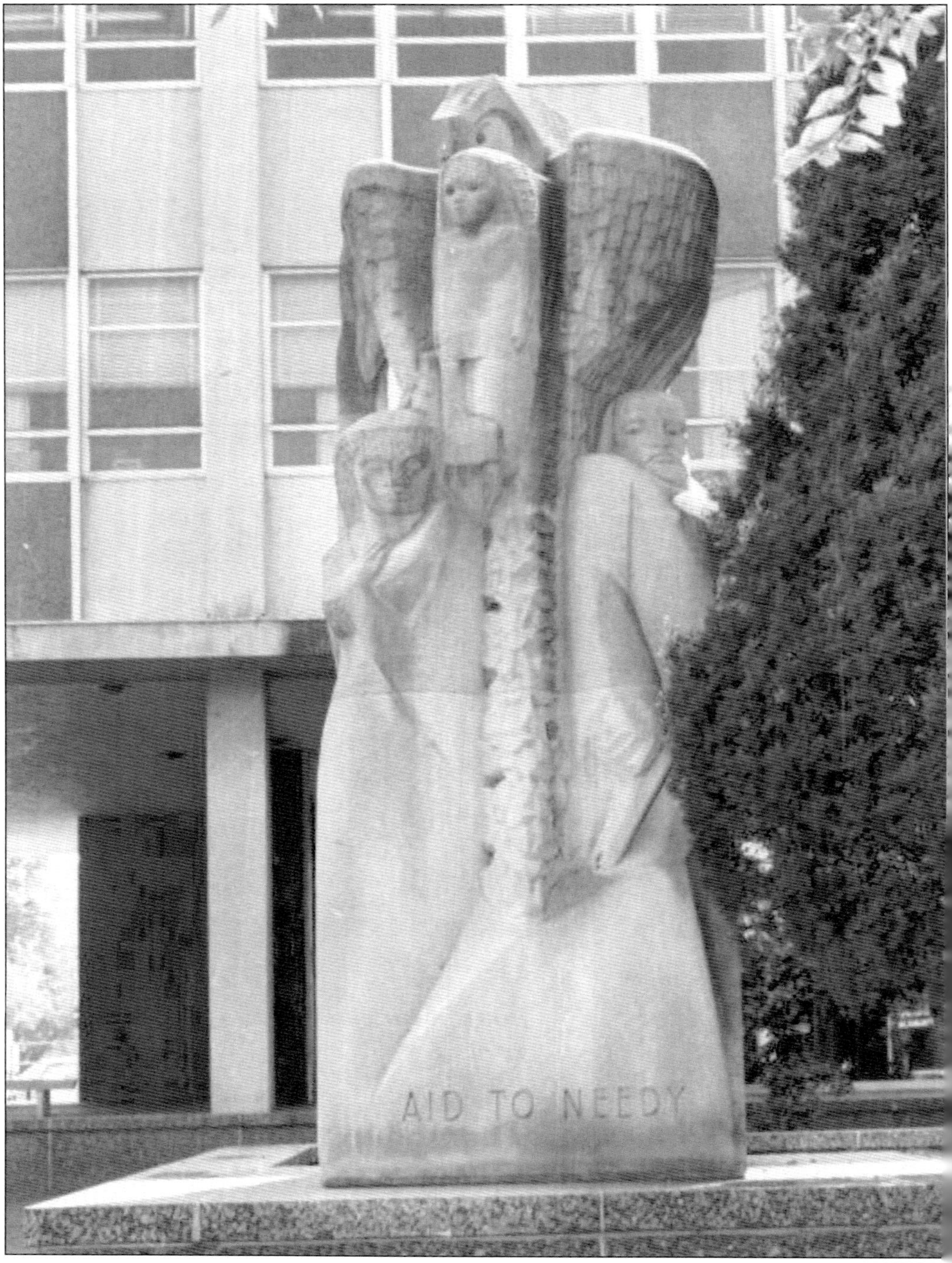

The Department of Public Welfare office building, named for civil rights leader A.Z. Young stood on the site of the Zachary Taylor home and the LSU Parade Ground and athletic fiel until 2007. This 1956 sculpture by Alfonso Iannelli, *The Welfare Rock*, was placed in front of th building and still remains in Capitol Park. (Courtesy of the Louisiana Collection of the Stat Library of Louisiana.)

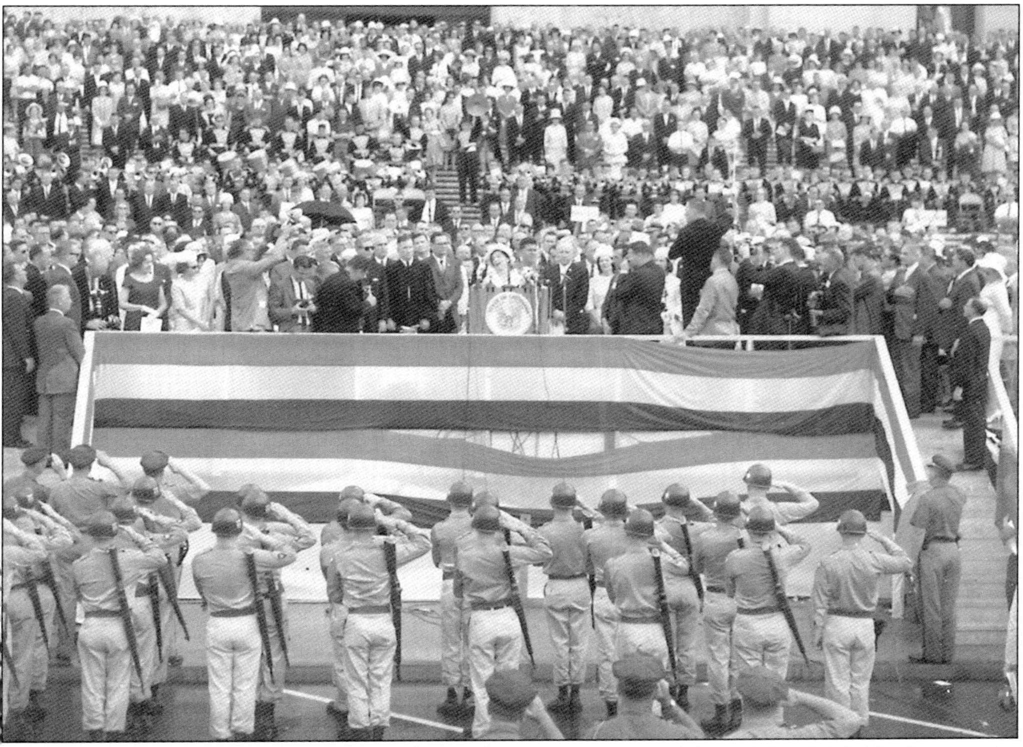

This photograph from May 12, 1964, shows the inauguration of Gov. John J. McKeithen at the capitol. McKeithen is best remembered for his efforts to ameliorate the racial politics of the 1960s and for his support for the construction of the Louisiana Superdome in New Orleans. (Courtesy of the Louisiana Collection of the State Library of Louisiana.)

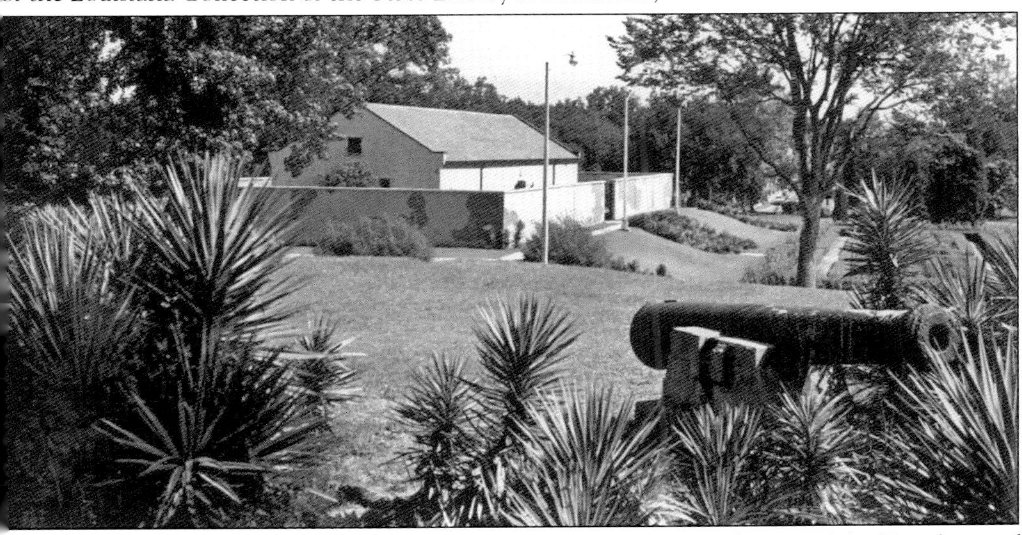

n 1932, the year that the capitol was dedicated, the Baton Rouge chapter of the Daughters of he American Revolution (DAR) began a campaign to restore the old powder magazine that had ecome known as the Arsenal, seen here in the 1960s. It would take 30 years for the campaign to ield success. (Courtesy of the Baton Rouge Room of East Baton Rouge Public Library.)

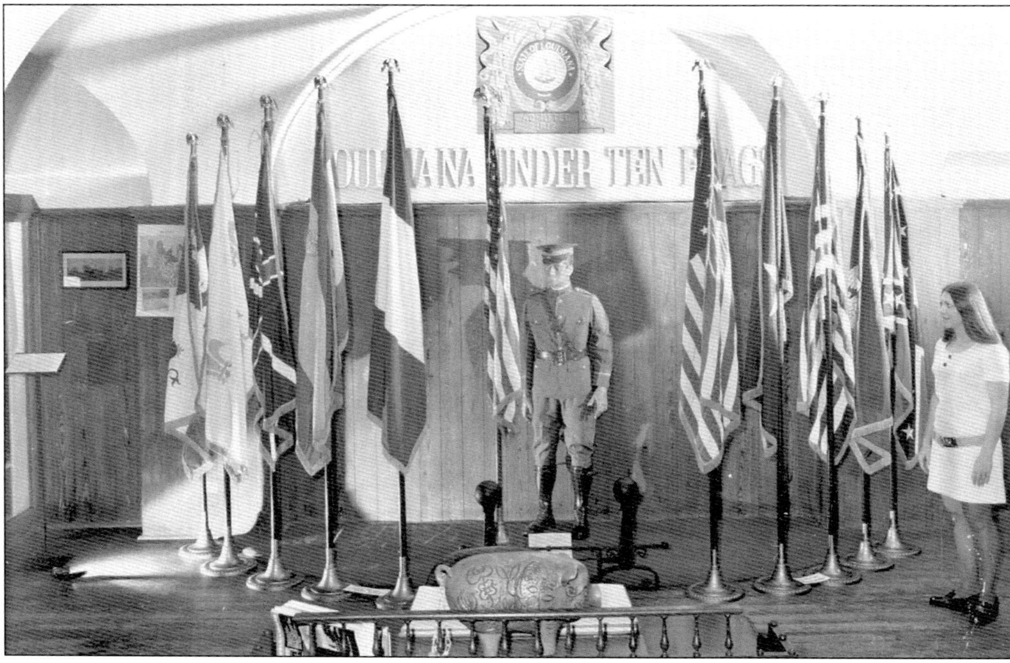

In its 1932 campaign to renovate the Arsenal, the DAR wrote letters to legislators stating that "no one knows" when the ancient landmark was built. In reality, it was not yet 100 years old. The Arsenal finally reopened in 1962 as "Louisiana Under Ten Flags," a historical exhibit designed to provide an overview of Louisiana's history. (Courtesy of the Louisiana Collection of the State Library of Louisiana.)

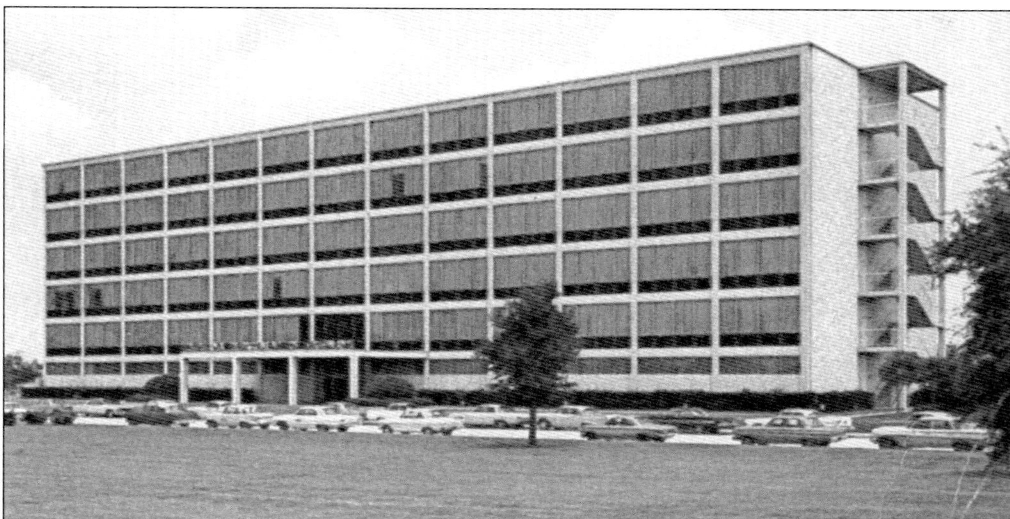

The easternmost outpost of Capitol Park is the Department of Highways (now Department o Transportation and Development, or DOTD) Building, constructed in the 1960s. DOTD grew ou of the Louisiana Highway Commission, which was established in 1921 under the administratio of Gov. John M. Parker, who pushed for the creation of more gravel roads throughout the state (Courtesy of the Baton Rouge Room of East Baton Rouge Public Library.)

In the 1960s, the demand for office space for state employees was temporarily eased by the construction of new office towers across Fourth Street from one another housing the Department of Natural Resources and the Department of Education, seen here. The building was razed in the early 2000s and replaced with the Claiborne State Office Building. (Courtesy of the Louisiana Collection of the State Library of Louisiana.)

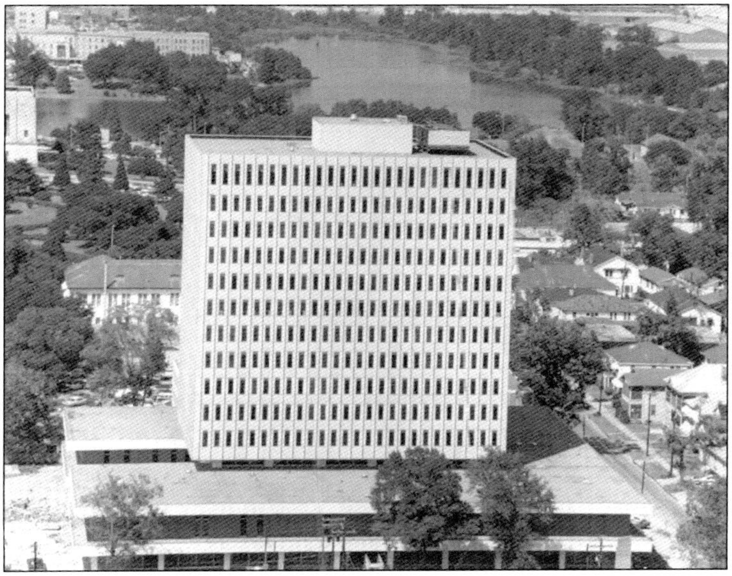

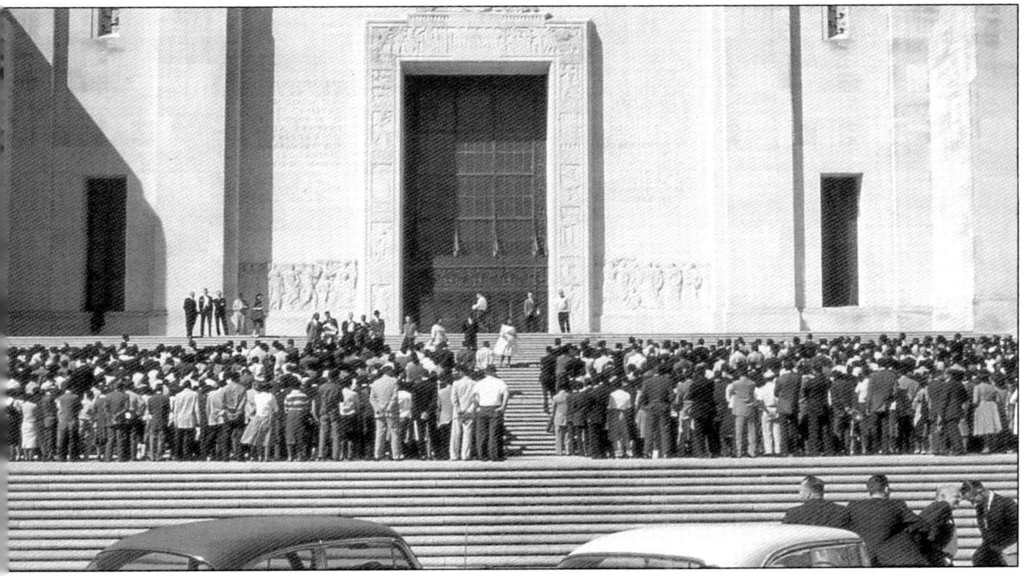

As Huey Long had intended, the broad steps of the State Capitol provide one of the state's grandest stages for political theater. Following demonstrations in downtown Baton Rouge to protest segregated lunch counters, more than 1,000 Southern University students marched on the capitol on December 18, 1961. Fifty students and others were arrested in the protest. (Courtesy of the Baton Rouge Room of East Baton Rouge Public Library.)

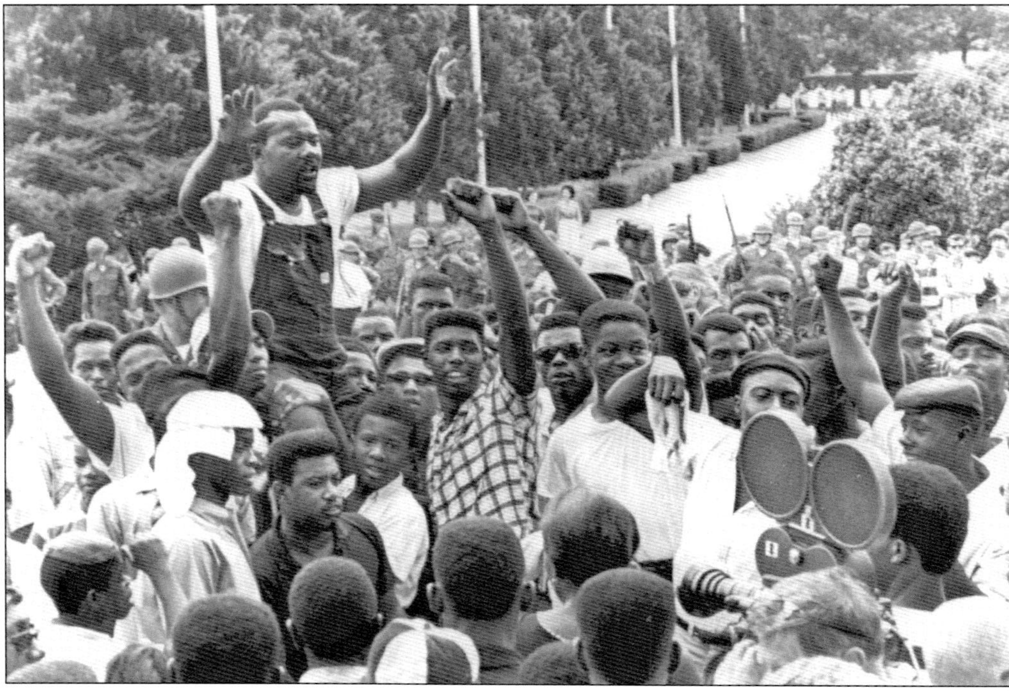

In August 1967, the capitol steps witnessed the dramatic ending of a 90-mile march led by civil rights leader A.Z. Young. By the time it reached the steps of the capitol, the group had grown from 25 to 600. The march, heavily protected by National Guardsmen and state police, was organized to protest ongoing racial injustice in Louisiana. (Courtesy of the Baton Rouge Room of East Baton Rouge Public Library.)

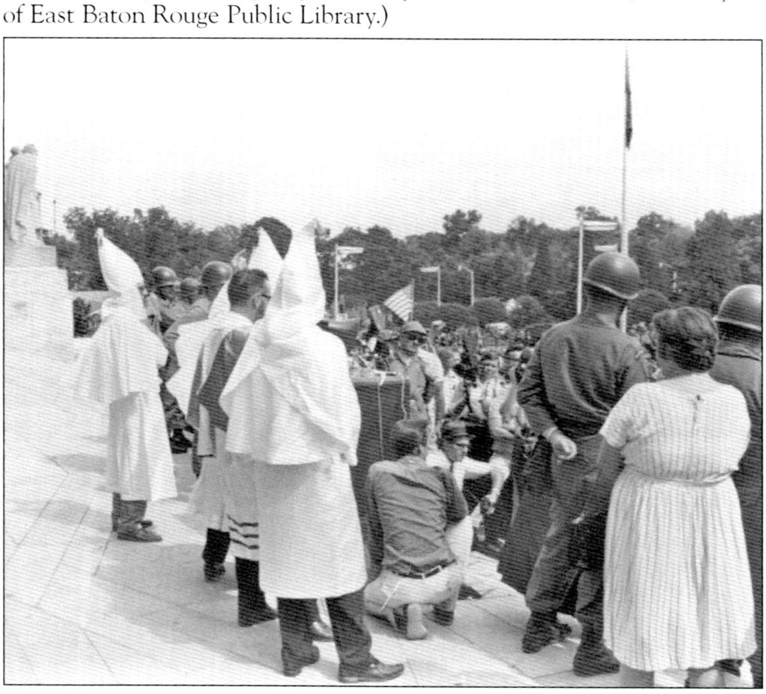

In August 1967, eight robed members of the Ku Klux Klan protested at the State Capitol. Three hundred spectators and over 2,000 National Guardsmen and policemen were on hand to watch and keep order. There were no reports of violence. (Courtesy of the Louisiana Collection of the State Library of Louisiana.)

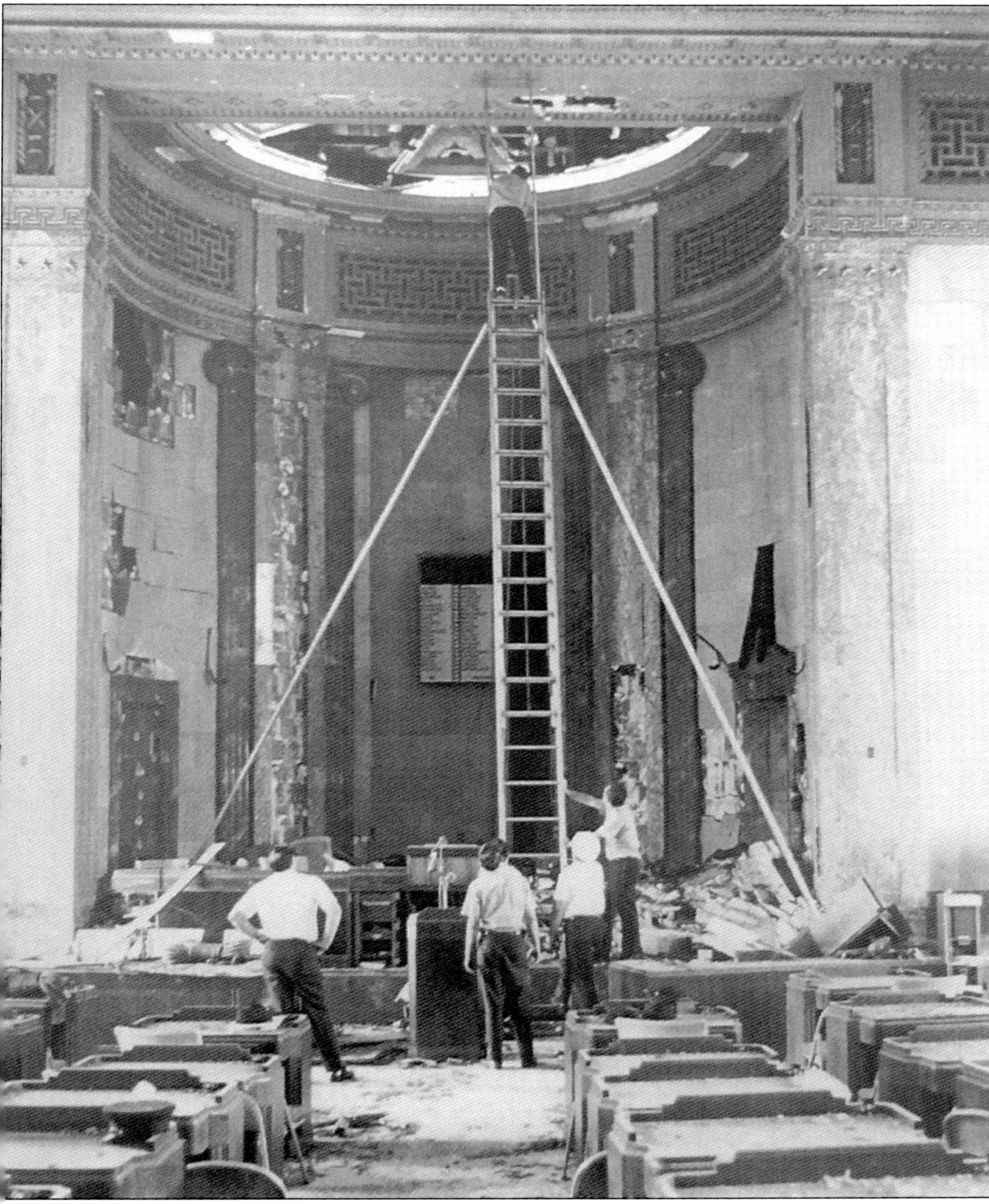

On Sunday, April 26, 1970, a bomb consisting of 20 to 30 sticks of dynamite was detonated in the Senate chamber. A note delivered to a Baton Rouge newspaper stated that the bombing was in retaliation for the shootings of three African Americans by police. A pencil thrown into the ceiling of the chamber by the blast has remained there for more than 45 years. (Courtesy of the Foundation for Historical Louisiana.)

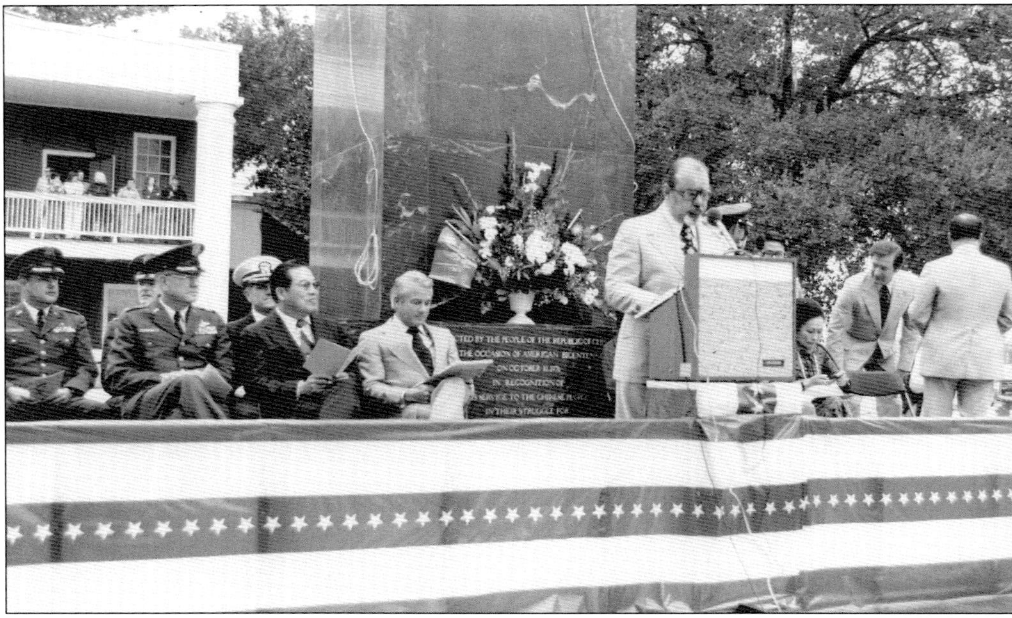

In 1976, Gov. Edwin W. Edwards and other national and international dignitaries gathered to honor Louisiana-born hero Gen. Claire Lee Chennault, who had led the famous "Flying Tigers" during World War II. The statue honoring Chennault that was dedicated in front of the Pentagon Barracks that day was later moved to another location on the Baton Rouge Riverfront. (Courtesy of Louisiana Collection of the State Library of Louisiana.)

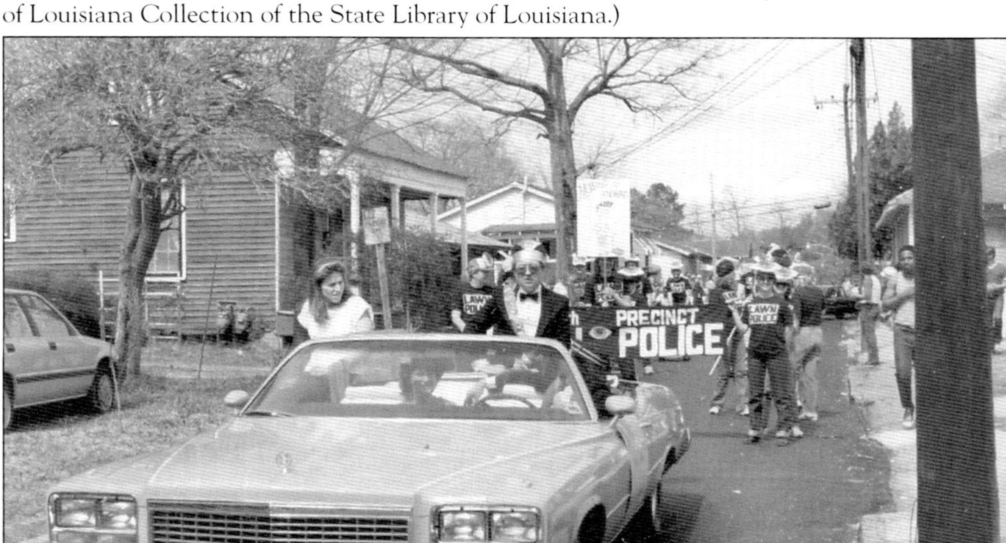

By the early 1970s, Spanish Town was a neighborhood in search of an identity. The Historic Spanish Town Civic Association was established in 1974 to provide a unified voice for the neighborhood. In 1981, residents established the Spanish Town Mardi Gras Parade in the neighborhood on the Saturday before Fat Tuesday. In 1984, local newspaper icon and Spanish Town resident Smiley Anders reigned as the parade's king. (Courtesy of Smiley Anders.)

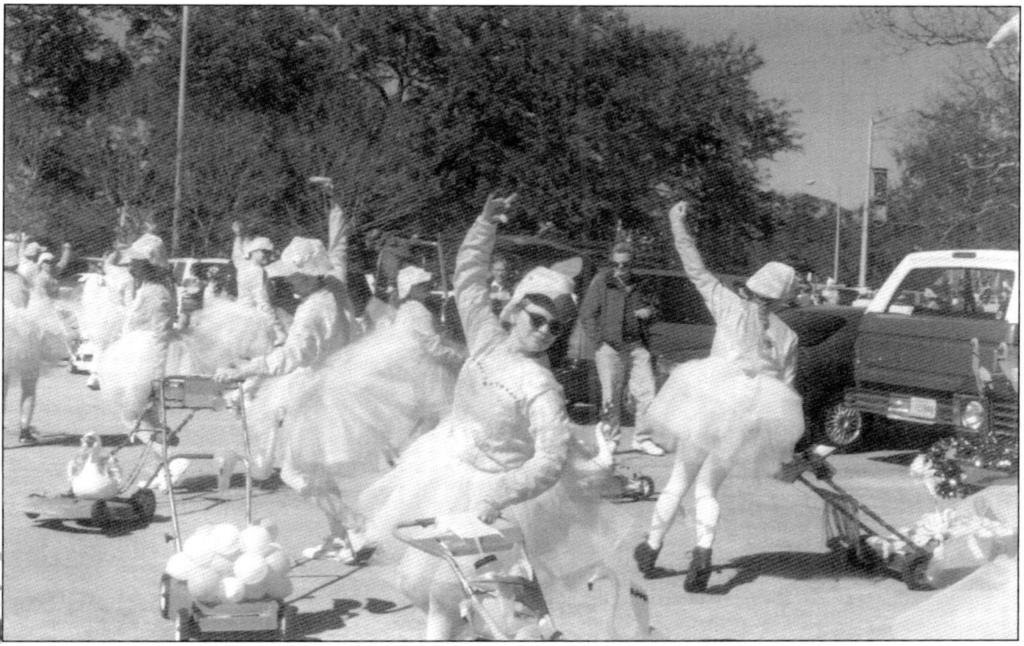

Throughout the 1980s, the Spanish Town Mardi Gras Parade continued to grow and spilled onto the streets of downtown Baton Rouge, where it remains a beloved annual tradition. In this photograph from the early 1980s, members of the Krewe of Yazoo execute an intricate lawn mower drill. (Courtesy of Donna LaFleur.)

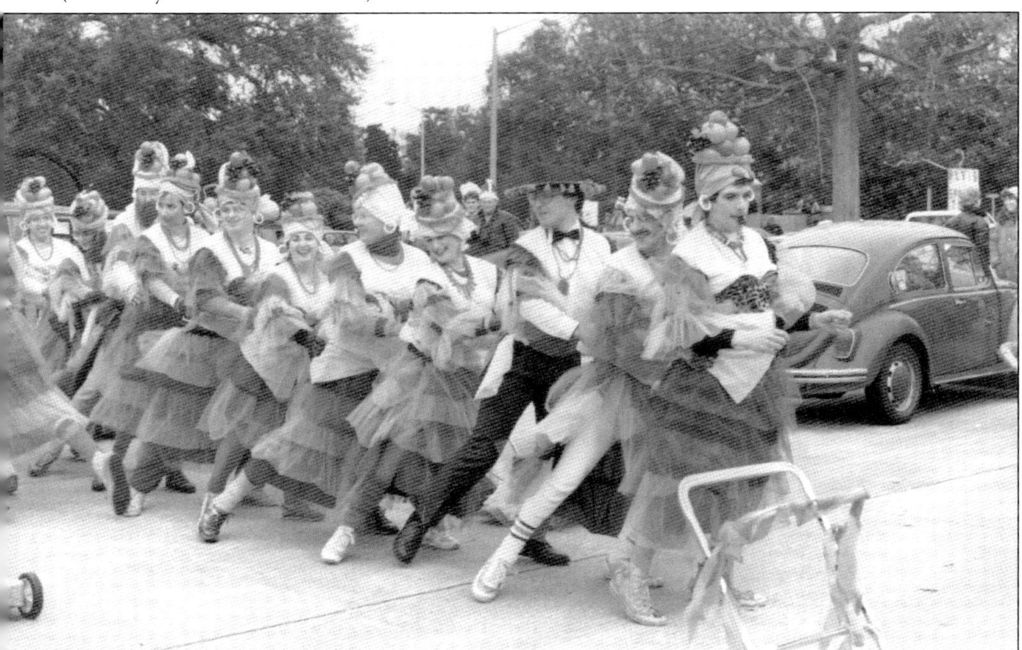

While the Spanish Town Mardi Gras Parade has grown over the decades, it still retains the character of a neighborhood party that it possessed when this conga line was photographed in the early 1980s. (Courtesy of Donna LaFleur.)

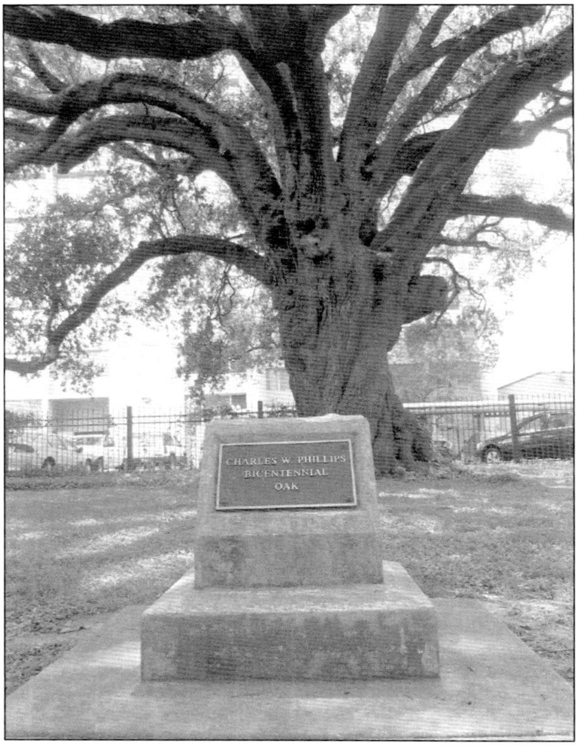

The oldest inhabitant of Capitol Park and Spanish Town is thought to be this live oak tree in Bicentennial Park, a pocket park on Seventh Street near the Catholic-Presbyterian Apartments. It is believed to be over 200 years old and received recognition during the dedication of the park in 1976. (Author photograph.)

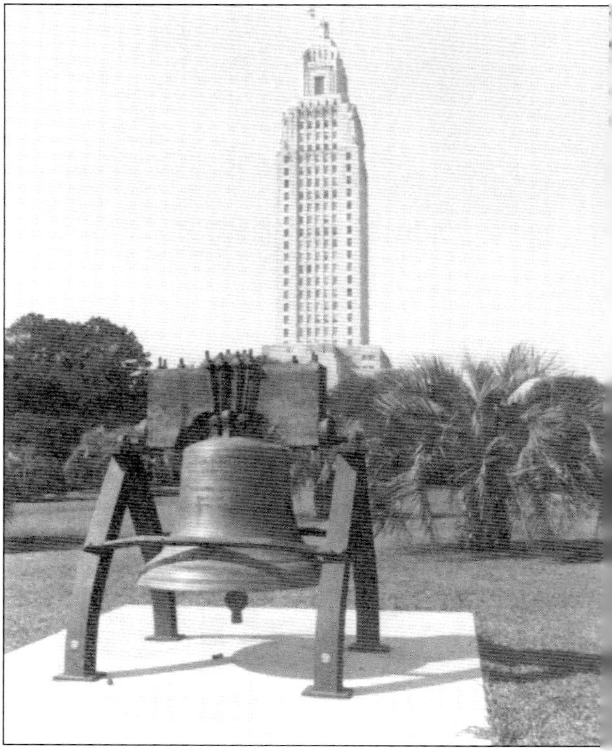

A replica of the Liberty Bell that was presented to the State of Louisiana in 1950 was moved from New Orleans to its current home at the Arsenal Museum in the 1970s. In recent years, ringing the bell at midnight on New Year's Eve has become a tradition for Spanish Town residents. (Courtesy of the Foundation for Historical Louisiana.)

Bibliography

Baton Rouge City-Parish Planning Commission. *Spanish Town: A Report on an Older Neighborhood in the Parish of East Baton Rouge, Louisiana*. Baton Rouge, LA: Baton Rouge City-Parish Planning Commission, 1973.

Carleton, Mark T. *River Capital: An Illustrated History of Baton Rouge, Revised Edition*. Tarzana, CA: American Historical Press, 1996.

Davis, John. *Travels in Louisiana and the Floridas in the Year 1802, Giving Correct Pictures of Those Countries*. New York, NY: I. Riley and Company, 1806.

Desmond, J. Michael. *The Architecture of LSU*. Baton Rouge, LA: LSU Press, 2013.

Franciscan Missionaries of Our Lady. *Celebrating Faith and Service, 1911–2011*. Baton Rouge, LA: Franciscan Missionaries of Our Lady, 2011.

Gleason, David King. *Baton Rouge*. Baton Rouge, LA: LSU Press, 1991.

Jolly, Ellen Roy and James Calhoun. *Pelican Guide to the Louisiana Capitol*. Gretna, LA: Pelican Publishing Company, 1980.

Kubly, Vincent F. *The Louisiana Capitol, Its Art and Architecture*. Gretna, LA: Pelican Publishing Company, 1977.

Le Page du Pratz, Antoine Simone. *History of Louisiana, or the Western Parts of Virginia and Carolina*. Reprint. Whitefish, MT: Kessinger Publishing, 2004.

Martin, Mark E. and Barry C. Cowan. *Historical Photos of LSU Football*. Nashville, TN: Turner Publishing Company, 2009.

Meyers, Rose. *A History of Baton Rouge, 1699–1812*. Baton Rouge, LA: LSU Press, 1976.

Richey, Thomas H. *The Battle of Baton Rouge*. 2nd ed. College Station, TX: Virtualbookworm Publishing, 2012.

Ruffin, Thomas F. *Under Stately Oaks: A Pictorial History of LSU*. Baton Rouge, LA: LSU Press, 2002.

Uter, Frank M. *A History of the Catholic Church in Baton Rouge, 1792–1992*. Baton Rouge, LA: St. Joseph Cathedral, 1992.

Wurzlow, Helen E. *Louisiana, Its Capitol*. Baton Rouge, LA: Ramires-Jones Publishing, 1932.